Gaza Yet Stands

Juan Cole

Informed Comment LLC

Ann Arbor

2024

Copyright © 2024 Juan Cole

ISBN – 13 - 979-8344288918

Cover design by: AI
Library of Congress Control Number: 2018675309
Printed in the United States of America

*Messenger: Gaza yet stands, but all her Sons are fall'n,
All in a moment overwhelm'd and fall'n.
Man: Sad, but thou knowst to Israelites not saddest
The desolation of a Hostile City.
Messenger: Feed on that first, there may in grief be surfet.*

MILTON,   SAMSON AGONISTES

Table of Contents

PART 5

October 7 and Colonial Revenge Genocide   202

PART 6

Iran, the Alliance of Resistance, and International Courts 254

1. Gaza in Modern History

October 23, 2024

The world's eyes were riveted to the video coming out of the Gaza Strip in 2023-2024 during Israel's massive total war on the small territory, still under Israeli occupation according to the International Court of Justice ruling of July 19, 2024. The Israeli assault was the most intense warfare thus far in the twenty-first century. The gut-wrenching violence of Hamas on October 7, 2023, rightly received wall-to-wall coverage, but the subsequent Israeli carnage and its victims were downplayed by the major corporate news organizations. Still, Palestinians and those sympathetic to them were able to get the word, and more importantly the video, out, via social media apps such as TikTok and "X" (formerly Twitter) — though, in contrast, Meta's Facebook algorithm allegedly deliberately suppressed news of Palestine. Some international outlets, such as Qatar's Al Jazeera and Turkey's TRT World also reported comprehensively on the conflict. The Arabic press covered the situation on the ground in Gaza in a far more detailed manner than did the Western or Israeli mass media, though Haaretz and +972 Mag published some excellent work. United Nations and aid agencies also presented masses of information, which was too little attended to by most journalists. A strong generational divide emerged in Europe and the United States, since older people got their news from the corporate media, whereas the young were more likely to see it in less curated form on their smart phones. Those paying attention were often outraged and disheartened that a high-tech genocide could be perpetrated against a people in the full view of the world and the great Powers in the twenty-first century. His unthinking and unstinting backing for the deadly Israeli campaign contributed to the unpopularity of President Joe Biden among the youths, which was among the considerations that led the Democratic Party to dump him as their candidate in 2024.

This book collects my public commentary about Gaza since 2006 and through the fall of 2024, for *Salon*, the Nation Institute's *Tomdispatch* and *The Nation*, *Truthdig*, and my own site, *Informed Comment*. Since for all its virtues, journalism generally does a poor job of providing the historical background and deep context for current events. I have therefore made a choice of pieces that shed light on the background and significance of the hot war that began in October 2023. Key inflection points, such as the fateful 2006 elections, which Hamas won, and the Israeli military campaigns of 2008-2009, 2012, 2014, and subsequent years are discussed. The lawfare of the Palestinians with the United Nations and the International Criminal Court are traced over more than a decade, an issue that reemerged powerfully in 2023-2024. The health and economic impact of Israel's cruel and illegal blockade of the Gaza civilian population is detailed. The Israeli sniping at unarmed protesters during the Great March of Return in 2018-2019 is considered. The rise of the extremist Israeli far right to power in Israel, which set the stage for the Gaza genocide, is traced, from the declaration that sovereignty is invested only in Israel's Jews (79 percent of the population) to increasingly racialist pronouncements in 2023.

Some of this writing was informed by my visits to Israel and East Jerusalem, and I am grateful to my Israeli and Palestinian interlocutors. I am an academic scholar of the Middle East, and despite the current events focus of these analyses, they inevitably reflect my own training and practice as a historian, including my extensive work on colonialism and Arab nationalism. They underline my conviction that the internet is itself a sort of postmodern archive, and that historians cannot afford to avoid commenting on an

increasingly rapid news cycle.[1] My treatment is distinctive in that I take into account the impact of these events on the wider Middle East, and the importance of Iran and its allies, one of the focuses of my scholarship.[2] Inevitably, these essays reflect my decades of involvement in the Middle East, giving them a perspective different from North American and European observers with a more North Atlantic set of concerns.

In some instances, I have taken advantage of this opportunity to carry out slight revisions to some of the essays, which were often originally written under tight deadlines, in order to clarify points or correct minor infelicities and errors. I have also added some citations where I think they may be of use to readers, or where the original hyperlinks are now dead. The bulk of the material, however, is presented here in print as it originally appeared on the internet, with all the advantages of an immediate, fresh reaction to developments and all the disadvantages of the fog of war. My rationale for collecting these essays into a book is that the internet is not very good at indexing itself, and observers such as Cory Doctorow have argued that the results of major search engines have declined in saliency because of the malign impact of advertising and search engine optimization schemes. Further, shadow-banning of Palestine-related postings has become a widespread practice on social media. In a revenge of the codex book on the internet, assembling these pieces into a book is the only way to allow them to be found reliably and read sequentially.

Gaza's story in the decades after 1948 has been one of shrinking horizons and ever-increasing misery. It was not always thus. Gaza has, despite its small extent, been an important trade and cultural crossroads for millennia. The literature on it is vast and this chapter is not the place for a detailed history. In the way of setting the context for these essays, let me instead offer an impressionistic overview and some vignettes, along with some limited citation of works that may be of use to general readers seeking more information.

Gaza was on the route between kingdoms in the Levant – Phoenicians, Canaanites, Syrians, later Israelites – and Pharaonic Egypt and was likewise on the way of invading Pharaohs who took and ruled those regions for centuries. Its harbor in ancient times,

Maiumas, connected the Mediterranean with the Near East. It was considered a prize by ancient monarchs. The Iranian prince, Pakur (Pacorus I) of the Parthian kingdom of Iran took it briefly from Rome in 40 BC. The people of Gaza adopted Christianity in large numbers from the 300s AD, giving up the worship of their local god Marnas, whom they had identified with the Cretan Zeus. Christian Gaza produced Greek-speaking theologians, philosophers and rhetoricians under the influence of Alexandria, who built early churches such as that of St. Porphyrius in 425.[3]

The Prophet Muhammad's father, Abdallah (who died in the late 560s AD), was said to have traded up to Gaza from western Arabia. Gaza became part of the Muslim empires from 636, and over the centuries its inhabitants gradually adopted Islam, though Christianity continued to have a significant presence.[4] As a trade and strategic route, it was viewed as an important possession by the sultans who ruled it, each in turn. On Dec. 29, 1516, it was taken from the Egyptian Mamluks by the Ottoman armies of Selim I and remained a district (*qaza* or *sancak*) of that empire, ruled from Istanbul, for four centuries. Local merchants, artisans, peasants and Bedouins strove to extract value from the area's resources, including the trading routes that ran through it. They sometimes came into conflict with Ottoman governors striving to monopolize those resources. The harsh governor Mehmet Pasha Kurd Bayram, appointed by the Sublime Porte over Jerusalem, Nablus and Gaza in 1701, doubled taxes and attacked recalcitrant peasants and Bedouin, including in Gaza. His campaign was said to have resulted in 200 deaths, and he displayed the heads of nine rebels in Jerusalem. In May of 1703 the entire region rebelled, and a citizens' council took over Jerusalem, establishing what sounds like a mini-republic for two years until Ottoman reinforcements could make their way from Damascus and reassert the sultan's administration.[5]

In the nineteenth century, another set of challenges was mounted to the rule of Istanbul, this time from the authoritarian, modernizing Ottoman vassal state of Egypt, which invaded the Levant in 1831. The new Egyptian order, with its administrative centralization, taxes, and expropriation of resources, provoked a rebellion in Jerusalem, Nablus and Gaza in 1834. The well-ordered Egyptian military commanded by Ibrahim Pasha quashed it within a matter of months, engaging in harsh reprisals against notables, sheikhs and clergymen who had supported it. The anti-Egyptian forces had their revenge in the late 1830s, when Egypt was forced from the region by the European Powers and a returning Ottoman army, with which the locals sided.

In the second half of the nineteenth century the Ottomans centralized their administration of the area and adopted policies that favored the growth of local big landlordism, which disadvantaged village farmers and urban artisans.[6] From 1850, the whole region of the Middle East began experiencing substantial population growth, which continues to this day in some countries, including Palestine. This growth created challenges for farming families, since because of Islam's inheritance laws each child got a portion of the estate, which shrank in each generation. Many village farmers ended up landless over time, forced to become sharecroppers on the increasingly large estates of the big landlords favored by reformed Ottoman land law.

Gaza under the later Ottomans not only had a governor of the *sancak* but also a local administrative council. With the first attempt to establish an Ottoman parliament, in 1876, Gaza's council was asked to send a delegate to the short-lived parliament in Istanbul.[7] One of the province's governors in the 1870s and early 1880s, the Jerusalemite Yusuf Diya' Efendi, had studied at the American missionary school, Robert College, in Istanbul, and was fluent in French, English, Greek and Ottoman Turkish as well as Arabic.[8] In 1893 Gaza City developed its first municipal council, with the mayor being Mustafa Muhammad al-`Ilmi. This family provided several mayors in the late nineteenth and early twentieth century, one of whom studied at the al-Azhar seminary in Egypt and became a scholar in his own right, as well as an inspector of Gaza's schools. Other mayors derived from big landlord families in Gaza City's hinterland, who often also engaged in commerce. The last of these Ottoman mayors, Sa`id al-Shawa, served 1907-1917, and was, like many other Gaza notables, a member of the Ottoman Committee for Union and Progress. When the British invaded in 1917, they imprisoned him briefly for his closeness to Istanbul.[9]

In the second half of the nineteenth century and into the twentieth century, farmers around Gaza grew wheat, barley, dates, olives and oranges, as well as cultivating bees for honey.[10] Bedouins in the area exploited marginal land that was unsuited for agriculture or did not receive enough rainfall, but which provided occasional pasturage for their goats, sheep, horses and camels. They traded meat and milk products for the grain of the peasants, though occasionally they took a shortcut through the bargaining process and instead raided village storehouses. Pastoralists, hard to police, also sometimes targeted the flocks of other Bedouins and engaged in feuds.

In the late nineteenth century Gaza City developed some industry. Gatt explained that "the pottery industry forms a separate quarter of considerable size on the western slope of the upper town, north of the road that leads out to the sea. There are about 16 workshops, each with three ovens and four wheels."[11] Potters depend on clay with special qualities, which Gaza provided. Their work also requires a vigorous athleticism. Gatt wrote, "The worker sits on the floor next to it, drives the lower wheel, which is much larger than the upper one, with his feet, and forms the clay with his hands on the upper wheel into large and small dishes." Families pitched in to work together in the workshops rather than hire laborers. "Children bring the clay and put the half or fully formed dishes in the workshop to dry," and women and girls worked as well. Dishes and pots were fired in locally made stone ovens. "During firing, a man sits at the lower entrance and continually throws chopped straw or brushwood into the lower compartment; this takes five to six days with interruptions." The aspect created by this lively manufacturing struck Europeans acquainted with their own smokestack industries as familiar: "When several kilns are in operation at the same time, the smoke billows as in many European factory towns." The distinctive grey-black Gaza dishes were more durable than those produced elsewhere in the region, and were prized and sought after, being exported by sea and over land. Bedouin and peasants bought them. Camel caravans transported them to Jerusalem, where they were displayed in front of Jaffa Gate, and further abroad up to Akka. Gazan potters were able to produce ceramic wares inexpensively, contributing to the demand for their goods, and although few were rich, none were needy.

Weaving was just as important an industry, with some 100 workshops, Gatt wrote, but less visible. He wrote that one found as many as six or more looms in each workshop. "The weaver sits in his pit all day and works just like weavers in Europe do." Linen weavers located their workshops in the Bani `Amr quarter. Wool weavers needed a less complicated set-up, while cotton weavers needed more sophisticated equipment. Gazan cotton weavers produced colorful fabrics in red and black or blue and yellow, which were used by women in Bethlehem to make their festive dresses. The weavers obtained local wool, but had to import flax and cotton from Egypt, since local peasants did not grow those crops. While men tended to work the looms, women often were the wool spinners, using spindles, since in Gaza at that time there were no spinning wheels. The weavers and spinners of Gaza were already facing stiff competition from European factory-made imported cloth, which was "ridiculously inexpensive." Like Nablus, Gaza produced soap, having access to local potash and lime brought in by Bedouin merchants, as well as village-produced olive oil.[12] Increasingly, cheap European manufactured goods led to the de-industrialization of Gaza, as they did in much of the global south.

World War I marked the beginning of the end of the cosmopolitan Gaza that had existed for millennia.[13] The Ottomans, afraid of Russian expansionism, threw in with Germany and Austria. The war did not go well during its first two years for France, Russia and Britain, which suffered massive losses on the battlegrounds of Europe. Their publics quickly became disillusioned with the hundreds of thousands of casualties and interminable trench warfare. The British government decided to attempt to make progress in the Ottoman front so as to give the weary public some victories. This initiative at first faltered as well, with a disastrous invasion of Iraq.[14] They also suffered a defeat at Gallipoli. The British, however, regrouped, and by 1917 they had taken Baghdad and Jerusalem. They had confronted the Ottoman contingents at Gaza in two major battles, which devastated the city.

At the Versailles Peace Conference after the war and more specifically at its San Remo satellite conference, Britain was awarded a League of Nations Mandate over Iraq and Palestine. Mandates were envisaged by the League of Nations as a temporary guardianship, such that the mandatory power had the responsibility to train up their wards for independent statehood. This plan, however paternalistic and imperialist, did give birth eventually to the new independent nations of Iraq, Syria, Lebanon, Togo, Rwanda and Tanzania. The Mandate of Palestine, however, did not lead to a state of Palestine in the same way.

In 1917, the British cabinet had been convinced by London Zionists, proponents of turning Judaism into a form of nationalism that sought to colonize a territory, to issue the Balfour Declaration to Lord Rothschild, saying, "His Majesty's Government view with favour the establishment in Palestine of a national home for the Jewish people, and will use their best endeavours to facilitate the achievement of this object, it being clearly understood that nothing shall be done which may prejudice the civil and religious rights of existing non-Jewish communities in Palestine, or the rights and political status enjoyed by Jews in any other country." It was a ridiculous pledge, since no such home for the Jewish people (even if the British then thought about it more as a community center than a new nation-state) could have avoided injuring the rights of the indigenous Palestinians. The British rulers of hundreds of millions of Asians and Africans thought nothing about moving people around to suit their imperial interests, and even at one point considered transporting millions of Punjabis to Iraq to relieve what they saw as India's dangerous population pressure. In 1915, two years before the tragic Balfour Declaration, 683,389 Arabic-speaking natives dwelled in the territory that the British would call Palestine, about 81,000 of them

Christians and the rest Muslims. There were only 38,752 Jews, most of them recent immigrants from Russia and Europe permitted to come into these provinces by the Ottoman sultan, some as pilgrims or retirees.[15]

The British in Palestine created a province of Gaza, separating it from the Bedouin-dominated area of Beersheba and the Negev, and permitted its notable families to administer it, though some refused to cooperate with the foreigners and others were distracted by local clan-based political faction-fighting. The war-time food crisis passed, probably helped more by the "highly fertile" land of Gaza than by laissez-faire British economic policies. Still, growing landlessness and poverty kept much of the population on the edge.[16] The influx of Jewish immigrants into Palestine, whom the indigenous viewed as illegal aliens sponsored by an illegitimate colonialism, created tensions. People in Gaza, as in the rest of Palestine, demonstrated annually against the Balfour Declaration. The Jews who colonized Palestine (their words) established a Jewish National Fund to buy land, which it forbade ever after to be sold to a non-Jew. The Palestinian population, in a largely agricultural country, doubled from 1915 to 1947, with multiple children splitting up the family farm in each generation, which had the effect of turning many Palestinian proprietors into very small farmers or landless laborers. At the same time, Jewish immigrants took six percent of the best land off the market. A riot against Jews in 1928 in Jerusalem had echoes in Gaza, where the 54 Jews who lived there were threatened by a mob. The former mayor, Said Shawa, and his clan intervened to protect the Jews. Some mayors in the 1930s, Filiu explained, undertook improvements, establishing a new hospital, a park, and a fancy neighborhood near the beach. He says that the French tourist magazine, *Le Guide Bleu*, in 1932 praised Gaza City's lively markets, its antiquities such as the ancient mosque, and its good communications, since it lay on the rail link from Haifa to the Suez Canal. It put Gaza City's population at 17,480, more than four times larger than Khan Younis. Deir al-Balah and Rafah were small.[17]

The pledge of the Balfour Declaration took on a significance beyond the relatively small Zionist movement in the 1920s and 1930s, with the rise of virulent European fascist movements that made Jew-hatred a centerpiece of their projects. Polish anti-Jewish measures and the antipathy to immigration in the United States caused Jews seeking to emigrate to go to British Mandate Palestine. The Jewish population there had swelled to about 175,000 by 1931. By 1939 it had nearly tripled to over 457,000.[18] These Jewish immigrants were refugees from an unprecedented paroxysm of murderous European racism, not for the most part committed Zionists with a program for settler colonialism. Once in Palestine, and given the horrors of the 1940s, however, some of them became available for mobilization by the ideological Zionists. This enormous influx of displaced Europeans created conflicts with indigenous Palestinians.

Notables and townspeople in Gaza joined in the strikes and demonstrations of 1936-1939, the "Great Revolt," which protested British colonial rule and the policy of allowing in thousands of European Jews. The uprising was begun by Ezzeddin al-Qassam, whom the British killed late in 1935, making him a martyr. Militias proliferated among Palestinians and immigrant Jews. The British military allied with the Haganah, one of the local Jewish militias, in putting down the revolt. Nevertheless, in May 1939 the Colonial Office under Malcolm MacDonald put forward a White Paper that laid out a plan to halt Jewish immigration and to create a Palestinian state by 1949 that would contain a Jewish minority.[19]

Instead, the British after World War II announced that they would abruptly depart Palestine. The Zionist militias took advantage of this looming power vacuum, undertaking attacks on British and Palestinian targets in hopes of reversing the MacDonald White Paper. The Mandate fell into civil war. A shockingly unbalanced and anti-Palestinian U.N. General Assembly advisory plan for partition issued in late 1947 made things worse by raising the hopes of the ambitious Zionists that they could defy expectations that they would become a model minority in an independent Palestine and instead establish a state for themselves on a territory far greater than the 6 percent they had managed to purchase and settle. As the civil war unfolded, the commanders on the ground were emboldened and began deliberately chasing out the Palestinian population. Joel Beinin, reviewing the findings of Israeli historian Benny Morris, observed that in July of 1948 the Arab Affairs director of the leftist Zionist Mapam party, Aharon Cohen, received a copy of a report from military intelligence. It explained why 240,000 Palestinian Arabs had fled from the regions awarded to the Jews by the 1947 U.N. General Assembly partition proposal and another 150,000 left the Jerusalem region and territories suggested for the Arab state. Beinin wrote, "Cohen was upset to read the report's conclusion that 70 percent of these Arabs had fled due to 'direct, hostile Jewish operations against Arab settlements' by Zionist militias, or the 'effect of our hostile operations on nearby (Arab) settlements.'"[20] The leftwing Mapam politicians had not aimed for this ethnic cleansing, but politicians by then were not in control of events on the ground.

Egypt, Jordan, Syria and Lebanon, with a little help from Iraq, came into the war, though often with relatively small forces. The sheer number of troops on each side was roughly equal. The green Arab troops, however, were no match for the well-organized Zionist forces some of whom had served in the anti-Nazi resistance or in the British Army, and who obtained good weaponry from Czechoslovakia. Jordan seemed mainly interested in grabbing the West Bank for itself and did not otherwise pose much of a challenge to the Zionists. The bureaucrats of the corrupt Egyptian government sold off equipment on the black market that should have gone to soldiers at the front. By the time of the 1949 Armistice, some 750,000 Palestinians had been ousted from what became Israel. In the south, around 250,000 of them were expelled to Gaza, where they swamped the 80,000 locals, becoming 70 percent of the population in what now was referred to as the Gaza "Strip," five miles wide and 28 miles long.[21] They never received any compensation for the property they lost or for having been made permanent refugees.

Egypt served as the caretaker for the Palestinians of Gaza for the succeeding decades. The Strip suffered from being cut off from its agricultural hinterland, which was usurped by the Israelis, and from its traditional trading markets in what became Israel and the West Bank, a separation that contained the origins of its long-term food insecurity. Egypt co-administered the territory, the population of which had been rendered stateless, with the U.N. Relief and Works Agency.[22]

During the 1967 Six Day War, which Israel's leadership launched in hopes of humiliating Egypt and vastly expanding its territory, Tel Aviv's armies captured Gaza, the West Bank, the Sinai Peninsula and the Golan Heights. By the 1970s, powerful elements of the Zionist establishment in Israel had decided to attempt to colonize the Occupied Palestinian Territories (OPT). In Gaza, Israeli economic policies, including restrictions on water use, began a process of "de-development."[23] While Egypt recovered the Sinai Peninsula with the 1979 Camp David Accords, the latter functioned as a separate peace. With the largest, best-armed and most capable Arab army out of the game, Israel could do as it pleased with the Palestinians in the OPT, and its hardliners pleased to colonize them and annex their land. Some Israeli governments at some points, as with Prime Minister Yitzhak Rabin in 1993 or Ehud Barak in 1999-2000, showed a willingness to compromise and to seriously consider a Palestinian state (though a very weak one that Israel could be sure to dominate). Their wiser instincts were overruled, however, by the rising Israeli right wing, embodied at first in the Likud Party. The rise in political power of conservative Jews from the Middle East (mizrahim), many of whose families had been expelled by mobs after the dispossession of the Palestinians in 1948, shifted the country to the right. So too did the arrival in the 1990s of a million Russian and other immigrant Jews from the old East Bloc, many of whom were hungry for living space and resources and opposed relinquishing the West Bank and Gaza.

Inside Gaza under Israeli occupation, a hothouse atmosphere of resistance grew up. Large numbers of people gave their loyalty to the umbrella group of secular and leftist parties, the Palestine Liberation Organization, which had many grassroots organizers and which sponsored institutions such as al-Azhar University (a secular school not related to the Egyptian seminary). The PLO, led by the Fatah Party, recognized Israel in 1993. Palestinians in Gaza were and are religiously and politically diverse. Hamas's narrow victory in the 2006 elections for the Palestine Authority has created an image of fundamentalism as more hegemonic in Gaza than it is, in part because of winner-take-all electoral rules. Aaron N. Bondar observed of the 2006 elections, "there were 170,021 votes for Hamas (Change and Reform) candidates in North Gaza and 146,818 votes for Fatah candidate; a total of 390,194 votes were cast. Hamas, despite receiving only 44 percent of the vote, gained 100 percent of the seats."[24]

The Muslim Brotherhood, a fundamentalist organization dedicated to political Islam, founded in Egypt in 1928, had established a small branch in Gaza in 1936. It was a decidedly minority taste for most Palestinians. Palestinian politics has often had a secular, nationalist or leftist overtone. Practicing Muslims among Palestinians were usually moderate traditionalists rather than fundamentalists, and mystical Sufi orders remain active in Gaza.[25] The Brotherhood gradually built a following, however, by constructing a network of mosques, clinics, soup kitchens in desperately poor Gaza, supplementing the work of UNRWA and other aid organizations.

A group drawn from the Brotherhood formed the core of the radical Hamas organization, founded in 1987. In response to Israeli strikes on Gaza and Tel Aviv's strangling of its economy, the Hamas paramilitary, the Ezzeddin al-Qassam Brigades, began conducting reprisal attacks on Israel in the 1990s. The non-state militia was straightforwardly committed to violence as a form of resistance, and it made no distinction between military and civilian targets. Hamas played a part in torpedoing the 1993 Oslo Accords, which it viewed as fatal to its maximalist (and wholly unrealistic) demands for an overthrow of Israel, with a series of high-profile attacks on civilians. In response to provocations and attacks by the government of Ariel Sharon, including the de-development of the Gaza economy, it engaged in another round of terrorist operations from 2000, killing hundreds of Israelis, though Israelis killed far more Palestinians with air strikes.[26]

Hamas was, however, capable of concluding and honoring a truce with the Israelis for a year or more at a time (sometimes it was the Israelis who violated such understandings). The extended family unit of the Palestinians is the Hamulah or clan, and Hamulahs make up a republic of cousins bound by loyalty, honor, and feuding with other clans. The impoverishment of these clans made it easier for Hamas to penetrate and tame them. It has been argued that Hamas subdued the Hamulahs in part through violence and in part through mobilizing them into an informal judicial system for settling conflicts.[27] Where even one member of a Hamulah joined Hamas and was subsequently killed by the Israelis, that person's male relatives – brothers, uncles and cousins – would feel a responsibility to declare a blood feud and take revenge on Israel.

Successive Israeli governments also used Hamas for their own purposes, to keep the Palestinians politically divided and to weaken the PLO, and to represent themselves as defending the Israeli public from (largely ineffectual) Hamas rockets. The Israeli economic boycott devasted the small Palestinian middle class in Gaza, the only force that potentially had the resources to resist Hamas, and some proportion of which favored the secular-minded PLO.

Notes for Chapter 1

[1] See e.g. Juan Cole,"Blogging Current Affairs History," *Journal of Contemporary History* 46 (July 2011): 658-670; Juan Cole, *Napoleon's Egypt: Invading the Middle East* (New York: Palgrave Macmillan, 2007): Juan Cole, *Colonialism and Revolution in the Middle East:*

Social and Cultural Origins of Egypt's `Urabi Movement (Princeton: Princeton University Press, 1993).

[2] Juan Cole, *Sacred Space and Holy War: The Politics, Culture and History of Shi`ite Islam* (London: I.B. Tauris, 2002)

[3] Jean-Pierre Filiu, *Gaza: A History*, trans. John King (Oxford: Oxford University Press, 2014), 3-16.

[4] Ibid., 17-34.

[5] Adel Manna, "Eighteenth-and Nineteenth-Century Rebellions in Palestine," *Journal of Palestine Studies*, 24, 1 (1994): 51-66, at 52-56.

[6] Ibid., 60-63.

[7] Alexander Schölch, "An Ottoman Bismarck from Jerusalem: Yusuf Diya' al-Khalidi (1842-1906)," *Jerusalem Quarterly* 24 (Summer 2005): 65-76 at 69.

[8] Malek Sharif, "A Portrait of Syrian Deputies in the First Ottoman Parliament," in *The First Ottoman Experiment in Democracy*, edited by Christoph Herzog and Malek Sharif (Istanbul: Orient-Institut, 2010), 285-311 at 300-301.

[9] Nasir al-Suwayr, "Ta'rikh baladiyyat Ghazzah," *Sama al-Akhbariyyah*, 4 September 2016. https://tinyurl.com/5n6s77xu

[10] `Arif al-Arif, *Ta'rikh Ghazzah* (Jerusalem: Dar al-Aytam, 1943), 287-292.

[11] This and further quotes from G. Gatt, "Industrielles aus Gaza," *Zeitschrift des Deutschen Palästina-Vereins,* 8 (1885): 69-79 at 70-71 and following. See also Alexander Schölch, *Palestine in Transformation, 1856-1882* (Washington, D.C. Institute for Palestine Studies, 1993).

[12] For the Palestinian soap industry see Beshara Doumani, *Rediscovering Palestine Merchants and Peasants in Jabal Nablus, 1700–1900* (Berkeley: University of California Press, 1995).

[13] Rashid Khalidi, *The Hundred Years' War on Palestine: A History of Settler Colonialism and Resistance, 1917–2017* (New York: Metropolitan Books, 2020); James Gelvin, *The Israel-Palestine Conflict: One Hundred Years of War* (Cambridge: Cambridge University Press, Third edn. 2014); Charles D. Smith, *Palestine and the Arab-Israeli Conflict: A History with Documents* (New York: Bedford/ St. Martin's, Tenth edn. 2020)

[14] Juan Cole, "British policy towards the Iraqi Shiites during the First World War," *Journal of Contemporary Iraq & the Arab World*, 15, 3 (2021):285-304.

[15] B.C. Busch, *Britain, India and the Arabs, 1914–21* (Berkeley: University of California Press, 1971), 22; Justin McCarthy, *The Population of Palestine: Population History and Statistics of the Late Ottoman Period and the Mandate* (New York: Columbia University Press, 1990), 12.

[16] Ilana Feldman, *Governing Gaza: Bureaucracy, Authority, and the Work of Rule, 1917-1967* (Durham: Duke University Press, 2008), 131-133.

[17] Filiu, *Gaza*, 40-43.

[18] "Demography and the Palestine Question," *Interactive Encyclopedia of the Palestine Question*, https://www.palquest.org/en/highlight/294/demography-and- palestine-question-i

[19] R. Orzeck, "Normative geographies and the 1940 Land Transfer Regulations in Palestine," *Transactions of the Institute of British Geographers*, 39 (2014): 345-359.

[20] Joel Beinin, "No More Tears: Benny Morris and the Road Back from Liberal Zionism," *Middle East Research and Information Project* (MERIP), 230 (Spring 2004), https://merip.org/2004/03/no-more-tears/;

citing Benny Morris, *1948 and After: Israel and the Palestinians* (Oxford: Oxford University Press, 1994), 83-102.

[21] Eugene L. Rogan and Avi Shlaim, eds., *Rewriting the History of 1948* (Cambridge: Cambridge University Press, Second edn., 2013); Avi Shlaim, *The Iron Wall: Israel and the Arab World* (New York: WW Norton, Second edn. 2014).

[22] Feldman, *Governing Gaza*, 135-140; Filiu, *Gaza,* 57-121.

[23] Sara Roy, *The Gaza Strip: The Political Economy of De-development* (Washington, D.C.: Institute for Palestine Studies, 1995).

[24] Aaron N. Bondar, "Breaking down the 2006 Palestinian elections vote-by-vote," *ProgressME Magazine*, Mar 15, 2016 https://medium.com/progressme-magazine/breaking-down-the-2006- palestinian-elections-vote-by-vote-cfc0ca2fd444

[25] Ala' al-Muqayyad, "Al-Tasawwuf fi Ghazzah: Tariq al-hurub min 'din al-siyasah' ila din al-ruh," *Raseef*, June 21, 2016. https://tinyurl.com/598hynej

[26] Beverly Milton-Edwards and Stephen Farrell, *Hamas* (Malden, Mass.: Polity, 2010); Tarek Baconi, *Hamas Contained: The Rise and Pacification of the Palestinian Resistance* (Palo Alto: Stanford University Press, 2018), chapters 1-3.

[27] Abdalhadi Alijla, "The (Semi) State's Fragility: Hamas, Clannism, and Legitimacy," *Soc. Science*, 10, no. 11 (2021): 437-455.

PART   1

The Rise of Hamas, and Israeli Bombardment

In 2005 the Israeli far right was disappointed when even the very conservative prime minister and war hero Ariel Sharon decided that the Israeli squatters on Palestinian land in Gaza could not be protected, pulling them out of the Gaza Strip, without, however, making any arrangements for what would come next. One of his advisers admitted that he took the step to freeze the political process and forestall progress toward a Palestinian state.[1]

In January 2006, elections for the Oslo-created Palestine Authority were held at the insistence of the Bush administration, in which Hamas pulled off a surprise victory. That is when I began commenting on Gaza at any length. It was the era of the Bush administration, of which I emerged as a major critic with regard to the invasion and occupation of Iraq and its ex post facto rationale for violent regime change of "democratization" in the region. I saw the Palestine elections through this lens, of the use of democratic forms and procedures for the purposes of imperial U.S. assertion in the region. The victory of Hamas in the elections set off a long-term crisis. In its wake came the 2007 joint coup by Israel, the PLO and the United States against Hamas, which overturned the election in the West Bank but failed to do so in Gaza, where Hamas fighters defeated Fatah cadres. The Hamas survival in the Strip was dealt with by a severe Israeli blockade on Gaza, a form of collective punishment that sought to provoke the population to turn against Hamas by making them miserable and keeping them on the verge of food insecurity. From 2006, Ilan Pappe has argued, Israel has pursued a policy of incremental genocide in Gaza, creating it as "the biggest prison on earth." 2 I was following Gaza's deteriorating public health situation because of the blockade with some astonishment that it was not more of an issue for America's newspapers of record and its cable news stations. The military campaign of 2008-2009 began an emerging pattern of what cynical Israelis called "mowing the lawn," keeping Hamas and the Palestinians of Gaza in line with brutal bombardments from time to time. I argued that this conflict put the lie to all of the pieties on the part of Bush administration officials about the virtues of regime change as a tool of muscular Wilsonianism and "democratization" in the Middle East.

In the teens of this century, Prime Minister Benjamin Netanyahu worked out a strategy of granting Gaza to Hamas as a fief, and of transferring to Gaza via Israeli bank accounts funds from Egypt and Qatar, in hopes that he could contain it and keep the Palestinians divided.[3] Many in the Israeli elite are so allergic to Palestinian self-determination that they pretend it is not necessary to deal with real Palestinians or to craft a sustainable future with them.

Notes

[1] Norman G. Finkelstein, *Gaza: An Inquest into its Martyrdom* (Berkeley: University of California Press, 2018), 31.

[2] Ilan Pappe, *The Biggest Prison on Earth: A History of Gaza and the Occupied Territories* (Oxford: Oneworld, 2019), 267-285.

[3] "Liberman: Netanyahu sent Mossad head, general to Qatar, 'begged' it to pay Hamas," *Times of Israel*, 22 February 2020. https://www.timesofisrael.com/mossad-chief-top-general-visited-qatar-begged-it-to-pay-hamas-liberman-says/.

2.   Hamas' stunning victory underlines the Contradictions and Hypocrisies in U.S. Mideast Policies

January 27, 2006

The stunning victory of the militant Muslim fundamentalist Hamas Party in the Palestinian elections underlines the central contradictions in the Bush administration's policies toward the Middle East. U.S. President George W. Bush pushes for elections, confusing them with democracy, but seems blind to the dangers of right-wing populism. At the same time, he continually undermines the moderate and secular forces in the region by acting high-handedly or allowing his clients to do so. As a result, Sunni fundamentalist parties, some with ties to violent cells, have emerged as key players in Iraq, Egypt and Palestine.

Democracy depends not just on elections but on a rule of law, on stable institutions, on basic economic security for the population, and on checks and balances that forestall a tyranny of the majority. Elections in the absence of this key societal context can produce authoritarian regimes and abuses as easily as they can produce genuine people power. Bush is on the whole unwilling to invest sufficiently in these key institutions and practices abroad. And by either creating or failing to deal with hated foreign occupations, he has sown the seeds for militant Islamist movements that gain popularity because of their nationalist credentials.

In Iraq, which is among the least secure and most economically fraught countries in the world, the Dec. 15 elections brought into Parliament a set of powerful Shiite fundamentalist parties and a new force, the Muslim fundamentalist Iraqi Accord Front, which gained most of the votes of formerly secular-minded Iraqi Sunni Arabs. Some IAF politicians are suspected of strong ties to Iraq's Sunni insurgency. In Egypt, last fall's election increased representation for the fundamentalist Muslim Brotherhood from 17 to more than 70 seats in Parliament, making that group a key political player for the first time in Egyptian history. Decades ago, the party once assassinated a prime minister and attempted to assassinate President Gamal Abdul Nasser, but now maintains it has turned to moderation. It aims at the imposition of a rigid interpretation of Islamic law on Egyptians, including Egyptian women.

Now Hamas, or the Islamic Resistance Movement, a branch of the Egyptian Muslim Brotherhood, has come to power in Palestine. In his press conference on Thursday, Bush portrayed the Palestinian elections in the same way he depicts Republican Party victories over Democrats in the United States: "The people are demanding honest government. The people want services. They want to be able to raise their children in an environment in which they can get a decent education and they can find healthcare." He sounds like a spokesman for Hamas, underlining the irony that Bush and his party have given Americans the least honest government in a generation, have drastically cut services, and have actively opposed extension of healthcare to the uninsured in the United States.

But the president's attempt to dismiss the old ruling Fatah Party as corrupt and inefficient, however true, is also a way of taking the spotlight off his own responsibility for the stagnation in Palestine. Bush allowed then Israeli Prime Minister Ariel Sharon to sideline the ruling Fatah Party of Yasser Arafat, to fire missiles at its police stations, and to reduce its leader to a besieged nonentity. Sharon arrogantly ordered the murder of civilian Hamas leaders in Gaza, making them martyrs. Meanwhile, Israeli settlements continued to grow, the fatally flawed Oslo agreements delivered nothing to the Palestinians, and Bush and Sharon ignored new peace plans -- whether the so-called Geneva accord[1] put forward by Palestinian and Israeli moderates or the Saudi peace plan[2]-- that could have resolved the underlying issues. The Israeli withdrawal from Gaza, which should have been a big step forward for peace, was marred by the refusal of the Israelis to cooperate with the Palestinians in ensuring that it did not produce a power vacuum and further insecurity.

Frustrated, the Palestinian public predictably swung to the far right. Their embrace of Hamas does not indicate that most Palestinians are dedicated to destroying Israel; polls show that most support a two-state solution and are weary of the endless violence. Rather, they are sick of the Palestinian Authority and believe that Hamas will be more effective negotiating partners with the Israelis. As a Saudi political talk show host told the Associated Press, "They [Hamas] will be the Arab Sharon. They will be tough, but only a tough group can snatch concessions from Israel."[3]

In a mystifying self-contradiction, Bush trumpeted that "the Palestinians had an election yesterday, the results of which remind me about the power of democracy." If elections were really the same as democracy, and if Bush was so happy about the process, then we might expect him to pledge to work with the results, which by his lights would be intrinsically good. But then he suddenly swerved away from this line of thought, reverting to boilerplate and saying, "On the other hand, I do not see how you can be a partner in peace if you advocate the destruction of a country as part of your platform. And I know you can't be a partner in peace if you have a -- if your party has got an armed wing."

So Bush is saying that even though elections are democracy and democracy is good and powerful, it has produced unacceptable results in this case, and so the resulting Hamas government will lack the legitimacy necessary to allow the United States to deal with it or go forward in any peace process. Bush's double standard is clear in his diction, since he was perfectly happy to deal with Israel's Likud Party, which is dedicated to the destruction of the budding Palestinian state, the charter of which calls for an Israel "from the river to the sea," and which used the Israeli military and security services for its party platform in destroying the infrastructure of the Palestinian Authority throughout the early years of this century. As Orwell reminded us in "Animal Farm," some are more equal than others.

President Mahmoud Abbas of Fatah had earlier been elected in a separate process and could continue in office if he chooses to work with a Hamas-dominated cabinet. He had earlier hinted that he would resign if his party lost. Asked about a possible resignation, Bush said in his typically tongue-tied way, "We'd like him to stay in power. I mean, we'd like to stay in office. He is in power; we'd like him to stay in office." Khaled Mashaal, the Hamas leader who is in exile in Syria, said that his party would be willing to work with Abbas as president, according to a party spokesman.

But then when Bush was asked if the United States would end aid to the Palestinian Authority if a Hamas government was formed, he implied that it would, unless Hamas changed its platform, which opposes the existence of the state of Israel on the grounds that the territory belongs to the Palestinians. He said, "Well, I made it very clear that the United States does not support political parties that want to destroy our ally Israel, and that people must renounce that part of their platform."

Bush implied that Hamas is dedicated to unremitting violence against Israel. And since 1994 its military wing has launched many suicide attacks against Israelis, killing hundreds of people, most of them civilians. But in fact it has observed a more or less effective truce for about a year -- indeed, as an important study carried out by the respected International Crisis Group pointed out, it has observed the truce far more reliably than Fatah[4] And Hamas' leaders have affirmed that they are willing to continue the truce if Israel refrains from aggressive violence toward them.

Despite Hamas' founding position that the Israeli state is illegitimate, violence is not foreordained. A Hamas leader, Mahmoud Zahar, told the Associated Press that his party would continue what he called its year-old "truce" if Israel did the same. "If not," he added, "then I think we will have no option but to protect our people and our land."[5] More fundamentally, even Hamas' charter could change. As the ICG points out, Hamas "has accepted the principle that there is no religious prohibition against negotiating or co-existing with Israel and that the provisions in its charter providing for Israel's destruction are not indelible." Even President Bush, in his measured response to the elections, seemed to hold out hope that Hamas would adopt a more pragmatic stance.

To be sure, many Israelis believe that Hamas is only using the truce to rearm, that it will never change its opposition to the very existence of Israel, and that any negotiations with the Islamist group will only weaken the Jewish state. And Hamas' failure to speak clearly about its intentions does nothing to allay such fears.

But no one has ever put Hamas to the test. Neither Bush nor Israel have ever made good-faith efforts to resolve the underlying issues, preferring to issue moralistic denunciations that ignore the reality on the ground. The bitter fruits of that shortsighted policy are now evident. In Iraq, Bush has been forced -- albeit too late -- to act pragmatically, negotiating with the leaders of Sunni insurgents whom his administration earlier denounced as "terrorists." He and Israeli leaders should follow the same course in Palestine and try to engage Hamas in a realistic, good-faith political effort to resolve the conflict.

There is no evidence that either party will do so. Bush announced early in his administration his unwillingness to do anything that would challenge Sharon. For his part, acting Israeli Prime Minister Ehud Olmert is following in Sharon's footsteps. He said that he would refuse to deal with the Palestinian Authority if it was led by Hamas or included Hamas as a partner, and that he would continue to take the high-handed unilateral actions planned by Sharon, including holding on to the large Israeli settlements in the West Bank and refusing to negotiate the status of Jerusalem.[6]

Bush has boxed himself into an impossible situation. He promoted elections that have produced results opposite of the ones he wanted. For all his constant rhetoric about his determination to hunt down and kill terrorists, in Palestine he has in effect helped install into power a group he calls "terrorists." His confusion over whether this is democracy, which should be legitimate, or is an unacceptable outcome -- and his unwillingness to address the underlying issues behind the Israeli-Palestinian conflict -- suggest that a fatal paralysis will continue to afflict the region.[7]

-Salon.

Notes

[1] "Geneva accord: The informal peace plan from Israeli and Palestinian moderates." http://www.salon.com/news/feature/2003/10/24/geneva/.

[2] Graham E. Fuller, "The Saudi Peace Plan: How Serious?" *Middle Eats Policy*, 9, no. 2 (June 2002): 27-30.

[3] Associated Press: Saudi political talk show host discusses Hamas - http://seattletimes.nwsource.com/html/nationworld/2002763522_webmideastarabs26.html.

[4] International Crisis Group: Study on Hamas' truce - http://www.crisisgroup.org/home/index.cfm?id=3886&l=1.

[5] Associated Press: Interview with Hamas leader Mahmoud Zahar - http://www.salon.com/wire/ap/archive.html?wire=D8FCEA1O7.html.

[6] *Haaretz*: Ehud Olmert's statement on refusing to deal with Hamas - http://www.haaretz.com/hasen/spages/675205.html.

[7] For the 2006 elections in Gaza, the role of Hamas and the aftermath, see now Milton-Edwards and Farrell, *Hamas*, 230-284; Tarek Baconi, *Hamas Contained: The Rise and Pacification of the Palestinian Resistance* (Palo Alto: Stanford University Press, 2018), 125-133.

3. The Situation in Gaza

June 19, 2007

The events of the past few days — Palestine Authority President Mahmoud Abbas's dismissal on June 14, 2007, with Israeli and U.S. support, of the Hamas government and the outbreak of fighting between PLO and Hamas fighters — have driven a nail into the coffin of Bush's "democratization" program for the "Greater Middle East." The Hamas government led by Ismail Haniyeh had come to power in free and fair elections, but was immediately boycotted, starved of resources, and its parliamentarians often simply kidnapped by the Israelis; and it is now being put out of office in a kind of coup. The people of the Arab world are not blind or stupid. If this is what the "Greater Middle East" looks like, it will too closely resemble, for their taste, the colonial 19th century, when Europeans dictated government to Middle Easterners.

It is to be expected that a lot of comment in the United States on these events will be rife with racist attitudes and polemical dismissals. The Palestinians have long been demonized by the Western media, apparently for not going along quietly with their expulsion from their homes, the large-scale theft of their land, and their reduction to an almost slave-like status of statelessness. Palestinians are not intrinsically more violent than anyone else, not essentially less able to administer or govern than anyone else. Few countries have not had civil wars or at least major civil conflicts. The question should be not "Why are Palestinians like that?"—which is a racist question—but what social and economic factors are driving the present conflict?

Why is it that so little analysis is offered of why things have developed as they have? Isn't anyone interested in the important differences between Gaza's economy and that of the West Bank? Gaza is much poorer and much more isolated from the world. Is it any big surprise that its population is more radicalized and might be drawn into supporting Hamas?

The Gazan population is being thrown into more misery by an Israeli blockade of electricity, fuel and even food.[1] (Israeli Prime Minister Ehud Olmert says that it will be a humanitarian blockade; if you believe that, I have a bridge over the River Jordan you can purchase inexpensively from me). The United Nations Relief and Works Agency is warning against the blockade on humanitarian grounds.[2] With an unemployment rate of 50 percent and widespread malnutrition, caused by the ordinary everyday Israeli pressure on Gaza, the territory's population can't take much more extra deprivation without an immense human toll being exacted.

If Bush and the Israelis couldn't live with a Hamas electoral victory, they should have excluded Hamas from running a year and a half ago. The Egyptians do not let explicitly religious parties contest elections, and a similar rule could have been made in Palestine. Holding an election, having people win it with whom you won't deal, and then overturning the election with militias, is a recipe for violence and instability. That's what happened in Algeria in 1992, when the generals allowed the Muslim fundamentalist Islamic Salvation Front to run. When it won, they cancelled the election results, enraging ISF supporters. It threw the country into a decade of civil war, and it caused untold suffering.

The Israelis may be sighing a sigh of relief that the Palestinian Fatah and Hamas paramilitaries are busy fighting one another for the moment. But what has happened is not good for Israel in the medium to long term, since I suspect it signals the end of the possibility of a viable Palestinian state. And, if you do not have a two-state solution, ultimately the likelihood is that Israel will be stuck with the Palestinians as citizens. The world is not going to look the other way forever as they are kept stateless, poor, landless and hungry.

[N.B. In the end the PLO won the struggle in the West Bank but Hamas retained power in Gaza.]³

\-   *Informed Comment* (rearranged and slightly revised).

Notes

¹ *The Age*: "Supplies low as Gaza blockade takes toll. https://www.theage.com.au/news/world/supplies-low-as-gaza-blockade-takes-toll/2007/06/18/1182019032232.html

² *Miftah*: "U.N. Warns on Gaza Economy and Blockade. http://www.miftah.org/Display.cfm?DocId=14524&CategoryId=5

³ For the Hamas-PLO civil war in 2007, see now Milton-Edwards and Farrell, *Hamas*, 284-294; Filiu, *Gaza*, 279-396; and and Baconi, *Hamas Contained*, 135-175.

4.   Israel's Bombardment of Gaza

December 29, 2008

The Israeli bombardment of Gaza entered its third day on December 29, 2008, as the prospect of a possible land invasion loomed, with Israel massing tanks on the border, in the Israeli Operation Cast Lead.[1]

What I can't understand is the end game here. The Israelis have pledged to continue their siege of the civilians of Gaza, and have threatened to resume assassinating Hamas political leaders, along with the bombardment. The campaign of brutal assassinations launched by Ariel Sharon earlier in this decade were, Sharon promised us, guaranteed to wipe out Hamas entirely. Do the Israelis expect the population at some point to turn against Hamas, blaming it for the blockade and the bombardment? But by destroying what was left of the Gaza middle class, surely they are throwing people into the arms of Hamas. The U.S. experience of bombing North Vietnam and mining Haiphong Harbor, etc., was that it only stiffened Hanoi's resolve. The massive Israeli bombardment of Lebanon in 2006 did not achieve any significant objectives. In fact, Hezbollah was politically strengthened; it now sits in the Lebanese cabinet and has been recognized as a formal national guard for the south of the country. Its stock of rockets has been replenished. There is a U.N. buffer now, but in the past such buffers have been removed when hostilities threaten.

If the Gaza population doesn't turn on Hamas, and Israeli measures do not destroy the organization (which they helped create and fund back in the late 1980s when they wanted a foil to the secular PLO),[2] then what? They'll just go on half-starving Gaza's children for decades? Malnourished children have diminished IQ and poor impulse control. That would make them ideal suicide bombers. Plus, sooner or later there will start to be effective boycotts of Israel in Europe and elsewhere over these war crimes. The Israeli economy would be vulnerable to such moves.

Of course, there were only 1.5 million Gazans in 2008, and they were increasingly being forced to live in Haiti-like conditions, so in the short term the Israelis can do whatever they want to them. But I can't see this ending well for the Israelis in the long term. Very few insurgencies end because one side achieves a complete military victory (I think it is about 20 percent). But by refusing to negotiate with Hamas, Israel and the United States leave only a military option on the table. The military option isn't going to resolve the problem by itself. Gaza is a labyrinth. Those Qassam rockets are easy to make. There is so much money sloshing around the Middle East and so many sympathetic Muslims that Gaza will be kept just barely afloat economically, making Hamas hard to dislodge. And the Israeli blockade of Gaza is so distasteful to the world that eventually there is likely to be a painful price to pay for it by the Israelis.

Among the 210 targets hit by Israeli airstrikes on December 27 and 28 was the campus of the Islamic University. Israel also bombed the Interior Ministry.[3]

The *Washington Post* reports a growing humanitarian crisis in Gaza, where the death toll from Israeli air strikes has reached 300 with 1,300 wounded, 235 of them serious, and humanitarian groups warned of shortages of medical supplies in the hospitals if the border checkpoints were not opened to allow them in. *The Post* writes: "'There are hundreds of wounded in the hospitals in the Gaza Strip, and what we have received so far has only been a fraction of our need. Our supplies have been depleted, and we are in desperate need for supplies,' said Iyad Nasr, a spokesman for the International Committee of the Red Cross in Gaza. 'We ask the parties to avoid striking the civilian population on both sides.'"[4]

Aljazeera English gives a video on Gaza hospitals struggling to treat civilians wounded by Israeli airstrikes. The hospitals' ability to treat had already been degraded by the long Israeli blockade of Gaza.[5]

- *Informed Comment*

Notes

[1] *Yahoo News/AFP*: "Israeli bombardment of Gaza enters third day" - http://news.yahoo.com/s/afp/20081229/wl_mideast_afp/mideastconflictgaza_081229060008; for Operation Cast Lead see now Finkelstein, *Gaza*, 31-188; Milton-Edwards and Farrell, *Hamas*, 298-309.

[2] *Information Clearing House*: "Israel's role in creating and funding Hamas in the late 1980s" - http://www.informationclearinghouse.info/article10456.htm

[3] *BBC News*: "Islamic University among targets hit by Israeli airstrikes" - http://news.bbc.co.uk/2/hi/middle_east/7802515.stm

[4] *The Washington Post*: "Report on humanitarian crisis in Gaza" - http://www.washingtonpost.com/wp-dyn/content/article/2008/12/28/AR2008122802111.html

[5] *Al Jazeera English* YouTube Video: "Gaza hospitals struggle" - https://www.youtube.com/watch?v=MTpWEtGgDJM

5. Gaza 2008: Micro-Wars and Macro-Wars

January 4, 2009

With regard to the Arab-Israeli conflict, we have entered the age of micro-wars.

The first wars that Israel fought with its Arab neighbors were conventional struggles in which infantry, artillery, armor and air forces played central roles.

Israel's enemies had few effective tools in the 1950s and 1960s. Abdel Nasser encouraged Palestinian resistance from Gaza in 1955, but it was more harassment than a serious military operation. The Egyptian, Jordanian and Syrian conventional armies were what Israel's leaders worried about. Jordan was no match for the Israelis and it had a history of secret agreements with the Zionist leaders, so its military was only a threat when, as in 1967, other Arab leaders convinced the Jordanian leadership to join in a collective effort.

Israel's policies were not merely defensive, contrary to the propaganda one constantly hears. Moshe Sharrett's diaries demonstrate conclusively the expansionist character of the regime. Israel's leaders badly wanted the Sinai Peninsula and therefore a commanding position over the trade of the Red Sea and the Suez Canal in the 1950s and 1960s. There was also some petroleum there. Israel used superiority in armor and air power in 1956 to take the Sinai, in conjunction with an orchestrated Anglo-French attack on Egypt's position in the Suez Canal (which Gamal Abdel Nasser had nationalized that summer). President Dwight D. Eisenhower, afraid that vestiges of Old World colonial thinking would push the Arabs into the arms of the Soviets, made Israel relinquish its prize. But hawks in Israel took the Sinai from Egypt again in the 1967 war, in which Israel again demonstrated that armor plus air superiority always defeats armor that lacks air cover. Israel managed to destroy the Egyptian air force early in the war.

Egypt could not accept loss of its sovereign territory. As the largest Arab state, with a third of the Arab population, and a developing economic, technological and military capability, Egypt could not be dismissed. Its leader from 1970, Anwar El Sadat, found a way of striking back. Egypt launched the 1973 war as a surprise attack and used sophisticated underwater sand-moving equipment to get across the canal and penetrate into the Sinai. By this time Egypt had Soviet SA-6 surface-to-air missiles that served as anti-aircraft batteries and was careful to keep its tanks under their umbrella. Had Egypt had a better air force, Egyptian armor could have rolled right into Israel proper in October of 1973. The Israeli cabinet is said to have feared it was the fall of the Third Kingdom. But even in the absence of a proper air force, the Soviet SAMs were a game-changer. I would argue that they were the difference between the crushing defeat of Egypt in 1967 and the draw-to-slight victory Cairo won in 1973.

The writing was on the wall. Israel could not have the Sinai. Egypt was too big and too increasingly powerful an enemy to continue to provoke it. The 1973 conflict settled that. The Egyptian public was tired of war and its expense, and so both sides were willing to conclude the Camp David Peace Treaty of 1978. Egypt got the Sinai back permanently. Israel escaped the most serious military threat in the region.

Israel's political tradition seeks expansion if possible; if not possible, it seeks a balance of power with its enemies. If that is not possible, it seeks to be held harmless from its avowed foes. If that is not possible, it is willing to wage total war to punish the enemy population until it accepts at least a cold peace. I mean by "total war" a war on the civilian population in which the guerrilla group is embedded, as for instance dropping a million cluster bombs on the farms of south Lebanon in 2006 or half-starving Gazan children in

2007-2008, methods illegal in international law but routinely deployed by Israeli leaders and defended by ardent partisans of Israel everywhere. Where necessary, Israel is willing to give up territorial expansion to get the cold peace.

The 1982 Lebanon War was a hybrid. Israel deployed a conventional army against the Palestine Liberation Organization and Lebanon. The PLO fought an unconventional struggle in Beirut, and reached out diplomatically to the U.S., France and Italy to achieve a negotiated outcome rather than an outright defeat. The PLO had to leave Beirut. But Israel's victory was pyrrhic. The Lebanon War was highly unpopular at home and abroad because it seemed unprovoked. The PLO was not destroyed. Israel's old expansionist tendencies kicked in and it was unwilling to relinquish South Lebanon, such that it began occupying yet another Arab country. Israel's occupation helped create the Shiite resistance we now call Hezbollah, which evolved into a highly effective unconventional military force.

Jordan's government was neutralized in the early 1990s with a peace treaty, just as Egypt's had earlier been with Camp David. The PLO also engaged in a peace process off and on, and with the death of Yasser Arafat on November 11, 2004, the old guerrilla PLO seemed to end, as Fatah became a political party.

That development left Israel with three main regional enemies: Syria, Lebanon's Hezbollah and Hamas in Gaza. Hezbollah in turn gradually attracted Iranian patronage. In the case of the Levantine players, the main issue was Israeli occupation of their land — south Lebanon and the Shebaa Farms for Hezbollah, the Golan Heights for Syria, and Gaza and the West Bank (the most vigorously colonized of the Occupied Territories) for Hamas.

The Arab-Israeli wars of the opening years of the 21st century have not been conventional wars. They have been micro-wars. Israel had demonstrated in the earlier Arab-Israeli wars that it could win a conventional struggle. The new repertoires of struggle against Israel had four dimensions. First, they depended on fundamentalist religious party organization (Hezbollah, Hamas), wherein cadres gained popularity in their own base by providing aid and services (e.g. hospitals, soup kitchens, etc.) This development marked a distinctive move away from the leftist romantic guerrilla model of the late 1960s and the 1970s, which was secular and less organic. Because they are religious and political communities, they can lace their guerrilla organizations and materiel through the civilian sphere. Guerrilla operations might be planned out in a civilian apartment building. Rockets might be stored in a mosque.

Second, they deployed new tactics such as suicide bombing, sophisticated tank-piercing explosively formed projectiles, and the launching of small rockets on Israeli settlements and nearby towns. Large rockets are vulnerable to the Israeli air force; small rocket launchers are mobile and hard to locate.

Third, the micro-warriors depended on regional-power backing (Syria, Iran) and technical help in the modification of rocket technology and in other areas, such as breaking Israeli codes and gaining the ability to monitor Israeli military communications.

Fourth, they targeted Israel's Achilles heel, its demographic vulnerability. Jewish communities are economically thriving and well-integrated in the industrial democracies, and there are significant pull factors encouraging Israeli emigration. Some Israeli demographers think that if one counts the second generation, there are 900,000 Israelis outside of Israel in 2009. There are as many as 200,000 Jews now in Germany, mostly from the former Soviet Union, who preferred to go there rather than to Israel. During the Second Intifada or Palestinian uprising, in some years Israel's retention rate of new immigrants fell to unheard-of low levels. Some 50 percent of American immigrants to Israel have returned to the U.S., and Israel has lost nearly ten percent of its one million Russian immigrants. All the violence is nervous-making. The micro-wars, the wars of the rockets, are intended to discourage in-migration to Israel by the Russians and other former East Bloc Jews, and to foster out-migration by Israeli Jews, which the Israeli leadership and Zionism view as a dire threat to the character of the Israeli state.

All four dimensions played a part in Hezbollah's success in forcing Israel to end its occupation of south Lebanon in 2000. That forced withdrawal was micro-war's first big success, and a more decisive victory than Egypt gained with conventional arms in 1973. Israel had to give up its claim on a slice of Arab territory without receiving any guarantees of peace or any advantage whatsoever.

All four dimensions were also at play in the summer, 2006 Israeli-Lebanese War. Hezbollah deployed its rockets so effectively that one fourth of Israelis were forced to flee their homes temporarily. Although the earlier Arab-Israeli wars did sometimes send Israelis to bomb shelters, I do not believe that as much of a fourth of the population was ever made to flee their own dwellings before. Hezbollah benefited from the loyalty to it of villagers and townspeople it had helped with clinics and other social services. Hezbollah was able to penetrate Merkava tanks and even hit an Israeli ship at sea. With Iranian and Syrian help, they had cracked Israeli codes and could listen in on their enemy's military communications. The Israelis had no idea where their caves and tunnels were. Israel lost the war with Hezbollah in the sense that the latter proved resilient. Only by ratcheting the struggle up to a total war, in which Israel hit Lebanese infrastructure in general and killed over 1,000 Lebanese, many of them not Hezbollah or even Shiites, was it able to convince the other Lebanese, the United Nations, and the Europeans to intervene to restrain Hezbollah. The Israeli attempt permanently to ethnically cleanse the Shiites from Lebanon's deep south near the Israeli border by the use of cluster bombs failed. The ensuing de facto truce allowed Hezbollah to re-arm with rockets and to gain local legitimacy as part of the Lebanese cabinet, but the European border patrols under the banner of United Nations Interim Force in Lebanon (U.N.IFIL) peacekeepers have forestalled further micro-warfare against Israel for the moment.

Even as the northern front quietened from fall of 2006, despite Israel having achieved few of its war goals, a new micro-war broke out in Gaza. The current Israeli military effort to substantially weaken Hamas in Gaza follows on the contradictions in the policy of the ruling Kadima Party, an offshoot of the far-right wing Likud. Hamas became popular in Gaza in part because of services and in part because of its rejectionism vis-a-vis Israel, and it won the January, 2006, elections for the Palestinian Authority. Because of its rejectionist ideology and its willingness to deploy terrorism and micro-war against Israel, Israel and the United States boycotted the PA under Hamas and strove to undo the results of the election.

Here is *Al Jazeera*'s timeline for what happened next:[1]

June 25, 2006: Palestinian fighters conduct an operation in Israel, killing two Israeli soldiers capturing another, Corporal Gilad Shalit.

June 28, 2006: Israel launches Operation Summer Rains in what it says is an attempt to recover the captured soldier. Israel launches air strikes against of bridges, roads, and the only power station in Gaza. Hundreds of Palestinians are killed during aerial and ground attacks over the following months.

June 29, 2006: Israel captures 64 Hamas officials, including eight Palestinian Authority cabinet ministers and up to twenty members of the Palestinian Legislative Council.

September 8: 2006 U.N. officials say Gaza is at "breaking point" after months of economic sanctions and Israeli attacks. By summer of 2007, the Israelis and the U.S. had managed to sponsor a coup in which the secular Fatah, led by Mahmoud Abbas, took back over the West Bank, and Hamas was confined to Gaza. Hamas pursued the tactic of sending small home-made missiles against nearby Israeli towns, mainly Sderot, emulating what Hezbollah had been doing to the Israeli colony in the occupied Shebaa Farms in 2005-2006. Israel responded primarily by squeezing the Gaza public, denying it enough food, fuel, electricity and services to function healthily, in hopes that it could be made to turn against Hamas. This punishment of the civilian population (half of which consists of children and some large proportion of which does not anyway support Hamas) is illegal in international law and failed in its purpose. Hamas became more entrenched.

Israel's current attack on Gaza is aimed at forestalling an ever more successful micro-war waged by Hamas. Its rockets were inaccurate and thousands fell uselessly in the desert. But they did do some property damage and killed 15 Israelis over 8 years, and they also inflicted psychological blows on the fragile Israeli psyche. The

Israeli leadership saw a danger that Hamas would become ever better entrenched, organically, in Gaza society and gain all the advantages such a social penetration offers, and that monetary aid from Iran and explosives smuggling through tunnels from the Egyptian Sinai would allow them eventually to wage a truly effective micro-war.

The Israeli leadership knew that it could not reply to Hamas's micro-war without engaging in total war on the Gaza population, and that this step would be unpopular with the world's publics. But the Israeli leadership has successfully thumbed its nose at world public opinion so often and so successfully that this sort of consideration does not even enter into their practical calculations, except to the extent that they are careful to do a lot of propaganda for their war effort. Their estimation that they will suffer no practical bad consequences of attacks on civilians is certainly correct in the short to medium term.

The Israel lobbies are wealthy and powerful, and the U.S. congress depends heavily on them for campaign funding.[2] Moreover, the Israeli project and the repression of the Palestinians resonates with the latent white Christian nationalism of many U.S. legislators. If the U.S. legislators voted on the Gaza operation, they would support Israel except for the same ten who objected to the war on Lebanon. The ten are mostly from congressional districts with a lot of Arab-Americans. Israel will suffer no practical sanctions from any government. Egypt and Jordan are afraid of Hamas and are more or less handmaidens of Israeli policy toward Gaza. Syria and Lebanon are weak. Iran, for all the hype it generates, is distant and relatively helpless to intervene. European governments have largely ceded the Palestinian-Israeli issue to the U.S. and Israel. UK Prime Minister Gordon Brown is publicly calling for a ceasefire while secretly supporting Bush's attempts to stop any such thing at the U.N.

The main immediate problem for the Israelis is that simply preventing Hamas from waging an ever more sophisticated micro-war is an extremely short-term and technical objective. It may or may not be achievable by the methods of the current war, which appear so far to be conventional methods. Its outcome is not very material to a settlement of the larger issues.

The big long-term problem Israel has is that its assiduous colonization of the West Bank has made a two-state solution almost impossible, turning it into an Apartheid state. And if you go on practicing Apartheid long enough, that begins to attract boycotts and sanctions. And forestalling a Palestinian state means that likely the Palestinians will all end up Israeli citizens.

I was on the radio recently with John Bolton, former U.S. ambassador to the U.N., and he expressed the hope that Egypt would take back Gaza, and Jordan what is left of the West Bank. You may as well dream of pink unicorns on Venus. It isn't going to happen. The Palestinians are Israel's problem. War on them, circumscribe them, colonize them all you like. They aren't going anywhere, and you can't keep them stateless and virtually enslaved forever, occasionally exterminating some of them as though they were vermin when they make too much trouble. That, sooner or later, will lead to boycotts by rising economic powers and by Europe that could be extremely damaging to Israel's long-term prospects as a state.

It may still be 10 or 20 years in the future. But because of Israel's economic and demographic vulnerabilities, for it to lose the war of global public opinion may ultimately be more consequential than either macro-war or micro-war.

- *Salon*

Notes

[1] "Timeline: Hamas in power," Al Jazeera, April 9, 2007. https://www.aljazeera.com/news/2007/4/9/timeline-hamas-in-power.

[2] John J. Mearsheimer and Stephen M. Walt, *The Israel Lobby and U.S. Foreign Policy* (New York: Farrar, Straus and Giroux, 2008); Kirk Beattie, *Congress and the Shaping of the Middle East* (New York: Seven Stories Press, 2015); Walter Hixson, *Israel's Armor: The Israel Lobby and the First Generation of the Palestine Conflict* (Cambridge University Press, 2019).

6.   Neoconservatism dies in Gaza

January 8, 2009

The Gaza War of 2009 is a final and eloquent testimony to the complete failure of the neoconservative movement in United States foreign policy. For over a decade, the leading figures in this school of thought saw the violent overthrow of Saddam Hussein and the institution of a parliamentary regime in Iraq as the magic solution to all the problems in the Middle East. They envisioned, in the wake of the fall of Baghdad, the moderation of Hezbollah in Lebanon, the overthrow of the Baath Party in Syria and the Khomeinist regime in Iran, the deepening of the alliance with Turkey, the marginalization of Saudi Arabia, a new era of cheap petroleum, and a final resolution of the Israeli-Palestinian conflict on terms favorable to Israel. After eight years in which they strode the globe like colossi, they have left behind a devastated moonscape reminiscent of some post-apocalyptic B movie. As their chief enabler prepares to exit the White House, the only nation they have strengthened is Iran; the only alliance they have deepened is that between Iran and two militant Islamist entities to Israel's north and south, Hezbollah and Hamas.

The neoconservatives first laid out their manifesto in a 1996 paper, "A Clean Break,"[1] written for an obscure think tank in Jerusalem and intended for the eyes of far right-wing Israeli politician Binyamin Netanyahu of the Likud Party, who had just been elected prime minister.[2] They advised Israel to renounce the Oslo peace process and reject the principle of trading land for peace, instead dealing with the Palestinians with an iron fist. They urged Israel to uphold the right of hot pursuit of Palestinian guerrillas and to find alternatives to Yasser Arafat's Fatah for the Palestinian leadership.

They called forth Israeli airstrikes on targets in Syria and rejection of negotiations with Damascus. They foresaw strengthened ties between Israel and its two regional friends, Turkey and Jordan.

They advocated "removing Saddam Hussein from power in Iraq," in part as a way of "rolling back" Syria. In place of the secular, republican tyrant, they fantasized about the restoration of the Hashemite monarchy in Iraq and thought that a Sunni king might help moderate the Shiite Hezbollah in south Lebanon.[3] (Yes.) They barely mentioned Iran, though it appears that their program of expelling Syria from Lebanon and weakening its regime was in part aimed at depriving Iran of its main Arab ally. In a 1999 book called *Tyranny's Ally: America's Failure to Defeat Saddam Hussein*, David Wurmser argued that it was false to fear that installing the Iraqi Shiites in power in Baghdad would strengthen Iran regionally.[4]

The signatories to this fantasy of using brute military power to reshape all of West Asia included some figures who would go on to fill key positions in the Bush administration. Richard Perle, a former assistant secretary of defense under Reagan, became chairman of the influential Defense Policy Board Advisory Committee, a civilian oversight body for the Pentagon. Douglas J. Feith became the undersecretary of defense for planning. David Wurmser first served in Feith's propaganda shop, the Office of Special Plans, which manufactured the case for an American war on Iraq, and then went on to serve with "Scooter" Libby in the office of Vice President Dick Cheney.[5]

The neoconservatives used their well-funded think tanks, including the American Enterprise Institute, the Washington Institute for Near East Policy (WINEP, an organ of the American Israel Public Affairs Committee), the Jewish Institute for National Security Affairs, and the Hudson Institute, among others, to promote this agenda of the conquest of Iraq as a solution of all ills.

They had cheerleaders and allies in major newspapers and political journals. Martin Peretz, owner of the New Republic, took up the neoconservative mantra on Sept. 5, 2002, writing that "The road to Jerusalem more likely leads through Baghdad than the reverse. Once the Palestinians see that the United States will no longer tolerate their hero Saddam Hussein, depressed though they may be, they may also come finally to grasp that Israel is here to stay and that accommodating to this reality is the one thing that can bring them the generous peace they require." (Peretz is a perennial embarrassment to his stable of often excellent journalists in that he occasionally hijacks the magazine for such pronouncements.)

Charles Krauthammer wrote in the *Washington Post* on Feb. 1, 2002, that "Iran is a deadly threat," insofar as it was trying "to establish a terrorist client state by arming and infiltrating Yasser Arafat's Palestine." How would he have us roll it back? "Overthrowing neighboring radical regimes shows the fragility of dictatorship, challenges the mullahs' mandate from heaven and thus encourages disaffected Iranians to rise." What did he mean by neighboring regimes? "First, Afghanistan to the east. Next, Iraq to the west." Leading neoconservative columnist William Kristol delivered himself of a daisy chain of false predictions, inaccurate pronouncements, and political wet dreams about Iraq and the Middle East, as David Corn itemized.[6] "Look, if we free the people of Iraq we will be respected in the Arab world," Kristol said in 2002.

The brutal Israeli war on the population of Gaza is the nail in the coffin of the neoconservative doctrine. Their policies have hardly strengthened ties between Turkey, Israel and the United States, as they had argued. Turkey had a special place in the thinking of figures such as Perle, who lauded it as a secular example for the Muslim world and a close ally of Israel. But in 2002 the Islamically tinged conservative Justice and Development Party (Turkish acronym AKP) of Recep Tayyip Erdogan swept to power and has ruled Turkey ever since. In 2003, the AKP dealt a cruel blow to the hopes of Perle and his colleague Deputy Secretary of Defense Paul Wolfowitz when its members of parliament voted against allowing the U.S. military to invade Iraq through Turkish territory. Erdogan more recently has been a profound disappointment to the Israeli right because of his willingness to talk with Hamas leaders. Hundreds of thousands of

Turks, many of them AKP supporters, have demonstrated in Istanbul against the Israeli bombardment of Gaza.

Erdogan drew anguished Israeli protests when he told an election rally in Ankara that Israel was "perpetrating inhuman actions which would bring it to self-destruction. Allah will sooner or later punish those who transgress the rights of innocents." Turkey has received Hamas leader Khalid Mashal and has worked for an early cease-fire in the current conflict, putting the blame for it on Israel. The right-wing *Jerusalem Post* observed ominously, "Turkey has just taken its seat as a non-permanent member of the Security Council and Ankara pledges to be Hamas's conduit to the United Nations," and urged Israel to recall its ambassador from Ankara.[7]

Massive demonstrations and protests in Jordan calling for the expulsion of the Israeli ambassador over the Israeli military's disregard for civilian life have caused Prime Minister Nader Dahabi to tell the parliament, "Jordan will look into all options, including reconsidering relations with Israel."[8] So much for Feith, Perle and Wurmser's plan to solidify ties between Israel, Turkey and Jordan.

But at least the new Iraqi government will support Israel rather than Hamas now that Saddam Hussein is gone, right? Think again.[9] The Islamic Da'wa Party of Prime Minister Nouri al-Maliki called last week for all Muslim countries to cut off diplomatic relations with Israel and to cease all public and behind-the scenes contacts with it. Large demonstrations have been staged against Israel in Mosul, Baghdad and the holy city of Karbala. The spiritual leader of many of the world's Shiites condemned Israeli aggression in Gaza and said that "mere verbal expressions of condemnation and disapproval" were not enough, calling instead for "practical steps" to break the Israeli blockade and stop the attack.[10] For a fatwa of the chief Shiite authority in Iraq to demand practical steps against Israel is a little noticed but ominous development for the Israelis that could help politicize Shiites even further on this issue.

Wurmser's conviction that Iranian Shiite influence would not spread if the Sunni bulwark were demolished in Mesopotamia has proved as wrongheaded as all the other neoconservative predictions.

The 2005 parliamentary elections were won by the most hard-line, pro-Tehran Shiite fundamentalist parties, who have ruled Iraq ever since. Iran has warm relations with the ruling Islamic Da'wa Party and the Islamic Supreme Council of Iraq, headed by Shiite cleric Abdul Aziz al-Hakim, whose party was founded by Ayatollah Khomeini in 1982.[11]

Iran's influence with Hezbollah in south Lebanon has grown from strength to strength, and was enhanced after Israel's disastrous 2006 war on that country when it sent extensive reconstruction aid.[12] Hezbollah has been able to rearm, and has joined a national unity government that recognizes its militia as a sort of national guard for the south of Lebanon. It gained new allies in Iraq. It had been formed in part by the Islamic Da'wa Party of Iraq, which naturally supports it, as does the large and influential Sadr Movement in Iraqi Shiism. Hezbollah, more popular than ever, was able to get out massive crowds in Beirut to protest Israel's assault on Gaza. And Gaza itself is now viewed by the Israeli establishment as an Iranian beachhead on the Mediterranean, the sort of development that the neoconservatives confidently predicted their policies would forestall.

Krauthammer's conviction that the overthrow of the Taliban in Afghanistan and of Saddam Hussein in Iraq would weaken the Iranian regime was wrong because it exalted ideology over power politics. Baathist Iraq and Sunni fundamentalist Afghanistan had walled Iran in. Destroying them no more weakened Iran than blowing up the Hoover Dam would tame the Colorado River. From an Iranian point of view, an elected Shiite parliament in Iraq morally guided by Ayatollah Sistani does not represent a significant departure from their own form of government, except that Iran is blessed with much greater stability, security and prosperity than its Mesopotamian sibling. Likewise, Syria's regime has been undisturbed by the changes in Iraq, and, recognizing at last that it would have to deal with Bashar al-Assad, the government of outgoing Israeli Prime Minister Ehud Olmert had initiated indirect negotiations with Damascus rather than, as the neoconservatives had insisted, bombarding it.

The neoconservatives made almost as big an error in working to destroy the peace process of the 1990s as they did in fostering a war on Iraq. A two-state solution was not far from being concluded in 2000, but negotiations were abruptly discontinued by the government of Ariel Sharon in spring of 2001 with the encouragement of the Bush administration. (It is not true that the Palestinian side had ceased negotiating, or "walked away," from the Clinton plan, nor is it true that the Israelis had as yet formalized a specific offer in writing.) In the past eight years, Israel has greatly expanded its settlements in the West Bank and around Jerusalem, fencing the Palestinians in with checkpoints, superhighways that cut villages off from one another, and a wall that has stolen from them key agricultural land. Ariel Sharon's 2005 withdrawal from Gaza made no provisions for what would happen next, and in any case Israel continued to control Gaza's borders. This tragic impasse, one phase of which is now playing out with sanguinary relentlessness, was avoidable but for the baneful influence of the neoconservatives and their right-wing allies in the U.S. and Israel.

The neoconservatives had prided themselves on their macho swagger, their rejection of namby-pamby Clintonian multilateralism, and on their bold vision for reshaping the Middle East so that the Israeli and American right would not have to deal with existing reality. In the cold light of day, they look merely petulant and arrogant. The ancient Greek poet Bion said that boys cast stones at frogs in sport, but the frogs die in earnest. The neoconservatives were the boys, and the people of Iraq, Israel, Palestine and Lebanon have been their frogs. The biggest danger facing the United States is that there will be no true "Clean Break" -- that the neoconservatives will somehow find a way to survive the Bush administration and continue to influence American foreign policy.

\-   *Salon*

Notes

[1] "A Clean Break." https://en.wikipedia.org/wiki/A_Clean_Break:_A_New_Strategy_for_Securing_the_Realm

[2] Think tank profile: http://rightweb.irc-online.org/profile/1493.html

[3] "A Clean Break," cited above.

[4] David Wurmser, *Tyranny's Ally: America's Failure to Defeat Saddam Hussein* (Washington, D.C.: AEI Press, 1999).

[5] Juan Cole, "All the Vice President's Men," *Salon*, October 28, 2005. https://www.salon.com/2005/10/28/vice_president_2/

[6] See now David Corn, "The Iraq War: A Personal Remembrance of Dissent," *Mother Jones*, March 21, 2023 https://link.motherjones.com/public/30899589

[7] "Turkey chooses sides," Jerusalem Post, January 5, 2009. https://www.jpost.com/opinion/editorials/turkey-chooses-sides

[8] "Jordan 'reconsidering Israel ties'," Al Jazeeera, January 5, 2009. https://www.aljazeera.com/news/2009/1/5/jordan-reconsidering-israel-ties

[9] "Iraqi cleric urges attacks on U.S. troops over Gaza," *San Diego Union-Tribune*, January 7, 2009. https://www.sandiegouniontribune.com/2009/01/07/iraqi-cleric-urges-attacks-on-us-troops-over-gaza/

[10] Juan Cole's blog on Sistani's fatwa: "Sistani's fatwa on Gaza" - http://www.juancole.com/2008/12/sistanis-fatwa-on-gaza.html

[11] Suzanne Maloney, "How the Iraq War Has Empowered Iran, *Brookings*, March 21, 2008. https://www.brookings.edu/articles/how-the-iraq-war-has-empowered-iran/

[12] Raed Rafei and Borzou Daragahi, "Iran builds a presence in Lebanon," *Los Angeles Times*, August 17, 2007. http://articles.latimes.com/2007/aug/17/world/fg-reconstruction17

7.   The Miseries of Settler Colonialism
January 9, 2009

The United Nations Security Council has now called for a ceasefire in the 2008-9 Israeli war on Gaza, which is probably a sign that it will wind down not so long from now.1 Despite assurances given by outgoing U.S. Secretary of State Condi Rice to her colleagues that the U.S. would sign off on the resolution, in the end the U.S. simply abstained. She appears to have been ordered into this humiliating about-face by President George W. Bush when she made the mistake of phoning him before the vote. The lack of unanimity may weaken the force of the measure, but it nevertheless is a signal that Israel's freedom of movement is now going to be increasingly constrained.

Since the Bush administration is diplomatically challenged, the primary work on the resolution was done by Egypt and Britain, among others.

It was little noticed that China dared break with Washington on the need for a ceasefire even before Thursday's vote. Chinese special envoy for the Middle East Sun Bi Gan said, "The Gaza conflict proves again that military means are not the way out for resolving Palestinian-Israeli disputes. Military force could only bring more hostility and enmity, without giving either side absolute safety."[2] China's explicit position is the early announcement of a Palestinian state, and immediate talks to that end. At the moment, China is not central to Middle Eastern diplomacy. But as it rises as a great power—and given that it is the second largest petroleum importer in the world after the U.S. (and so increasingly close to Saudi Arabia, Sudan and Iran) — it may become a player over time. China is usually so taciturn in these matters that I was surprised to see Sun Bi

Gan speak out forcefully and before he had the cover of a U.N. Security Council resolution. Less surprising is that France and Russia had begun calling for a ceasefire. Both have long been assertive in foreign policy, unlike the Chinese.

Israel's immediate reaction to the ceasefire call was to intensify its bombardment of Gaza.[3] The Israeli leadership thinks of itself as in a race against time to destroy as much of Hamas and its infrastructure as possible before they are forced to implement a ceasefire. The U.S. was earlier helping prolong the campaign, but even the tepid abstention at the U.N., which allowed the ceasefire call to go through, shows an increasing impatience in Washington with Israel's tactics.

I do not know of any analyst of counter-insurgency techniques who thinks Israel's blunt instruments are suited to effectively removing Hamas in anything but the short term. Aside from the argument from inefficacy, there are troubling ethical issues in the way Israel has proceeded.

The best explanation for why Israel is on weak ground in its current operation appeared as a letter to the editor at the *New York Times*. Columnist Nicholas Kristoff had written that "Israel's right to do something doesn't mean it has the right to do anything." A Marine who had recently gotten out of the service and had served in Iraq vehemently agreed with this sentiment: "I am dismayed by the rhetoric from U.S. politicians and pundits to the effect that 'if the U.S. were under rocket attack from Mexico or Canada, we would respond like the Israelis.' This a gross insult to U.S. servicemen; I can assure you that we would NOT respond like the Israelis... Americans do not, I repeat DO NOT, respond to that fire indiscriminately . . ."[4]

I think the writer has a point, though he is probably exaggerating the difference between the U.S. military in Iraq and the Israeli military in Gaza. But it is true that in November 2004 before the Marines went into Fallujah after fundamentalist guerrillas, they allowed and even encouraged civilians to leave the city. Of 200,000 or so, fewer than ten percent chose to stay. In contrast, Israel has the Gazans bottled up and would never consider allowing the civilians to come in Israel to stay in tent cities while Gaza was being bombard. Israel thus insisted that the civilian population remain in the line of fire, in a way that the Marines did not do with regard to Fallujah. Indeed, letting so many people depart was contradictory to the war aim of killing or capturing as many guerrillas as possible, since the smart ones put on civvies and slipped out with the women and children. That was a price the Marine commanders were willing to pay to reduce civilian casualties.

Likewise, in August of 2004 when the U.S. military was battling the Mahdi Army in Najaf, it stopped firing when Grand Ayatollah Sistani sent tens of thousands of civilians walking into the city center. If a Palestinian cleric convinced tens of thousands of civilians to stream into Gaza City and they were in the way of the Israeli war aims, they would likely just be mown down.

Note that I am not alleging, and neither is the letter writer, that Israeli troops are deliberately killing civilians. I am alleging that Israeli troops do not care very much if they happen to kill civilians while getting at what they think of as Hamas targets. They are not doing due diligence to avoid civilian deaths and casualties.

The difference between Israeli military action in Gaza and most U.S. operations in Iraq is not a matter of national character or some other essentialist attribute. It is the difference between imperial occupation for specific purposes and settler colonialism. The Israelis are both an army and a settler movement. The U.S. never considered flooding Iraq with colonists from Alabama and Mississippi.

When threatened by an indigenous population trying to expel it, settler colonialism is vicious. It is after all facing an existential threat. The U.S. can withdraw from Iraq with no dire consequences to the U.S. In 1954-1962, the Algerians claim that the French killed at least half a million, and maybe as much as 800,000 Algerians, out of a population of 11 million. That is between nearly 5 percent and nearly 10 percent! The French military had been enlisted to fight for the interests of the colonists, who were in danger of losing everything. (In the end they did lose almost everything, being forced to return to Europe, or choosing to do so rather than face the prospect of living under independent Algerian rule).

The brutality with which the British put down the Mau-Mau revolt in Kenya in the 1950s is another example of massive human rights violations on behalf of a settler population.

This latest sanguinary episode is a further manifestation of Israel's insecure brand of settler colonialism, in which the lives of the indigenous population are viewed as worthless before the interests of the colonists. The Israelis have not killed on the French scale, but I would argue that they kill, and disregard civilian life, for much the same reasons as the French did in Algeria.

Settler colonialism is unstable in the contemporary world because of the facilities subject populations have for mobilization and resistance. Conflict between colonizer and colonized has only ended in one of three ways: 1) The expulsion of the colonists, as in Algeria; 2) the integration of the colonists into a nation that includes the indigenous population, as happened in South Africa; or 3) the expulsion of the indigenous population, as with the Trail of Tears in the nineteenth-century United States.[6]

Prominent journalist Bob Simon told Charlie Rose that the 'two-state solution' in Israel-Palestine is dead, which is likely correct.[6] He suggested that the most likely outcome is Apartheid. However, I would argue that Apartheid is a phase and is itself an unstable situation, and that only one of the above three outcomes is actually permanent. Given that the Arabs are becoming more technologically sophisticated and wealthier over time, and given their demographic advantage, I do not expect a transferist or trail of tears policy to be implemented or succeed. In the long term, over several decades, I think that either there will be a gradual outflow of Israeli emigrants that leaves Jews a plurality in Israel, or there will eventually be a single state. The other possibilities, of either a century-long Apartheid or another expulsion of Palestinians like that of 1948 seem to me less likely. The Gaza operation is intended to extend the life of an incipient Apartheid. But that is sort of like giving a heart transplant to a man diagnosed with terminal cancer.[7]

- *Informed Comment*

Notes

[1] United Nations calls for ceasefire in Gaza: https://news.un.org/en/story/2009/01/287162

[2] China's stance on the need for a ceasefire: http://lr.china-embassy.gov.cn/eng/majorevents/200901/t20090109_6258624.htm

[3] Israel intensifies bombardment after ceasefire call: http://news.bbc.co.uk/2/hi/middle_east/7819371.stm

[4] Marine's letter agreeing with Nicholas Kristoff on Israel's military conduct: http://community.nytimes.com/article/comments/2009/01/08/opinion/08kristof.html?permid=141#comment141

[5] Ann Byers, *The Trail of Tears: A Primary Source History of the Forced Relocation of the Cherokee Nation* (New York: The Rosen Publishing Group, 2004).

[6] Bob Simon on the 'two-state solution' being dead: https://mondoweiss.net/2009/01/heres-bob-simon-on-charlie-rose/

[7] See now also Sara Roy, *Unsilencing Gaza: Reflections on Resistance* (London: Pluto Press, 2021), 67-73 and Baconi, *Hamas Contained*, 196-207.

PART 2

The Creepy Blockade

In 2010-2012, the full implications of the Israeli blockade on the civilians of Gaza were beginning to become clear. As I note below, the release of thousands of U.S. State Department cables by Wikileaks included a few that shed loads of illumination on Israeli policy, which was to put the Palestinians of Gaza on a "diet" that left them no body fat but would not produce obvious signs of malnutrition. As I pointed out at the time, the likelihood was that the Israeli officials in charge of this creepy policy missed their mark, such that there were actually signs of anemia in Gaza. Anyway, there was an enormous amount of misery, with among the highest rates of unemployment in the world and shortages of essential medications. It seemed clear to me that these Israeli policies devastated the Gaza middle classes and made people dependent on the Hamas-run public sector, and so strengthened the party's hands. The experiment in limiting the nutrition of an entire people to the minimum required calories also, however, struck me as morally reprehensible and as creepy. It reminded me of those totalitarian regimes that did experiments on living human beings. In 2010, aid activists to attempt to mount a seaborne mission to bring relief to Palestinian civilians, an effort that was met with deadly force by Israeli commandos, who imprisoned hundreds of them. The Israeli blockade of Gaza and the attack on the aid flotilla was declared illegal by the U.N., which also demanded that the activists be released.

In late 2012, we saw another brief Israeli air campaign against the Strip, more "mowing the grass." I pointed to its indiscriminate character and deleterious effects on health, with 39 aid organizations pointing out that since Israel kept Gaza on the edge of hunger and of public health disasters as a matter of course, even a brief indiscriminate military campaign could result in a disaster.

Even as this humanitarian disaster unfolded, behind the scenes the Palestine Authority, increasingly styling itself the "State of Palestine," pulled off a diplomatic and legal coup during Israel's brief "Operation Pillar of Defense" operation, when Palestine succeeded in being recognized by the U.N. General Assembly as a non-member observer state at the United Nations, a status enjoyed by the Vatican. The acceptance, vigorously opposed by the United States, gave Palestine access to positions on U.N. committees and implicitly made an argument for more countries to recognize it as a state. It also gave a firmer platform to the Palestinian civil society campaign for Boycott, Divestment and Sanctions with regard to Israel, especially in Europe, where international law is held in greater respect than in the United States.

8. Historic UNSC

Condemnation of Israel

June 1, 2010

In a rare public denunciation of Israel, the United Nations Security Council on Monday condemned the Israeli raid on the Gaza aid flotilla and deplored the loss of innocent life that attended it.[1] The world body insisted that Israel immediately release the hundreds of humanitarians it had taken captive and demanded that it also let their ships go. The UNSC also instructed Israel to lift its blockade of the Gaza Strip, calling the siege "not sustainable." Although the statement was weaker than the text urged by Turkey and the Arab world,[2] it was brutal compared to the anodyne language usually insisted upon by Washington when it comes to Israel.

This development is head-spinning in its implications. The United States almost never allows UNSC resolutions condemning Israel to go forward (though this text was admittedly a presidential statement rather than a full resolution). But here it is clear that President Barack Obama instructed his ambassador to the U.N. to join in the condemnation of the Israeli "acts." Since Turkey is currently a non-permanent member of the UNSC and led the charge on the condemnation of Israel, it is possible that the U.S. felt it had to trade horses with Ankara if it has any chance of still getting a UNSC resolution tightening sanctions on Iran (a step that Turkey opposes, as does Brazil, though neither has a veto). It is also possible that Israel's rash attack has sabotaged the Obama administration's push for increased U.N. sanctions on Iran, hardening opposition to an Israel-driven policy toward Tehran.

The U.N. Assistant Secretary General for Political Affairs, Argentina's Oscar Fernandez-Taranco, gave us some idea of the UNSC's thinking when he called on Israel on Monday to end its "counterproductive" and "unacceptable" blockade of the Gaza Strip.[3] He pointed out that the fiasco around the Israeli commando attack on the civilian aid flotilla would not have occurred had there been no blockade in the first place. The demand that Israel give up the siege of Gaza was repeated by the United Kingdom and by Brazil. Nick Clegg, the new LibDem deputy prime minister of the UK, has long been a vocal critic of Israeli policies toward the Palestinian West Bank and Gaza.

As long as Israel, therefore, continues its blockade of the general Gaza population, it is no less in contravention of the United Nations Security Council instructions than Saddam Hussein was with regard to his weapons programs in the early 1990s.

While gathering the details of how some humanitarian aid activists were killed and dozens were wounded by Israeli soldiers is important, above all for the sake of justice toward the idealistic persons mown down, it is far more important that the episode produce an end to the lockdown of the 1.5 million Gazans, who have been placed by the Israeli government in a sort of open-air penitentiary.

Contrary to the assertions of far-right Israeli foreign minister Avigdor Lieberman, the Palestinians of Gaza, stripped of any citizenship and lacking any basic human rights, face continual shortages of medicine, medical equipment, electricity and even of food.[4] They face crushing poverty and unemployment, along with inadequate hospitals. Many are still homeless after the Israelis destroyed their homes in the Gaza War, and they are being denied cement for rebuilding. They are cut off from the market for their goods in Egypt, Jordan and the rest of the Arab world. As Uri Avnery points out, Israel pledged in the Oslo accords 18 years ago to allow a deep-water port for Gaza on the Mediterranean.[5] Instead, it is assaulting even small aid vessels attempting to land at the pitiful excuse for a port.

The blockade is shameful. It is a gross violation of the international law governing the treatment of Occupied populations. And now the Security Council has roundly condemned it and insisted that it be lifted.

The Israeli peace organization, Gush Shalom, demonstrated in front of the detention center where the aid activists were being held.[6]

There are no new details of the Israeli assault on the humanitarian aid flotilla early Monday morning, largely because the 480 eyewitnesses had been sequestered by the Israelis. Some, including an 81-year-old former U.S. ambassador, a Turkish woman with a baby, and a former U.S. navy sailor who had been on the U.S.S. Liberty when the Israelis attacked it in 1967, are now trickling home.[7] The whereabouts and condition of many others is unconfirmed, including European parliamentarians, Nobelists, and Swedish mystery writer Henning Mankell (whose anti-imperialist novel *The Man from Beijing* I just read and enjoyed).[8]

The incident could have implications for the future relationship of Israel to the European Union. Irish Minister of Foreign Affairs Micheal Martin hinted that Dublin might go so far as to expel the Israeli ambassador, thus cutting off diplomatic relations with Tel Aviv. Some 8 Irish citizens are among Israel's prisoners, and one of these humanitarians, Fiachra O'Luain, is said by his father to have been wounded by Israeli gunplay. Martin thundered, "These citizens did not enter Israel illegally -- they were essentially kidnapped from international waters, taken into Israel and are being asked to sign documents saying they entered illegally."[8]

The other big casualty of the Israeli raid may well be the special relationship between Turkey and Israel, as the BBC says. Turkish Prime Minister Recep Tayyip Erdogan condemned the raid as "state terrorism."[10]

In late May 2010, thousands of demonstrators also gathered to chant against Israel in Baghdad, inspired by Shiite cleric Muqtada al-Sadr. Interior Minister Jawad Bulani, serving in the government of Prime Minister Nuri al-Maliki, said, "We want to send a message to the Palestinians to let them know they are not alone and that the

Iraqis are with them . . . What is going on is a vicious crime. The international community must condemn it and take responsible action against them. This is the stand of all Iraqis, officially and publically."[11]

Historians may look back on the Marmara raid as the moment a new order began emerging in the Middle East, grouping Turkey with Iran, Syria, Iraq and Palestine rather than with Washington and Tel Aviv. *Al Jazeera* English has video on the world condemnation of the Marmara raid.[12]

The enforced silence of the flotilla activists, in Israeli custody, has allowed Israeli spokesmen to shape the narrative of events for American news media. Former CIA analyst Ray Close blames President Obama for not being tougher with Israeli PM Binyamin Netanyahu to begin with, arguing that coddling the Likud leader led to this atrocity. As Jonathan Cook points out, the Israeli authorities have still not announced a definitive list of those killed and wounded by their commandos.[13]

In response to Israeli official pronouncements, Amnesty International said, "Israel says its forces acted in self-defence, alleging that they were attacked by protestors, but it begs credibility that the level of lethal force used by Israeli troops could have been justified. It appears to have been out of all proportion to any threat posed."[14]

Raw video posted to YouTube from the initial phase of the Israeli boarding of the Turkish vessel, *Mavi Marmara* demonstrates that as the Israeli commandos approached the ship, they were laying down suppressive fire and at that point killed two individuals aboard the ship. Even after the ship ran up a white flag, the Israelis continued to use live ammunition along with stun grenades and tear gas. See Stephen C. Webster's analysis of this video of the boarding.[15]

If the crew and passengers of the *Mavi Marmara* were coming under fire and had taken casualties in the initial phase of the Israeli approach, that horror would help explain why some actively resisted the boarding and that in turn would explain the contextless snippet of video released by the Israeli army of Israeli commandos being fought as they commandeered the vessel. If the passengers thought the

Israeli military had murderous intentions toward them, some would obviously attempt to forestall the boarding. It is also possible that there were no deaths on the other ships because they were boarded later and after the Israeli helicopter gunship crews had learned that suppressive fire during the initial approach was unnecessary and counterproductive, and so they ceased that tactic.

It is unclear why the commandos behaved in this way with regard to the Mavi Marmara in the first place, but it is possible that they believed their own propaganda. The Turkish aid ships were supported by a Muslim fundamentalist charity in Turkey, IHH, that has been accused of being sympathetic to the Muslim Brotherhood and to Hamas, and in Israeli eyes that orientation would make them terrorists. So perhaps the commandos assumed they were boarding a ship full of Hamas operatives. It was just idealistic humanitarians. But even they could be provoked to active resistance if they thought they were about to be shot down.

It is a sign of to what depths the pride of the Israeli military has fallen that it is complaining of attempts to "lynch" its soldiers (none of whom was killed, while [nine] humanitarian aid workers appear to be dead).[16] This is the Israeli army of the 1967 Six Days War and of Entebbe? They were in danger of being lynched as they boarded a small civilian vessel? Of course, they could have avoided this menace by simply not being uninvited on a ship in international waters. And, it is pretty obvious who is actually being lynched-- the people of Gaza and anyone who objects to them being half-starved by the Israeli blockade.[17]

- *Informed Comment*

Notes

[1] United Nations Security Council condemns Israeli raid: http://www.cnn.com/2010/WORLD/meast/06/01/gaza.raid.resolution/?

hpt=Sbin

[2] Security Council statement weaker than Turkey, Arab world's text: http://www.hurriyet.com.tr/dunya/14897147.asp?gid=373

[3] U.N. Assistant Secretary General for Political Affairs calls on Israel to end Gaza blockade: http://www.hindustantimes.com/rssfeed/americas/U.N.-asks-Israel-to-end-blockade-on-Gaza/Article1-551447.aspx

[4] Avigdor Lieberman's assertions: http://communities.canada.com/shareit/blogs/reality/archive/2010/05/31/more-than-10-dead-as-israeli-navy-storms-gaza-aid-ship_.aspx

[5] Uri Avnery on Israel's 18-year old pledge for deep water port for Gaza: http://www.americanchronicle.com/articles/yb/145624394

[6] Gush Shalom protest: http://www.americanchronicle.com/articles/yb/145624394

[7] Eyewitnesses being sequestered by Israelis after aid flotilla assault: http://www.irishexaminer.com/breakingnews/world/former-us-ambassador-on-gaza-aid-ship-459908.html

[8] Henning Mankell, *The Man from Beijing*, trans. from the Swedish by Laurie Thompson (New York: Knopf, 2010).

[9] Irish possible diplomatic actions: http://www.independent.ie/world-news/middle-east/wave-of-fury-erupts-over-israeli-killings-2202006.html

[10] Turkish PM Erdogan condemns raid as "state terrorism": http://www.irishtimes.com/newspaper/breaking/2010/0531/breaking25.html

[11] Demonstrations in Baghdad against Israel: http://www.reuters.com/article/idU.S.TRE64U3C520100531

[12] Aljazeera English video on global condemnation of Marmara raid: http://www.youtube.com/watch?v=Scf5K0ZHdxE

[13] Israeli narrative of events: http://www.consortiumnews.com/2010/060110a.html

[14] Amnesty International's response to Israeli official statements: http://www.uscatholic.org/blog/2010/05/view-mavi-marmara

[15] Stephen C. Webster's analysis of the boarding video: http://rawstory.com/rs/2010/0531/raw-video-reporter-claims-israelis-fired-activists-boarding-ship/

[16] In my original text, based on early reports, I mentioned 16 dead, but it later transpired that the Israeli military had killed nine.

[17] For a retrospective on this episode see Moustafa Bayoumi, ed., *Midnight on the Mavi Marmara: The Attack on the Gaza Freedom Flotilla and How It Changed the Course of the Israel/Palestine Conflict* (Chicago: Haymarket Books, 2010), in which I have a chapter; and Finkelstein, *Gaza*, 189-276.

9.   Wikileaks: Israel Plans Total War on Lebanon, Gaza

January 2, 2011

The Norwegian newspaper Aftenposten has summarized an Israeli military briefing by Israeli Chief of Staff Gen. Gabi Ashkenazi of a U.S. congressional delegation a little over a year ago and concludes that "The memo on the talks between Ashkenazi and Congressman Ike Skelton, as well as numerous other documents from the same period of time, to which Aftenposten has gained access, leave a clear message: The Israeli military is forging ahead at full speed with preparations for a new war in the Middle East."

This war preparation is serious and specific, according to the paper, and clearly is not just a matter of vague contingency planning.

The paper says that U.S. cables quote Ashkenazi telling the U.S. congressmen, "I'm preparing the Israeli army for a major war, since it is easier to scale down to a smaller operation than to do the opposite."

The general's plans are driven by fear of growing stockpiles of rockets in Hamas-controlled Gaza and in Hezbollah-controlled Southern Lebanon, the likely theaters of the planned major new war. Ashkenazi does not seem capable of considering that, given a number of Israeli invasions and occupations of those regions, the rockets may be primarily defensive.

Ashkenazi told the visiting delegation that Israeli unmanned drones had had great success in identifying rocket emplacements in southern Lebanon, and that it had been aided in this endeavor by the U.S. National Security Agency, which spies on communications.

The new, major war will be a total war on civilians, Ashkenazi boasted: "In the next war Israel cannot accept any restrictions on warfare in urban areas." (*I den neste krigen kan Israel ikke godta noen restriksjoner på krigføring i byområder* in Norwegian . . .) Mind you, the civilian deaths deriving from this massive and unrestricted bombing campaign on targets in the midst of civilian urban populations will be branded "a mistake." But planning to bomb civilian areas with foreknowledge that you will thereby kill large numbers of civilians is a war crime.

Ashkenazi also admitted to then Rep. Kirsten Gillibrand (D-NY) that Hamas is not in control of even more radical groups, which had infiltrated cells into Hamas itself, and which had rocket-making capabilities. In public, Israeli officials routinely demonize Hamas for every rocket fired from the lawless, besieged territory of Gaza, but here in private Ashkenazi was admitting the opposite. He even admitted that Israeli intelligence had no means to distinguish the even-more-radical from the merely Hamas.

Other State Department documents on the same theme say that last year this time Hezbollah had about 20,000 rockets, some of which can now reach Tel Aviv, and that the Shiite militia will attempt to stretch out its supplies for a two-month-long war and would try to lob about 100 rockets at Tel Aviv per day.

In the 2006 Israeli war on Lebanon, one fourth of the Israeli population was be forced to move house. It will be more this time, and for longer.

The memos reveal that none of the goals of Israel's 2006 war on Lebanon and its 2008-9 war on little Gaza were achieved, and that both Hamas and Hezbollah have effectively re-armed. What makes Ashkenazi think things would be different this time? Israel hawks have doomed themselves to the particular hell of Sisyphus, forced to roll the same stone up the hill over and over again with no hope of ever balancing it on the summit.

You know, Israel could have a peace treaty with Syria and Lebanon tomorrow by giving back the Golan Heights and the Shebaa

Farms, and by accepting a two-state solution. Instead, its Dr. Strangeloves are planning out massive bombings of areas thick with innocent civilians and willing to subject Tel Aviv to two months' worth of rocket fire.

Nor will the United States be held harmless from the blowback in the region caused by another Israeli war of aggression. Before September 11, Israel hawks used to make fun of Americans who warned that eventually there would be hell to pay for the Israeli strangulation of the Palestinians.[1] And, imagine what a war would do to gasoline prices and to the world economy. My deepest fear is that U.S. support for Israeli militarism, and the terrorism that support inevitably engenders, will be what finally finishes off the civil liberties enshrined in the American Constitution.

Note

1. Juan Cole, "Jerusalem and Terrorism," *Informed Comment*, July 11, 2005. https://www.juancole.com/2005/07/jerusalem-and-terrorism-ariel-sharon.html

10.   Wikileaks: Israelis "Intend to Keep the Gazan Economy on the Brink of Collapse"

January 5, 2011

The Norwegian newspaper Aftenpost has released a March, 2008, U.S. embassy cable describing the Israeli blockade and siege of Occupied Gaza as an attempt to reduce the society to the lowest possible level of functioning without provoking a "humanitarian crisis" (presumably mass starvation).[1]

"Israeli officials have confirmed to Embassy officials on multiple occasions that they intend to keep the Gazan economy functioning at the lowest level possible consistent with avoiding a humanitarian crisis."

And, with regard to taking money out of circulation in Gaza, a deflationary policy used as a tool of oppression:

"As part of their overall embargo plan against Gaza, Israeli officials have confirmed to econoffs on multiple occasions that they intend to keep the Gazan economy on the brink of collapse without quite pushing it over the edge."

It seems to me the Israeli right-wingers missed their mark, since 55 percent of Palestinians in Gaza are food-insecure and 10 percent of children show signs of stunting from malnutrition.[2] I'd call that a humanitarian crisis. What the despicable Israeli officials meant by their phrase, of course, is that a mass die-off should be avoided that would bring to bear world pressure to abandon this criminal policy. The Israeli blockade of Gaza is illegal in international law and violates explicit United Nations Security Council resolutions.[3] (Wasn't defying UNSC resolutions given as a reason by the American Right for invading and overthrowing the Iraqi government?)

Although the mainstream media is putting the blockade in the past tense ("Israel intended"), it is still very much being pursued. Virtually no Palestinian-made goods are allowed to be exported. A very slight easing of imports has been permitted, and Egypt is letting in some volunteer aid, as with the recent Asian flotilla.[4] You wouldn't want your own child to live as Palestinian children are mostly living in today's Gaza.

This Israeli policy also violates the Fourth Geneva Convention of 1949 on the treatment of populations in Occupied Territories (yes, Israel still occupies Gaza even though it is not actively colonizing it any more):

> Art. 55. To the fullest extent of the means available to it, the Occupying Power has the duty of ensuring the food and medical supplies of the population; it should, in particular, bring in the necessary foodstuffs, medical stores and other articles if the resources of the occupied territory are inadequate... Art. 59. If the whole or part of the population of an occupied territory is inadequately supplied, the Occupying Power shall agree to relief schemes on behalf of the said population, and shall facilitate them by all the means at its disposal. Such schemes, which may be undertaken either by States or by impartial humanitarian organizations such as the International Committee of the Red Cross, shall consist, in particular, of the provision of consignments of foodstuffs, medical supplies and clothing. All Contracting Parties shall permit the free passage of these consignments and shall guarantee their protection.[5]

The Convention did not envisage a situation where the population of the occupied territory is deliberately left "inadequately supplied" by the Occupying Power, apparently not able to imagine the full sadism of the Likud Party. Israel is in violation of both the Geneva Convention of 1949 (passed to prevent a repeat of the kinds of policies toward occupied populations pursued by the Axis Powers) and of the Hague Convention of 1907 on the treatment of populations in occupied territories. The Israeli officials who told the U.S. embassy what they were doing are war criminals. While the cable is not sympathetic to these Israeli policies, neither does it note their criminal nature.

By the way, Art. 59 clearly vindicates the Turkish aid flotilla to Gaza of last May. I believe you will find that no American media ever cited it in that regard, since the United States increasingly resembles a mob rather than a Republic.

The cable reveals that the Israelis deliberately starved the Fatah-dominated Palestine Authority of funds in Gaza, preventing them from paying their loyalists, and so inevitably strengthened Hamas rule. These officials are not only sadists, keeping children on the brink of starvation, but are also, like, terminally stupid, to boot.

Another document shows that even before the blockade, in 2006, corrupt Israeli officials were making money off the misery of the Palestinians in Gaza by insisting on large bribes to let in American goods past the checkpoint.[6] There must be a special place in hell . . .

Notes

[1] URL to the released U.S. embassy cable on the Norwegian newspaper Aftenpost:
http://www.aftenposten.no/spesial/wikileaksdokumenter/article3972840.ece; also reprinted at https://www.juancole.com/2011/01/wikileaks-israelis-intend-to-keep-the-gazan-economy-on-the-brink-of-collapse.html

[2] URL describing malnutrition among children in Gaza:
https://www.juancole.com/2009/08/no-health-reform-for-gaza-but-death.html

[3] URL of UNSC condemnation of Israel and of Gaza blockade:
https://www.juancole.com/2010/06/historic-unsc-condemnation-of-

israel-and-of-gaza-blockade-world-body-demands-release-of-aid-activists-ships.html

[4] URL to the news about the Asian flotilla: http://www.google.com/hostednews/afp/article/ALeqM5ixOMcCW4EKCKHkuFnk0XXyXvc3Sg?docId=CNG.813cab6bb3cc5a132ebd8bd97f225bb3.2f1

[5] URL to the Fourth Geneva Convention of 1949: http://www.icrc.org/ihl.nsf/385ec082b509e76c41256739003e636d/6756482d86146898c125641e004aa3c5

[6] URL to another document regarding corrupt Israeli officials: http://www.aftenposten.no/spesial/wikileaksdokumenter/article3974066.ece

11. Gaza Unemployment among Worst in World: U.N.

June 14, 2011

The illegal Israeli blockade of little Palestinian Gaza (pop. 1.5 million in 2011) has produced a situation in which real income has fallen by a third in the past five years. This according to a new report by the United Nations Relief and Works Agency.[1] The bad economy, caused by an Israeli policy of blocking all exports from Gaza and severely limiting imports, has an especially severe impact on refugee families who had been ethnically cleansed by Israelis from what is now Israel in 1948, who make up about 70 percent of the Gaza population.[2] *Al Jazeera English* did a video report on the report.[3]

The Gaza Strip's stock of medicine has also fallen to dangerously low levels. *Al Jazeera English* reports that: "Dr Basim Naim, the minister of health in the de facto government of Gaza, says 178 types of necessary medications are at near zero balance in stock. He says more than 190 types of medicine in stock are either expired or are close to their expiry date, which has forced his administration to postpone several medical operations."[4]

Israeli officials say the blockade targets arms imports, but in fact it targets the Palestinians of Gaza in toto. Why ban all exports of things produced in Gaza if the aim is to stop arms imports? Why did they ban import of chocolate if that was the aim? Wikileaks State Department cables reveal that Israeli officials have admitted privately that their goal in Gaza is to make Palestinians there live on the absolute edge, without tipping the situation over into clear humanitarian disaster.

I heard a BBC reporter point out that private sector employment has fallen, but public sector employment numbers are not so dire. Since Hamas controls the public sector, Israeli policy is essentially pushing the Gaza population into their arms.

The victory in Sunday's election of the Justice and Development Party in Turkey was proclaimed by Prime Minister Tayyip Erdogan as a "victory for Gaza." Turkey opposes the blockade and a Turkish aid flotilla was attacked by Israeli commandos last year this time with lethal force, leaving nine aid workers dead (including one American). There are plans for more aid convoys. A U.N. commission found that the Israeli attack on the Mavi Marmara was illegal in international law, as is the blockade of the civilian population in general.[5]

The new transitional government in Egypt has slightly opened the Rafah border crossing, but mainly for certain categories of Gaza residents who need to travel outside the Strip. The new Foreign Minister (and incoming head of the Arab League) Nabil Alaraby has called the Israeli blockade 'disgusting," which is about the least harsh thing a civilized person could say about it. Israel has been in violation of international law on this issue for so long and so egregiously that I think a case could be made that its occupation of Palestinian territory is by now itself illegal.

Notes

[1] U.N.RWA report: http://www.unrwa.org/userfiles/201106083557.pdf

[2] URL to the Guardian article on U.N.RWA report and Gaza unemployment: https://www.theguardian.com/world/view-from-jerusalem-with-harriet-sherwood/2011/jun/15/gaza-palestinian-territories

[3] Aljazeera English video report: http://youtu.be/FQONfQmoofs

[4] Aljazeera article on Gaza's dangerously low medicine stock: https://www.aljazeera.com/features/2011/6/12/gazas-hospital-stock-running-on-near-empty.

[5] U.N. commission finding on the Mavi Marmara attack:
https://digitallibrary.un.org/record/720841?ln=en&v=pdf

12. Creepy Israeli Planning for Palestinian Food Insecurity in Gaza Revealed

October 18, 2012

An Israeli human rights organization, Gisha, sued in Israeli courts to force the release of a planning document for "putting the Palestinians on a diet" without risking the bad press of mass starvation, and the courts concurred. The document, produced by the Israeli army, appears to be a calculation of how to make sure, despite the Israeli blockade, that Palestinians got an average of 2279 calories a day, the basic need. But by planning on limiting the calories in that way, the Israeli military was actually plotting to keep Palestinians in Gaza (half of them children) permanently on the brink of malnutrition, what health professionals call "food insecurity". And, it was foreseeable that sometimes they would slip into malnutrition, since not as many trucks were always let in every day as the Israeli army recommended (106 were recommended, but it was often less in the period 2007-2010).

Planning for keeping people on the edge is nearly as bad as planning actually to starve them. A prudent person would know that a blockade is a blunt enough instrument, with shipments up and down in a given week, that such a policy would from time to time produce real misery. Were any physicians involved? They should be boycotted by the international community.

And, the Israeli army's way of trying to minimize the document must be the worst example of propaganda in history! They are saying that the plan was produced but not consulted. But this document aimed at making sure just enough trucks got in to keep people on the edge. If the government didn't consult it, does that mean it did not care if the food shipments slipped below the basic calorie allowance? Wouldn't it have been better if they had known about the 106-truck recommendation?

The food blockade had real effects. About ten percent of Palestinian children in Gaza under 5 have had their growth stunted by malnutrition.[1] A recent report by Save the Children and Medical Aid for Palestinians found that, in addition, anemia is widespread, affecting over two-thirds of infants, 58.6 percent of schoolchildren, and over a third of pregnant mothers.[2]

I mean, do not those figures make you want to do something for those mothers and children? Wouldn't they melt anyone's heart?

Although, under international pressure, the Israeli government eased its blockade slightly in 2010, and foodstuffs are no longer interdicted, it still limits imports into Gaza, and its wide-ranging ban on exports has thrown Palestinians into unemployment at Depression levels, imperiling their ability to afford food even when it is available.

A U.N. Report out last month predicts that if Israel does not change its policies toward Gaza, the strip will be uninhabitable by 2020, when the population will likely be 2.1 million (think Houston). The deterioration of the water, and the sharp downward mobility of the Palestinians, are only some of the problems the territory will face.[3]

Note that the Israeli government did not voluntarily cease its policy of keeping Palestinians on a diet in 2010. It was forced to by Turkish and European aid activists, and nine people, one an American citizen, were martyred for this change when Israeli commandos illegally boarded a civilian, unarmed ship in international waters and shot it up. In any case, there are other ways to starve out the people of Gaza than bluntly preventing food from coming in. Nobel-prize-winning economist Amartya Sen showed that the real cause of famines is not lack of food but that the price of the food rises above the ability of people to pay for it. By keeping Gaza on the edge of economic collapse, the Likud government has continued the food blockade by other means.

The Israeli members of Gisha, who are Mensches, care that their government is contributing in a systematic and deliberate way to damaging children's health because of the way their parents voted in 2006! And they want to embarrass it into ceasing this illegal and inhumane treatment of people who are under Israeli military Occupation. Al Jazeera English did a video report, valuable because unlike CNN or other Western cable news channels, it actually interviews the Palestinians affected.[4]

It is precisely because the Israeli blockade of Palestinian non-combatants in Gaza is considered creepy and evil not just by me but by any ethical person that a number of European members of parliament have boarded the aid ship Estelle and will make another attempt to deliver food and other aid to Gaza, despite Israeli threats.[5]

The blockade has medical as well as nutritional bad effects. Palestinians in Gaza have to get Israeli permission (!) to leave the strip for medical care. Palestinian hospitals, having been starved of funds and materiel by Israel, are dilapidated. A study published this month in *The Lancet* found that ten percent of such requests were delayed or rejected by Israeli authorities (the rejection or delay rate for the Palestinian territories over all is nearly a fifth). Israel's delays murdered 6 Palestinians in Gaza last year, as surely as though they had been taken out and shot twice behind the ear. How would you like to have to apply to an arbitrary foreign government for permission to go next door to a neighboring country for medical care?

The *Lancet* article says,

> In 2011, 1082 (10%) of 10,560 applicants in the Gaza Strip had their access permits denied or delayed, with no reason given, and 197 (2%) were called for security interview. Patients aged 18–40 years had the highest rate of denied or delayed permits. Tracer interviews with Gazan families of patients who had their permits denied or delayed showed that six patients died while waiting for the permits.[6]

From 2007, the Israeli government had decided to wage economic and nutritional warfare against the Palestinians.

Obviously, allowing them to become malnourished would raise an outcry even in an international community that typically allows Israel's settler colonialism to get away with murder toward the Palestinians. So, the policy was to keep the Palestinians "food insecure." That is, they wouldn't be starved, but they'd be one step away from starving -- if they lost a source of income, for instance.

Wikileaks revealed a U.S. embassy cable that confirmed, "As part of their overall embargo plan against Gaza, Israeli officials have confirmed to [U.S. embassy economic officers] on multiple occasions that they intend to keep the Gazan economy on the brink of collapse without quite pushing it over the edge . . ."[7] Note that the cowardly U.S. government went along with this policy of ruining the lives of civilian non-combatants as a way of trying to defeat the Hamas party-militia (five years later, I think we can safely pronounce the policy a failure).

The most horrible thing is that the Israelis, and the international community, have no long-term plans for Gaza. There is no light at the end of the tunnel. There is no vision for how this blockade of innocents will ever end. People pay lip service to a "two state solution," but everyone knows that Israel won't allow the Palestinians to have a state! Although Qatar has just announced a multi-million-dollar aid program, it remains to be seen whether Israel will allow it. And, aid is secondary to the dignity of being citizens in a state, which is what Palestinians really need (the economic efflorescence would come from that statehood better than from outside charity). The people of Gaza are apparently to be kept in a large out-door concentration camp forever. Unless the world cares enough to rescue them from that fate.

- *Informed Comment*

Notes

[1] About ten percent of Palestinian children in Gaza under 5 have had their growth stunted by malnutrition: http://www.ibtimes.com/israels-blockade-gaza-puts-palestinian-childrens-health-risk-report-702821

[2] A report by Save the Children and Medical Aid for Palestinians on widespread anemia in Gaza: https://www.slideshare.net/slideshow/gaza-health-report/13363928

[3] U.N. Report predicts Gaza uninhabitable by 2020: http://www.unrwa.org/etemplate.php?id=1423

[4] Aljazeera English video report interviewing Palestinians affected by blockade: http://youtu.be/DbL_ViP8dks

[5] European members of parliament have boarded the aid ship Estelle to attempt to deliver aid to Gaza: http://www.anphoblacht.com/contents/22352

[6] Study published in *The Lancet* on Palestinians in Gaza denied or delayed permits for medical care: http://www.thelancet.com/health-in-the-occupied-palestinian-territory-2012

[7] Wikileaks U.S. embassy cable on Israeli embargo plan against Gaza: http://www.aftenposten.no/spesial/wikileaksdokumenter/article3972840.ece

13.   Gaza's Health Crisis and Israel's Crimes Against Humanity

November 20, 2012

Israeli air strikes in its "Operation Pillar of Defense" for the past 6 days have killed over 100 Palestinians in Gaza, many of them women and children; one strike deliberately targeted a media building that the Israeli government knew to house journalists.[1] Medics announced Monday that they are running out of key medicines (Gaza is under Israeli blockade). Military strikes are also interfering in the delivery of medical and other aid by international organizations in the Strip.

An Arabic-language report says that Israeli warplanes targeted the Jordanian field hospital late on Monday.[2] I have not been able to find confirmation for this report, but if it is true, and deliberate, it would be a war crime. A World Health Organization spokesman reported Monday that injured individuals showing up at Gaza hospitals had "dramatically increased in the last 24 hours."[3] Some 700 have come to hospital, 252 of them children. Nurses at Shifa Hospital, who work 12-hour shifts, say that the injuries they are seeing are unprecedented. One said, "It's very hard now, with many injured people coming every hour. Women and children outnumbered men, especially with the new wave [of attacks] targeting houses and civilian buildings." In a statement, the World Health Organization worried about lack of medicine: "Many of the drugs at zero stock are lifesaving. Gaza hospitals are now having to deal with the growing number of casualties with severely depleted medical supplies."

Since small homemade rockets coming out of Gaza in 2012 had killed no Israelis before the Israeli Air Force started bombing the Gaza Strip last week, there is no doubt that Israel is engaged in a disproportionate use of force and a reckless disregard for the well-being of civilian non-combatants in its own occupied territory. Israeli army spokesmen claim they are precisely targeting only Hamas paramilitary personnel and blame Hamas for hiding among non-combatants. However, it is the Occupying power's responsibility to do due diligence in ensuring the safety of the occupied population, and if Israeli pilots do not have a clear shot at an enemy combatant, they simply should not take it.[4]

These hostilities are deepening a longstanding crisis in Gaza health care that has resulted from deliberate Israeli policies. The Reuters Foundation's Trust.org reported that 39 aid organizations are warning of humanitarian disaster in Gaza if there is no ceasefire soon. Nishant Pandey, director of Oxfam Country is quoted as saying: "We urgently need to enforce a ceasefire. The present conflict threatens to perpetuate and worsen the humanitarian impact on Palestinian civilians in Gaza of over five years of Israeli blockade and the 2008-2009 Israeli military operation 'Cast Lead.'"[5]

Physicians in Occupied Gaza are attempting to treat head injuries, serious burns, and injuries from falling buildings and debris caused by Israeli pilots. Al Jazeera English reports on the difficulties faced by paramedics in Gaza during the Israeli bombardments.[6]

A spokesman for the Israeli army tweeted on 19 November, "We continue to transfer goods & gas to #Gaza", saying that on 18 November some 16 trucks carrying medical supplies entered Gaza, and 26 Palestinian patients were taken to Israel for treatment.[7] Although Israel is now letting in some supplies, they were inadequate to the need even before these attacks. Medhat Abbas, head of Shifa Hospital, reported that his institution lacks 40 percent of the needed drugs: "The shortage, of course, affects the quality of our work.

However, our staff are working to the maximum to fulfill needs in this catastrophic situation."[8]

Morocco is setting up field hospitals in Gaza to treat the wounded. Jordan has had one there for 3 years, and all the personnel are Jordanian.[9] Some 500 Egyptian activists, from the same youth groups that overthrew Hosni Mubarak in February 2011, brought food and medical aid to Gaza on Saturday. Egypt is keeping its Rafah checkpoint with Gaza open for the transport of wounded to El Arish Hospital.[10]

The Gaza Strip, home to some 1.7 million Palestinians (about half of them children and minors) in 2012, has been the victim for a long time of Israeli colonial oppression, including policies that deliberately harm the health and well-being of its residents. Stunting in children, along with widespread anemia in pregnant women and children, are one result of the economic blockade imposed on Israeli-occupied Gaza by the far-right-wing Likud government of Israel. Israeli strangulation of the Gaza economy has led not only to poverty and food insecurity but also to threats to the availability of potable water and access to medicine and hospital care.

A recent World Health Organization report worries that in just 8 years, in 2020, if current Israeli policies continue, Gaza will be virtually uninhabitable.[11] Since Israeli policies of Apartheid, discrimination, exile, restriction of movement, and infliction of harm on Palestinians in Gaza are long-standing, deliberate, and systematic, Israeli leaders are guilty in this regard of crimes against humanity.[12] The WHO report says: "Ms. [Jean] Gough [of UNICEF] said that demand for drinking water was projected to increase by 60 percent while damage to the aquifer, the major water source, would become irreversible without remedial action now. Mr.[Robert] Turner [of U.N.RWA] added that more than 440 additional schools, 800 hospital beds, and more than 1,000 doctors would be needed by 2020."

Israeli airstrikes are exacerbating what had already been a parlous health care situation for Palestinians in Gaza.[13]

Notes

[1] Photos and accounts of Palestinian casualties due to Israeli airstrikes in Gaza. http://electronicintifada.net/content/photos-gaza-buries-its-children-israeli-attacks-intensify/11914

[2] Jordanian field hospital reported being targeted by Israeli warplanes. http://www.ammonnews.net/article.aspx?articleno=137216

[3] WHO spokesman highlights increased casualties and the burden on Gaza's medical infrastructure. http://www.irinnews.org/Report/96823/OPT-Gaza-hospitals-need-more-drugs

[4] Analysis of the disproportionality of Gaza rocket attacks and Israeli retaliatory measures. http://mondoweiss.net/2012/11/dissecting-idf-propaganda-the-numbers-behind-the-rocket-attacks.html

[5] Aid organizations warning of a humanitarian disaster in Gaza amidst escalating conflict: Trust.org quoted at Alarabiya. http://english.alarabiya.net/articles/2012/11/19/250590.html

[6] Aljazeera English's coverage on the challenges faced by Gaza paramedics during bombardments. http://english.alarabiya.net/articles/2012/11/19/250590.html

[7] Israeli Defense Forces' communication about transferring medical supplies to Gaza and treating Palestinian patients in Israel quoted at the U.N.'s Irinnews. http://www.irinnews.org/Report/96823/OPT-Gaza-hospitals-need-more-drugs

[8] Ibid.

[9] Morocco's support to Gaza with the establishment of field hospitals. http://www.african-bulletin.com/news/967-morocco-to-dispatch-field-hospital-to-gaza.html

[10] Egyptian activists delivering aid and Egypt's facilitation of medical transportation at the Rafah checkpoint. http://english.ahram.org.eg/NewsContentP/1/58631/Egypt/Eyewitness-from-Gaza-Historic-convoy-breaks-the-si.aspx

[11] World Health Organization Report on the dire state of the future of Gaza if Israeli policies remain unchanged.

http://www.unrwa.org/etemplate.php?id=1423

[12] Rome Statute defining crimes against humanity.
http://www.preventgenocide.org/law/icc/statute/part-a.htm

[13] For Operation Pillar of Defense see now Finkelstein, *Gaza*, 279-291 and Baconi, *Hamas Contained*, 243-248.

14. Palestinian Legal strategy against Israel: The Real Prize is Europe

November 30, 2012

The United Nations General Assembly voted overwhelmingly to accord Palestine the status of "Observer State" on Thursday, with 138 countries voting in favor of the measure, 41 abstaining, and only 9 voting against. The U.S. and Israel were decisively marginalized, as Italy and Sweden joined France, Spain, Portugal, Ireland, and several other European countries in voting for the new status. Continental Western Europe and Scandinavia were almost unanimous in supporting the Palestinians, in a kind of declaration of independence from the Obama administration. Even Germany, which for historical reasons is typically reluctant to buck Israel, voted to abstain rather than to oppose.

From the Israeli press, it appears that many government and press figures are absolutely stunned and in a state of angry disbelief over the magnitude of this diplomatic defeat.[1] The Israeli Right wing is so out of touch with how its aggressive policies are seen by the outside world and so self-righteous and arrogant that it even launched a Facebook page urging a boycott of Israeli supermodel Bar Rafaeli merely for tweeting during the recent Gaza war, "I pray for the safety of the citizens on both sides and for the day when we will live in peace and harmony. Amen." Caring about human beings from the other side or praying for peace are apparently verboten in "Strong

Israel."[2] (Somehow I think Ms. Rafaeli's fan base is secure, inside and outside Israel).

The UNGA vote will not have a big immediate effect on the lives of Palestinians toiling under Israeli occupation. But over time, if the Palestinian leadership deploys it wisely, the new status could have an incremental effect, especially affecting Israel's relationship to Europe. Europe itself now has the opportunity to play the kind of honest broker between the two sides that the U.S. pretended to but almost never did (with Jimmy Carter a partial exception).[3]

Many European countries have elevated the Palestine mission in their capitals to the status of full embassy. Palestine's new status as U.N. observer state could well become a basis for it being given further embassies in Europe. Being an embassy rather than a mission strengthens the legal status of Palestine, including in national courts and EU tribunals.

Israel's economy is deeply dependent on its relationship to Europe, the largest single source of imports into Israel and the second-largest market for exports (after the United States). European investment in Israel is also significant, as are various agreements giving Israel access to European technological advances and promoting scientific and technological exchange.[4]

The European Union imports 15 times more goods from Israeli settler enterprises in the Occupied West Bank than from the Palestinians themselves. Europe is therefore a major, hidden support for Israeli crimes against the Palestinians.[5]

Much speculation has focused on whether Palestine will attempt to take Israel to the International Criminal Court, getting specific Israeli officials or officers indicted for war crimes or crimes against humanity. Such cases may well be brought, and if successful might more or less imprison the individual inside Israel, since traveling abroad would risk arrest by Interpol.[6]

But actually, gaining the standing to provoke resolutions and statements from various United Nations bodies and committees is also important. Such documents can then be cited in the European Parliament and in national parliaments in Europe. Over time, a latticework of human rights law on the treatment of the Palestinians can be erected that might well cause Europeans to boycott settler-made goods or even Israel proper (after all, the squatters are being sent into Palestine by the Likud government). One Israeli strategy over the years has been to attempt to prevent the creation of such a body of resolutions, findings, and judgments. The U.S. veto on the Security Council and the lack of Palestinian standing as a state to bring matters before the UNGA aided in this Israeli quest for impunity.

A big problem with international law, such as the Geneva Convention on the treatment of Occupied populations (1949), the Apartheid convention, etc., is that they typically do not have attached to them any court in which a practical judgment of guilt can be rendered. The European Court of Human Rights and the International Criminal Court are steps toward achieving such arenas of adjudication for claims of rights violation. But the European Court of Human Rights, e.g., has no mechanism for enforcing its rulings.[7]

It seems to me that any court rulings against Israel will have their major effect through providing a basis for civil society organizations (unions, businesses, associations, NGOs) and parliaments to punish Israeli war crimes, Apartheid crimes, and crimes against humanity through boycotts. Over time, such steps could begin having a major impact on settler enterprises and even on the Israeli economy itself (which is fragile and highly dependent on foreign trade with Europe, since its goods are often shunned in the Middle East).

An example is the recent demand of the youth wing of the Swedish Social Democratic Party that Sweden boycott all settler-made goods. (Sweden, a little unexpectedly, voted for the UNGA resolution yesterday). If such demands proliferate, and the next generation of Europeans feels so strongly on this issue, the settlers could end up bankrupted.[8]

How this could work is clear on a small scale is apparent in the 2010 European Court of Justice ruling that goods from the Occupied West Bank do not fall under the European Union's preferential trade provisions for Israeli goods. What is important here is that German authorities declined to allow the British firm Brita to import mineral water tariff-free into Germany because they believe it originated with a squatter company in the West Bank. The German decision was upheld by the European Court of Justice.[9]

Expect to see more such decisions by governments in Europe, and by its courts. The Palestinian victory at the U.N. will likely begin creating a whole set of new opportunities for the Palestinians to make their case in the most important Israeli market.

Notes

[1] Reaction from Israeli government and press to the U.N. vote. https://www.juancole.com/2012/11/israeli-reaction-to-un-vote-politicians-burn-palestinian-flag-pundits-fear-international-criminal-court.html

[2] Backlash against Israeli supermodel Bar Rafaeli for expressing hope for peace. http://www.ynetnews.com/articles/0,7340,L-4310596,00.html

[3] New possibilities for Europe to mediate between Israel and Palestine. http://www.europesworld.org/NewEnglish/Home_old/Article/tabid/191/ArticleType/articleview/ArticleID/21782/language/en-U.S./Default.aspx

[4] The significance of Europe to Israel's economy in terms of trade and investment. http://ec.europa.eu/trade/creating-opportunities/bilateral-relations/countries/israel/

[5] EU's contribution to the Israeli economy and indirect support of occupation through trade with settlements. http://www.guardian.co.uk/world/2012/oct/30/european-union-trade-west-bank

[6] The potential for Israel to be taken to the International Criminal Court for war crimes. http://www.theglobeandmail.com/news/world/palestinians-potential-access-to-international-criminal-court-worries-israel/article5831228/

[7] C. Hillebrecht, "Implementing International Human Rights Law at Home: Domestic Politics and the European Court of Human Rights," *Human Rights Review* 13 (2012):279-301.

[8] Calls within Sweden for boycotting settler-made goods. http://www.maannews.net/eng/ViewDetails.aspx?ID=543399

[9] The European Court of Justice decision on goods from Occupied West Bank not being part of EU trade agreement with Israel. http://www.alhaq.org/advocacy/topics/settlements-and-settler-violence/285-european-court-of-justice-israeli-settlement-goods-do-

15.   Israel's Apartheid Deepens, Along With Its Global Isolation

December 12, 2012

The real threat to Israel comes not from tiny, impoverished Gaza, but from the policies of the country's increasingly right-wing politicians.

Palestinian leaders are responding to the aggressive policies of Israeli Prime Minister Benjamin Netanyahu, deploying new legal strategies, and, in Gaza, a mass rally reminiscent of Arab Spring protest tactics. Palestinian Authority President Mahmoud Abbas is reportedly considering taking Israel to the International Criminal Court over Netanyahu's recent announcement that Israel will build 3,000 new dwellings for settlers in the E-1 area of the West Bank. Abbas indicated that this step would be a last resort, but it is a threat to be taken seriously.

With the round of Israeli bombardments over, Hamas leader Khaled Meshaal.[1] joined a celebration of tens of thousands in Gaza over the weekend and repeated his long-standing opposition to ever giving up an inch of Palestinian land to Israel. Israeli politicians condemned him for refusing to recognize, and wanting to destroy, the Israeli state. Israeli opposition leader Shaul Mofaz of the Kadima Party said that Meshaal should have been assassinated while in Gaza.

By denying the Palestinians a state, Israelis are actively destroying the Palestine they agreed to create in the Oslo Accords that Israel signed in 1993, and they are now keeping Gaza from exporting most of what it makes.[2] Meshaal's 2012 triumphant visit to Gaza underscored the new limitations on Israeli power. Netanyahu's recent attack on Gaza remained a brief air war, and, unlike in 2008-2009, could not be escalated into a land incursion because of opposition to that step in Washington, Brussels and Cairo. Egypt's fundamentalist president, Mohamed Morsi, played a key role in negotiating a cease-fire, but those talks themselves limited the scope of Netanyahu's ability to act unilaterally.

Netanyahu stubbornly refuses to get the message. His settlement project in E-1 would cut the West Bank in two and forever forestall the emergence of a Palestinian state. U.N. Secretary-General Ban Ki-moon referred to the plan as "an almost fatal blow" to any two-state solution.

The declaration came just after the United Nations General Assembly humiliated Israel and the Obama administration by elevating Palestine's status to "nonmember observer state," with 138 delegates in favor of the upgrade, nine against and 41 abstaining. That overwhelming sentiment in favor of the Palestinians had been stoked by Israel's attack on Gaza in November. Netanyahu moved quickly to remind the world that while the General Assembly might be able to play symbolic political games, he controls the land, water and air of the Palestinian West Bank, and intends permanently to annex all three to Israel, even as he keeps the entire population of the Gaza Strip under an economic blockade. Abbas has riposted by reminding Netanyahu that Palestine's new status gives it access to international forums in which he can press his case.

Think of the Palestinian West Bank as a peanut with a curve in it in the middle on the left. Jerusalem is in the crook of that curve. After the Israelis invaded and occupied Arab East Jerusalem and the West Bank in 1967, they gradually annexed part of the latter territory to their "district of Jerusalem." In the last few decades, they have aggressively constructed Israeli housing projects on Palestinian land around Jerusalem, encircling the city to the west.

Building a new, large settlement in the E-1 area between west Jerusalem and the big settlement of Maale Adumim just nine miles from the Dead Sea border with Jordan would virtually slice the West Bank in two, making a contiguous Palestinian state impossible. The West Bank was already carved up by checkpoints and highways (some Jewish-only) into a set of tiny Bantustans. But now the whole territory is to be sundered, just as Solomon offered to cut the disputed newborn in two.

That Netanyahu and his partners intended to make a Palestinian state impossible was never in doubt, but their boldness in pressing forward to implement this plan has shocked the capitals of Europe. In response to the announcement about E-1, the British and French foreign ministries took the unusual step of summoning their Israeli ambassadors for a dressing-down, and there were rumors that they were considering withdrawing their own ambassadors from the country.

British Foreign Secretary William Hague was reportedly furious at Netanyahu, feeling betrayed because he had expended a great deal of political capital on behalf of Israel in opposing "observer state" status for Palestine.[3] French President Francois Hollande warned Israel that this proposal was not the way forward to peace, but denied that he was considering sanctions against the nation.[4] That anyone even asked such a question, however, is a sign of the incredible shift in world opinion against Israel's policies.

The public pressure on European governments for some sort of sanctions in response to apartheid policies will only grow. Already, courts have found that goods imported into the European Union from Israeli companies on the occupied West Bank are not eligible for tariff discounts, unlike those coming in from Israel proper. The major Unison labor union in Britain is boycotting Israel, and the country's fifth-largest food chain, the Co-Op, is declining to import agricultural goods from Israeli settler farms on Palestinian territory.[5] Throughout Europe, labor unions, pension funds and universities are increasingly divesting from firms seen as profiting from or enabling the occupation of the West Bank.[6] In response to Israel's attack on Gaza in November, 52 prominent activists and artists, including Nobel laureates, called for an international military boycott of Israel.[7]

Netanyahu's 2012 Gaza War fizzled out and its quick end seems mainly to have resulted in greater popularity for Hamas and for its new patron, Morsi. Netanyahu's campaign to prevent the nations of the world from recognizing Palestine as an observer state was an epochal failure. Palestine's new status as a U.N. observer state gives it potential access to the International Criminal Court, a way possibly to fend off aggressive Israeli colonization of its territory. Netanyahu's announced intention to annex more Palestinian land in E-1 and chop the West Bank permanently in two resulted in his ambassadors being called on the mat and a clear recognition that he is not so much unserious about a peace process as dead set against one.

- *Truthdig*

Notes

[1] Khaled Meshaal's opposition to Israel:
http://www.guardian.co.uk/world/2012/dec/08/hamas-gaza-palestine-khaled-meshaal-israel

[2] Prevention of Gaza's exports:
http://www.juancole.com/2012/11/gazas-health-crisis-and-israels-crimes-against-humanity.html

[3] British Foreign Secretary William Hague's fury at Netanyahu:
http://www.itv.com/news/2012-12-03/british-foreign-secretary-furious-with-the-israelis/

[4] French President Francois Hollande's denial of considering sanctions: http://www.reuters.com/article/2012/12/03/us-palestinians-israel-france-idU.S.BRE8B20ML20121203

[5] Unison labor union boycotting Israel:
http://www.ejpress.org/article/news/western_europe/58197

[6] Increasing divestment from firms involved in the occupation of the West Bank:
http://www.israelnationalnews.com/Articles/Article.aspx/12550.#_UMVYFqzhdBl

[7] Call for international military boycott of Israel:
http://www.guardian.co.uk/world/2012/nov/28/nobel-laureates-call-israel-boycott

PART 3

Stateless!

In 2008, my colleague in the Sociology Department at the University of Michigan, Margaret ("Peggy") Somers, published her pathbreaking book, Genealogies of Citizenship. I had been in a biweekly interdisciplinary reading group with her and read her book not long after it came out. It came as a revelation to me when thinking about the Palestinians, because it helped me think about their plight and the legal framework within which it had become virtually insoluble. In that light, the issue seemed clear: The Palestinians were without citizenship but the Israelis had achieved it. The stateless Palestinians had no real rights, and no standing in any court to pursue their rights. No treaty with them needed to be abided by, since they were abject and without the rights of citizenship in a state. When I was asked by the Jerusalem Fund and the Palestine Center in Washington, D.C., to give the 2013 Hisham B. Sharabi Memorial Lecture, I felt it would be a good opportunity to reflect at some length on this problematic. I have revised that lecture for publication here.

In 2014, the government of Prime Minister Benjamin Netanyahu attacked Gaza again, in order to degrade Hamas paramilitary capabilities and to punish it for launching rockets at Israel, though the latter motivation was as always overblown, since few of the rockets ever did any real damage. They were symbolic defiance, but Netanyahu appears to have felt it politically advantageous to punish these symbolic actions with a massive campaign of effective bombardment. These periodic Israeli campaigns against Gaza, which always managed to kill far more civilian noncombatants than members of the Hamas paramilitary, the al-Qassam Brigades, do not appear to have been intended to solve any problem. The blockade and the bombardments guaranteed that ordinary people in Gaza would be radicalized and that Hamas would remain in power. The knocking out of the Strip's power plant, endangering water purification and therefore risking high infant mortality, was a bad look.

Israel in the 1950s and 1960s had portrayed itself as a plucky David confronting the Goliath of the large Arab frontline states. But these governments were neutralized in the twenty-first century by the American outfitting of Israel with the most advanced weaponry and by the American security commitment to Tel Aviv. The 2014 campaign was not a war, since the Palestinians of Gaza had only small arms but faced advanced armor, artillery, and F-16s. In European civil society, a movement to boycott Israel over its colonization of the Palestinian West Bank and its periodic slaughter in Gaza began to grow, as the Palestinians began looking more like David and the Israelis like Goliath. Palestinian lawfare also progressed, as in early 2015 Palestine signed the Rome Statute and joined the International Criminal Court for which it served as a charter. This move, as Israeli leaders recognized at the time, created genuine legal period for Israel and was a bellwether for things to come. In 2018-2019, Israel responded to peaceful marches by civilians in Gaza by assigning snipers to shoot them in the knees, and crippled thousands of them.[1] This tactic was even creepier than trying to keep the Palestinians thin by limiting the calories to which they had access. In response, in the same year, the Palestine Authority filed a case against Israel at the International Criminal Court. The plot thickened.

Notes

[1] Hilo Glazer, "'42 Knees in One Day': Israeli Snipers Open Up About Shooting Gaza Protesters," *Haaretz*, March 6, 2020. https://www.haaretz.com/israel-news/2020-03-06/ty-article-magazine/.highlight/42-knees-in-one-day-israeli-snipers-open-up-about-shooting-gaza-protesters/0000017f-f2da-d497-a1ff-

f2dab2520000; Lena Obermaier, "Disabling Palestine: the case of Gaza's Great March of Return," *Race & Class*, 65, 3 (October 2023): 27-46. https://doi.org/10.1177/03063968231203485.

16. The Palestinians as Stateless Subjects

*2013 Hisham B. Sharabi Memorial Lecture:
The Jerusalem Fund & Palestine Center, Washington, D.C.*

May 2, 2013

I want to make an argument about the character of the Palestine issue. I am not going to argue that it is a unique problem, but I am going to argue that it is almost unique in contemporary affairs, and that there are some aspects of it that explain why it is so seemingly intractable. I am going to start with an increasingly important field of study, citizenship studies. There are journals now devoted to it; it has become a big thing in academia.1 My colleague at the University of Michigan, Margaret Somers, wrote an important book on citizenship.2 And as she points out, Chief Justice Earl Warren of the U.S. Supreme Court in 1958 wrote: "Citizenship is man's basic right, for it is nothing less than the right to have rights. Remove this priceless possession and there remains a stateless person disgraced and degraded in the eyes of his countrymen."3 Warren is drawing here implicitly on the work of Hannah Arendt but this is the key point that I want to make today. Citizenship is the right to have rights. People who lack citizenship in a state ipso facto have no right to have rights.

Now citizen-ness, the quality of being a citizen, is of course not one data point, not one thing. It exists as with all social phenomena on a spectrum. It is like "coolness." In popular culture, you can be more or less cool. There are attributes that contribute to one's coolness. Citizen-ness likewise is on a spectrum. Somers brings in several things that make for citizenship—the intersection with the state, how strong the state is, how much recognition by the state is there of a particular group as citizens, their relationship to the market. I come from the Detroit area where there are a very large number of young people who have no access to the market. They do not live where there are jobs and they are not suited to the jobs that are in their neighborhoods, if there are any. They are disconnected from the market. Somers argues that that is also a problem of citizenship, of full citizenship. And then there is the issue of civil society, of non-governmental organizations of various sorts. How thick are they are the ground? How much do they interact with local people? Somers argues that what we discovered after the Katrina Hurricane was that very large numbers of people in New Orleans were not actually full citizens. They had low levels of citizenship in American terms. The state did not do much for them and they were not connected to the market. She puts these criteria of citizenship on a scale of low to high.

If we took the Palestinians, the Israelis, and the Jordanians as test cases and looked at their relationship to these three factors, the Israelis have a relatively strong state, and Israeli citizens have a strong relationship to that state. Obviously, the Palestinian Israelis do not have as much citizenship as Jewish Israelis, but they do have rights of citizenship. For instance, the Israelis set things up so that they only recognize municipalities if they have been incorporated in a certain way. They do not give permission to a lot of the Palestinian Israeli villages to incorporate, and without that permission then they cannot do repairs or get permits. In fact, the Likud party in the 1970s came to some of them and said, 'We will recognize you as proper Israeli municipalities only if you will vote for us.' There is a reliable Likud vote to this day in some of these places. Still, on the whole and by and large, the Israelis have citizenship and they have a strong state. Obviously, it is a country with a vigorous market and a strong relationship of people to that market, and a very active non-governmental organization sector. That is a normal distribution for citizenship according to Somers.

The Jordanians have a much weaker state. The Palestinian Jordanians are not as connected to it as the East Bank population. In addition, there are non-citzens — some two hundred thousand Iraqis and now ten percent of the residents are Syrian refugees. Jordanian citizens, nevertheless, do have citizenship. Their form of citizenship is not as robust as that in Israel, but it exists. The market is complicated in Jordan because so much of it is off the books. But if you counted the black market, then people are pretty connected to it. And then there is a fairly lively NGO scene. We would say the Jordanian chart is a little distorted from Somers' point of view— with a weaker state and a strange kind of market. Still, all three categories are there.

The sort of citizenship we find among the Palestinians in the Occupied Territories is obviously deformed. There's no state. They are lacking an entire category. Their market is not very robust and in Gaza there is no market to speak of since the Israelis have Gaza under siege. Mostly the export market does not exist in Gaza. The market and the separation wall and the politics of the neighboring states are such that the Palestinians do not have a strong relationship to the market. There are a lot of NGOS, and so for the Palestinians, the NGO sector is the one place where there is a little glimmer, perhaps, of some citizenship. But that is a weird situation, unparalleled in the world. There's no other group of people that look like that, right now.

This problem of citizenship and the Palestinians of course goes back to the early twentieth century. The Palestinians, the Iraqis, and the Syrians were recognized after World War I as Class-A Mandates, coming out of the old Ottoman Empire. The League of Nations had a paternalistic rhetoric that nations were kind of like persons and they were at various ages of development. The Syrians, Iraqis, and Palestinians were considered the political equivalent of adolescents, not ready to run their own affairs. The League of Nations engaged in a paternalistic juvenilizing of people. George W. Bush said at one point during the U.S. occupation that the Iraqis were just about ready to take off the training wheels, as though they were three years old. That rhetoric is not new, and its equivalent existed among the Europeans in 1920 after WW I. The French and the British were designated to be mentors, the way Robin is Batman's ward. They were supposed to raise them up to the point where they could stand on their own feet.

Not all the territories detached from the defeated Powers after the Great War were given the status of Class-A mandate. There were Class-B mandates. The Syrians, the Iraqis, and the Palestinians were relatively well thought of by the Europeans in this regard. The diplomats at San Remo thought there would be a period of mandatory rule by the Europeans and then eventually these territories would gain independence. That was the charge, unlike in previous projects of colonization, which simply consisted of organized looting. When the British went into India, there were no promises that they were going to "mature the Indians." They were mainly interested in taking money out of the country. In the mandates, they were given a responsibility to set these countries up on their own feet and let them become proper members of the League of Nations. It was complicated in the case of Palestine because of the Balfour Declaration made in the course of World War I. This crackpot Englishman thought Jews ruled the world and wanted to make the Jews happy so that the British would win World War I. Therefore, he promised them a "home" in Palestine without saying what a "home" was and simultaneously promising at that it would not "inconvenience" the Palestinians. You see why I used the word "crackpot."

The mandatory documents about Palestine from the League of Nations are weird in the sense that all the other charters for the Mandatory states talk about this process of preparing them for independence, but in Palestine there is a lot of language about the Jews, of which at that time there weren't very many. The Italians and the French, if you go back in correspondence to the League of Nations, pressed the British on this.[4] They said, you cannot just disregard the rights of the local people.

The problem of statelessness in the early twentieth century was severe. Nations as a matter of course used statelessness as a ruthless political tool. And so, when the White Russians lost the

Rebellion against the new Soviet regime, the Soviets took away their citizenship in the millions. The Armenians were deprived of citizenship. The Hungarians were deprived of citizenship. The Spaniards on the Left who fought Franco, when they lost, often were denaturalized . . . Of course, it was a policy of the Nazis when they came to power to start depriving people of citizenship. We tend to forget this now—that millions of Europeans in the 1930s were deprived of their citizenship, were denaturalized, and were left without the right to have rights.

Hannah Arendt points out that the Nazis viewed this policy of denaturalizing people, or leaving them without citizenship rights, was a demonstration project. That is to say, the Nazis began by thinking that Gypsies and Jews and other groups were the scum of the earth and a kind of infection in the body politic, and by taking away their citizenship, they demonstrated that they were abject. Goebbels said that depriving the Jews of citizenship made the Jews mere flotsam and he said, you know, let us see – everybody's criticizing us on how we treat our Jews, but will they take them? Does America want them? Does Britain want them? And of course they did not, once they were stateless. By marking them as non-German, by taking away German Jews' citizenship, the Nazis were thereby demonstrating the worthlessness of their Jews.

And so ironically enough Mandatory Palestine, Palestine under British rule, served the function of being a refuge for stateless Jews at this point and in fact, this was one of the arguments that proponents of Jewish immigration to Palestine made. So, for instance in 1939 when you had a British MacDonald White Paper after the 1936-39 Palestinian uprising, which argued that henceforward Jewish immigration in Palestine should be limited, the Zionists in Europe raised an outcry that in 1939, the Sudetenland in Czechoslovakia was taken over by the German Nazis and they denaturalized a hundred thousand Jews there. And people said, where will they go if you do not let them go to Palestine? Palestine was a solution to the increasing statelessness of European Jewry.

Let me stop at this juncture and consider some possible twists on or objections to this theory of citizenship. Many people have said to me that there are lots of people in the world who do not have proper rights, for instance undocumented immigrants. Well, undocumented immigrants do not have rights of citizenship in their country of residence because they are did not arrive there legally. They nevertheless still do have citizenship. In 2013, the United States deported 400,000 of them back to their countries of origin, where they are citizens. When Palestinians are deported from the West Bank by the Israelis, where are they deported to? Jordan? They are not being deported in the technical sense of going back to their country of origin. They are being expelled to other places. They remain stateless.

Then people say, well what about the Basques and the Kurds and the Catalans? They have the citizenship they have. I agree that it is unfortunate not to have the citizenship that you want, but it is different from not having any at all. The Turkish Kurds may suffer some disabilities from being Kurdish in Turkey, but they still are Turkish citizens. They vote. In fact, they are influential in the elections. They can work. An aspiration for separatism is a different situation than statelessness. It is not the same thing.

Then there are citizens of states that do not amount to much. I mean, I do not know how much good it does you to be a Somali citizen. And then there was Iraq under American rule, what kind of a citizen were you there? But still, it doesn't have the same implications for you as statelessness.

Statelessness means the complete lack of citizenship in a recognized state. It means you do not have a passport; you have a laissez-passer. That means a lot of countries will not accept your travel documents. It means you cannot travel freely, you do not have constitutional protections, you often cannot get a work permit, your property is not secure because people can take it away from you, and you do not have access to national courts that could adjudicate those disputes. It is different.

After World War II, this problem of the inter-war period of millions of stateless was resolved. The bias in international law was against people being denaturalized, and against statelessness. Statelessness became rare. Out of the billions of human beings today, the United Nations High Commission on Human Rights estimated in 2013 that perhaps twelve million are stateless. There are 90,000 Bidun in Kuwait, tribes that used to wander amidst states and then got caught on the Kuwaiti side of the border and cannot move now, and are not recognized by the emir as Kuwaiti. The Kuwaitis have hired them as their policemen, on the theory, I suppose, that they will not be loyal to other tribes.

Some 300,000 Syrian Kurds were denaturalized by the pre-Baath Arab nationalists, in the 1960s, who have grown to probably over a million, today. People have alleged to me that the situation of Kurds under the Baathis in Syria, say in the 1990s, was actually worse than the situation of Palestinians there, though both were stateless in Syria.

There were a hundred thousand Taiwanese in Japan in 1971 when Japan unrecognized the Taiwanese government. For all practical purposes, the Taiwanese in Japan suddenly became stateless. That issue has been resolved over time.

But the very largest group of stateless people in the world, the largest single group, are the Palestinians. There were over a million Palestinians in 1943 in Mandatory Palestine, about half a million Jewish settlers who had bought up out about six percent of the land. Then in 1947-48 the British prepared to withdraw, and a civil war broke out between the two communities in which the Yishuv, the budding community that became Israel, conducted a campaign of ethnic cleansing against the Palestinians, which displaced them in very large numbers. Probably on the order of 730,000, out of the 1.3 million Palestinians of that time, were displaced. Many of them went to the West Bank or Gaza, Jordan, Lebanon, Syria, a few to Egypt. In 1967, many of those who had been displaced to the West Bank and Gaza were again displaced.

Take a place like Lebanon. The Palestinians who came into Lebanon grew over time. Demographically, the U.N. estimates on the order of 400,000-450,000 Palestinian refugees from Israel there. Probably there are actually less, since many of them have surreptitiously emigrated to Europe. Whatever their number, most still live in camps. Lebanese law does not allow them to have property rights, for the most part—there's been a slight adjustment of this—but generally speaking they cannot get work permits, they cannot get business permits. If you visit the Palestinians in their camps in Lebanon, you find that they are in jail, they are like prisoners. They cannot get out. Other countries won't accept their travel documents for fear that they will stay.

The camps themselves are lawless. If you think about it, in such a place Lebanese sovereignty does not extend very far. It is not as if there are police. People organize militias for self-protection. But the militias can be armed and predatory. It is a horrible situation and it has been going on now since 1948. I visited the former Palestinian camp of Nahr-el-Bared [in 2010]. I met an old man there who told me the story of how in 1948 he was with his mother in an apartment in Haifa and the Zionists came and told them to leave at gunpoint. So, they went north and they waited there on the Lebanese border to go back and then of course Ben-Gurion announced that he would close the borders and they couldn't go back. They were there for a year. And then the U.N. put them on trains and took them up to Tripoli, very far away from their homes. They have been there ever since in camps. Nahr-el-Bared was such a camp. And because frankly, of the lawlessness of camp life, nevertheless there are some opportunities there that do not exist elsewhere for unregulated commercial exchange, let us say. Over time Nahr-el-Bared started to have some money and there was a lot of commerce there, maybe some commerce that could not be conducted elsewhere. People gentrified their buildings and there were shops, and it became a town of 70,000 and it was a relatively nice town. But then because there were no police and there was lawlessness, in the middle of the past decade about 50 men formed a gang and started robbing banks in nearby Tripoli, which angered the Lebanese government. And then these bank robbers, for reasons that I cannot entirely understand, announced they were an al-Qaeda affiliate. What do you get from doing that? I mean, does al-Qaeda give you a gold star or what benefit is there in saying that? Well, I know the downside is that all of a sudden U.S. Vice President Dick Cheney is on the phone with the Lebanese government saying, "you have to go in there." And anyway, these men were robbing banks and causing trouble. So, the Lebanese army invaded Nahr-el-Bared, a civilian settlement of 70,000 people. I am showing slides of it, it is destroyed now. It is gone. People are again refugees, and they are living in pre-fab U.N. little apartments. The old man who had been expelled from Haifa took me by the arm and brought me to one of the rooms and there were two old women lying there on oxygen and he asked, "Is this a way to live?"

When you are stateless, you do not have the right to have rights. Everything is unstable. It is a little bit like being a child of an alcoholic, abusive family. Such children suffer from everything always being interrupted. You never know what is going to happen and therefore you cannot make plans. A parent might suggest in the morning, "Let's go for a picnic today;" -- but then the picnic does not happen because the parent got drunk. If you're stateless you do not know what is going to happen to you. Your property is unstable, your rights are unstable. Even if you had been stateless and you managed to gain citizenship, your citizenship is unstable. Jordan gave citizenship to the West Bank Palestinians at one point and then because of the Rabat Accords after Israel conquered it, they took the Jordanian citizenship back away. They have just denaturalized about 30,000 or 40,000 Palestinians from Gaza in Jordan.

If you were ever stateless, the stigma of statelessness seems to attach to you even if you gain citizenship and then that is unstable and can be taken back away. You never know when you may be a refugee again. Palestinians in Gaza, on the other hand, were not granted Egyptian citizenship, though they were ruled by Egypt 1949 to 1967. And then they were directly ruled by Israel from 1967 to 2005, during which time the Israelis thought it would be a good idea to try to put Israeli settlers into this densely populated, resource-poor area. In 2005, the Israelis felt as though they could not protect those settlers, and so took them back out. But they did not make any agreement with the Palestinians in Gaza about the post-withdrawal situation, leaving the Palestinians in limbo.

Then from 2007 they slapped a boycott on Gaza. The Israeli Ministry of Defense actually sat down and figured out that each adult person needs 2200 calories and how many trucks of food would you let in everyday to keep them svelte. Not starving to death but not with any baby fat, either. No chocolate for the children. This is creepy! This is weird. I mean, it is repulsive! Actually one of my victories in life was that I called it "creepy" at my blog and the *National Review* at one point published an article trying to refute me and it quoted me as saying that the blockade is "creepy". So, I inserted that meme into the *National Review*, even though they were trying to wriggle out of it.

This is a population that has been without citizenship for 61 years as of 2013 and apparently if you are without citizenship, you not only do not have a right to have rights, you do not have a right to have chocolate, or more than 2200 calories a day. Your body becomes an experimental field for planners on the part of your enemies. On the West Bank, as I said, the Jordanians did grant citizenship to the Palestinians but after 1967, and after Jordan and the Arab League recognized the PLO as the Palestinian spokesman, Jordanian citizenship ultimately was revoked and so they are formally stateless.

The implications of this situation are that the Palestinians lack control. Because what does a state do? It controls land, water, air. If a North Korean MiG flew over San Diego, all hell would break loose. Why? It would have penetrated the airspace of the United States of America. The airspace is owned by the federal government. If an Israeli plane flies over the West Bank . . . meh. Not a state. If substantial water resources, a river or something, were expropriated from the U.S. by Canada, there would be trouble because that is America's water, it is owned by the federal government. But if 85 percent of the water on the West Bank is diverted to Israeli settlers, that is alright because there is no Palestinian state. The water does not belong to anybody. It is a no-man's land.

States control immigration. I said the United States nowadays deports 400,000 people a year for coming here without proper procedures or documentation. It was a million a year not so long ago. It is really a vast bureaucracy. But the Palestinians would deport somebody, how? There are lots of undocumented people on the West Bank, i.e. the Israeli squatters, but their state is behind them.

Aquifer rights are interfered with. The Israeli settlers can dig their tube wells deeper than the Palestinians and cause the aquifer to fall and so the old wells of the Palestinian villages dry up. The Israelis have set up a vast network of checkpoints, of special highways on which Palestinians cannot drive. They have made it difficult to get from one part of Palestine to the other. There must be a whole class of post-modern novelists who should write about the cohort of Palestinians born at checkpoints because their mom could not get through in time to the hospital. There's difficulty of travel and a lack of speedy hospital access. There are no proper medical facilities for many diseases in Gaza and Palestinians there have to apply to the Israeli government to get permission to leave for treatment. In a few cases the permission has not quite come in time. They are stateless. They have no right to have rights; they have no right to have medical care.

Palestinians rate low on citizenship state. One of the ripostes to my argument sometimes, is that there is the Palestine Authority. It is alleged that the Palestinians have a state, it is just not a very good one. Well, the Palestine Authority doesn't look like a proper state in most regards; it doesn't have control of the things that a state controls. So, Palestinians rate low on citizenship in a state, they rate low on access to or incorporation into a market. There is some civil society, although that is circumscribed by the Palestine Authority and by the Israelis.

One of the things you have seen in the past couple years is that the Palestine Authority, which has now changed its name to just Palestine (I approve), has gone to the United Nations and asked for the status of an observer state. Some journalists have said they asked for recognition of the state, as a state. This is not true, they already believed that they were a state. They were not asking for recognition of that. They were asking for a particular kind of status that the U.N. would just call an "observer state status." It was enjoyed previously only by the Vatican. The United States and Israel fought tooth and nail against recognition. And of course, the United Nations Security Council hasn't signed off on it. But the General Assembly last fall did recognize the State of Palestine in this way. The reason that the Palestinians wanted this status is that as international law has evolved, an International Criminal Court has been established. There begin to be — because of the Rome Statute — some ways of adjudicating certain kinds of sorts of torts, of wrongs done by a state, one state to the people of another, that can only be accessed by another state. In the law, standing is very important. If you have standing to sue, you have standing to participate in a legal settlement of some sort. The Palestinians, being stateless, did not have standing in international law. That is another problem with being stateless. No tort can be committed against you because you have no standing. Or, no tort can be adjudicated.

So what Palestine was doing in seeking U.N. observer state status was to begin to establish standing to pursue tort cases against the Israelis, who are constantly breaking international law, The Israelis are breaking the Hague Convention of 1907, they're breaking the Geneva Convention on Occupied Territories of 1949, on a daily basis. They are also contravening large numbers of U.N. Security Council Resolutions. At one time or another, the Americans have occasionally let things such resolutions be passed without vetoing them, and there is quite a body of U.N. Security Council resolutions about Jerusalem, about the West Bank and Gaza, which the Israelis disregard. There is a set of cases to be made, but the Palestinians were not able to make that case as long as they did not have standing — as long as they did not have this state observer status. And as you can tell, I think that this is exactly the right strategy. It is the strategy of beginning to establish Palestinian claims on citizenship.

The statelessness of the Palestinians is virtually unknown as an issue in the United States. If you did a poll of Americans, asking "are Palestinians without citizenship rights?" — almost none of them would know this. And on the other hand, everybody in the Middle East knows it. It is one of the problems for American foreign policy. American foreign policy towards the Palestinians on the whole and by and large, is to screw them over. Not because the United States hates Palestinians — although maybe some officials do — but because it pleases their ally, Israel, to have these policies. So, the

Wikileaks revelation of State Department cables about Israeli policy and the blockade of Gaza demonstrate that these Americans and the U.S. Embassy in Tel Aviv were gung-ho. They were perfectly willing to help half starve the Palestinian children in Gaza. I was taken aback by the language of these cables. They were very harsh. They may as well have been written by the Likud party. And I am sure there are officials in the U.S. government who know the score, but practically speaking and de facto, the U.S. is complicit in Palestinian statelessness and in keeping them in that status. And this stance obviously causes problems for the U.S. in the region. Nobody can understand why the U.S. would want to do that to these poor people.

What is the end game here? What is the solution? I am arguing that it is unacceptable in international law, in international diplomacy, to have millions of people permanently kept in a status of statelessness, which is to say kept in a status where they have no right to have rights, taken off the human rights table entirely. It is unacceptable for that to continue. So when a prime minister of Israel comes out and says, it is not the time yet to establish a Palestinian state, that needs to be translated. What does it say? It is saying Palestinians must remain stateless for the time being. They must remain without rights for the time being. Well, that's not acceptable. It is not acceptable for any group of people to be deprived of basic human rights. I think, not so much in the United States but in the world at large, this problem is coming to the fore and people are beginning to mobilize. You see entire governments like the government of Ireland, the government of Norway, beginning to highlight this issue. There are moves among some European countries to raise the status of the Palestinian representation in the country to that of full embassy status. What does that do? It recognizes a Palestinian state. It is one more step toward recognizing the Palestinians as having citizenship.

There are increasingly boycotts of, especially of West Bank Israeli enterprises that are making money off the exploitation of the statelessness of the Palestinians, and I expect those boycotts to grow. Israel does 50 percent of its foreign trade with Europe and the Israeli economy is actually quite fragile and very dependent on international trade, and international technology transfers. If the European countries have a meeting on technology, they invite the Israelis. That gradually could end if the Israelis go on like this, as people become more and more aware that the Israelis are actively depriving so many people of citizenship rights.

I know many Palestinians feel strongly about the need for a two-state solution, the need for a Palestinian state of the West Bank and Gaza. But frankly, I think the time has probably already passed when that's plausible. There are so many Israeli squatter-settlements in the West Bank, it looks like Swiss cheese on a map and it is not going to happen. And then what's left is probably long-term apartheid, which, however, is not stable. I do not think that the world will put up with apartheid forever. So, there will be increasing boycotts, increasing pressure, increasing economic problems. Ultimately it seems to me very likely that you end up with a single state. I am not arguing for it, I am not saying it is desirable, I am not saying it is the best outcome. But I think somebody has to give citizenship to the Palestinians. Increasingly, the only one that could plausibly do that is the Israelis, and the Israelis increasingly own all of Palestinian territory so they are responsible for the people that live on that territory even though they do not think they are. I do not really care how this problem is solved. From my point of view, it is all the same to me. The important thing, as you can tell, is that I insist that the Palestinians must end up with the right to have rights. Thank you.

Notes

[1] E.g. the peer-reviewed *Citizenship Studies* at Taylor & Francis.

[2] Margaret R. Somers, *Genealogies of Citizenship: Markets, Statelessness, and the Right to Have Rights* (Cambridge University Press, 2008).

[3] Clemente Martinez PEREZ, Petitioner, v. Herbert BROWNELL, Jr., Attorney General of the United States of America, decided March 31, 1958. https://www.law.cornell.edu/supremecourt/text/356/44.

[4] Lord Curzon wrote in 1920, "As regards the Palestine Mandate, this Mandate also has passed through several revises. When it was first shown to the French Government it at once excited their vehement criticisms on the ground of its almost exclusively Zionist complexion and of the manner in which the interests and rights of the Arab majority (amounting to about nine-tenths of the population) were ignored. The Italian Government expressed similar apprehensions. It was felt that this would constitute a very serious, and possibly a fatal, objection when the Mandate came ultimately before the Council of the League. The Mandate, therefore, was largely rewritten, and finally received their assent. It was also considered by an Inter-Departmental Conference here, in which the Foreign Office, Board of Trade, War Office and India Office were represented, and which passed the final draft.

"In the course of these discussions strong objection was taken to a statement which had been inserted in the Preamble of the first draft to the following effect:— "Recognising the historical connection of the Jewish people with Palestine and the claim which this gives them to reconstitute Palestine as their National Home.

"It was pointed out (1) that, while the Powers had unquestionably recognised the historical connection of the Jews with Palestine by their formal acceptance of the Balfour Declaration and their textual incorporation of it in the Turkish Peace Treaty drafted at San Remo, this was far from constituting anything in the nature of a legal claim, and that the use of such words might be, and was, indeed, certain to be, used as the basis of all sorts of political claims by the Zionists for the control of Palestinian administration in the future, and ;2) that, while Mr. Balfour's Declaration had provided for the establishment of a Jewish National Home in Palestine, this was not the same thing as the reconstitution of Palestine as a Jewish National Home—an extension of the phrase for which there was no justification, and which was certain to be employed in the future as the basis for claims of the character to which I have referred. On the other hand, the Zionists pleaded for the insertion of some such phrase in the preamble, on the ground that it would make all the difference to the money that they aspired to raise in foreign, countries for the development of Palestine. Mr. Balfour, who interested himself keenly in their case, admitted, however, the force of the above contentions, and, on the eve of leaving for Geneva, suggested an alternative form of words which I am prepared to recommend." (Memorandum of Lord Curzon, British Secretary of State for Foreign Affairs, concerning League of Nations "Class A" Mandates in November 30, 1920. British National Archives, Catalogue Reference: CAB/24/115.)

[5] Antonio Cazorla Sánchez, *Fear and Progress: Ordinary Lives in Franco's Spain, 1939-1975* (London: John Wiley & Sons, 2009), 114.

17.   Israel's Groundhog Day: Reverse Snowballs and the Horrors of Lawn-Mowing
July 12, 2014

A gut-wrenching video is circulating on social media, of a Palestinian father in Gaza who is bringing a toy to his four-year-old son, only to find once he enters his home that his son's head has been crushed by Israeli shrapnel. That is the face of Israel's current 2014 military operation, "Operation Protective Edge," against Gaza to the outside world.

But from the point of view of Israeli hawks, the point of a campaign like the present one against the Gaza Strip is to degrade the military and organizational capabilities of the enemy. They clearly do not care if they are thereby killing dozens of women, children, and non-combatants (they are). The important thing for them is to accomplish what they see as a narrow military and counter-terrorism objective.

It is a bizarrely ahistorical quest, as though the Israeli leadership lives in a bubble isolated from the demographic and political realities of its neighborhood. They seem to think they are hanging by their fingers from a cliff, that Hamas is prying their fingers loose, and that if only they can push Hamas back, they can go on clinging to the cliff for another period of time, avoiding falling. They do not seem to realize that if this is their situation, it is untenable in the long run. The current campaign will end in failure and likely will help doom the Israeli enterprise over the next few decades.

The Israeli hawks have been trying to destroy Hamas since the late 1990s, when it went from a favored client of the Israeli state (having received support from Tel Aviv in the 1980s to offset the Palestine Liberation Organization) to enemy. The military wing of Hamas launched a vicious campaign of terrorism inside Israel in response to the doubling of the Israeli squatter population on Palestinian land in the 1990s. In the early zeroes, the Israelis conducted a campaign of murder against Hamas leaders, including against civilian party leaders with no operational role. They assassinated Sheikh Yasin, the spiritual leader of the movement, with a rocket fired from a helicopter gunship at his wheelchair as he was issuing from a mosque, killing and injuring people around him, as well. Sheikh Yasin had spoken of the possibility of a decades-long truce with Israel even though he rejected its legitimacy. In his absence, the truce talk rather declined, though Hamas has proved itself willing and able to negotiate long-lasting cease-fires with Israel; most often it has been the Israelis who violated them.

The theory behind the murders of leaders is that leadership is a rare quality and that if you inflict attrition on leaders, you will fatally weaken the organization. Israeli intelligence operatives drew on social science research about how many top-level managers a Western corporation could lose before it collapsed. In societies where kinship systems remain relatively strong, however, you do not have a hierarchical GM corporate flow chart for leadership, and if you kill someone's cousin, the republic of cousins comes together for revenge. This whole theory and the whole operation vindicate the old saw that "Government Intelligence" is an oxymoron.

Because of the Israeli attacks on Hamas figures, the party became more popular both in Gaza and the West Bank. So, I think we can pronounce the serial murders committed by then-Prime Minister Ariel Sharon an abject failure. From 2007 the Israelis put a severe blockade on the Gaza Strip, in hopes of making Hamas unpopular, figuring people in Gaza would blame it for the consequent collapse of the Gaza economy.[1] In response, Palestinians in Gaza just got really good at smuggling, developing an extensive tunnel network into the Sinai desert. My guess is that despite the Israeli naval blockade, things must get brought in sometimes by sea, as well.

Among the things they imported were small rockets, with which to harass the Israelis who had moved into the homes in what is now southern Israel that used to belong to the Palestinians of Gaza.

Israel's 2008-2009 and 2012 episodes of what hawks call "mowing the lawn" in Gaza were aimed, as well, at inflicting attrition on the rocket stock and at killing Hamas leaders and disrupting their institutions. (Since Hamas had been democratically elected in 2006, the police in Gaza had to report to the party after that, so the Israelis bombed the police stations; but most police were not Hamas cadres).

Hamas had received some support from Iran and Syria. My guess is that it has been exaggerated, but it was there. The attempted Syrian revolution and then the outbreak of civil war in Syria posed a problem for Hamas. The Syrian Muslim Brotherhood is a kindred movement, and it is opposed to the Baath government in Damascus. So, Hamas's dependence on Iran and on Bashar al-Assad was, let us say, awkward.

When Muhammad Morsi was elected president of Egypt in summer 2012, Hamas gravitated to him as its preferred sponsor and mostly broke with Syria and Iran. Unfortunately for Hamas, Morsi was overthrown in July of 2013, leaving Hamas high and dry and with no sponsor.

Worse, current Egyptian President Abdel Fattah al-Sisi and the officers who back him really, really hate political Islam. They banned the Muslim Brotherhood, killed over a thousand members in crackdowns on sit-ins, and imprisoned perhaps 20,000 to 30,000 members and sympathizers. Al-Sisi sees Egypt's security problem with Bedouin and fundamentalists in the Sinai Peninsula as a side-effect of Hamas activities.

So the Egyptians have been unusually energetic in closing off the smuggling routes and tunnels into Gaza from Sinai. This move has, along with the vigorous Israeli blockade, contributed to fuel shortages and water and sewage problems as well as economic distress. At the same time, young Palestinians in Gaza have rebelled against Hamas and some say they want to see it overthrown the way Morsi was.

My guess is that Israeli Prime Minister Binyamin Netanyahu and other Likud leaders see Hamas as unusually vulnerable. In essence, al-Sisi is shoring up Israel's western flank. The Israeli hawks no doubt believe that if they can destroy, or get Hamas to fire off, large numbers of its rockets, that they can deplete that stock and that al-Sisi will help ensure that it is not replenished, and that Syria and Iran might not be so eager now to help their fair-weather friend.

With leaders killed and rockets depleted, the Israeli hardliners probably believe, Hamas may be fatally weakened. At the very least, it will be less able to resist future episodes of lawn mowing in Gaza.

The theory behind this campaign, however, is incorrect. Hamas is perfectly capable of building more rockets, even if they are smaller and have less range than the imported ones. And killed leaders can be replaced by their cousins.

Gaza's population has grown to about 1.7 million in 2014. It has a high rate of population growth and will likely double over the next two or three decades. Egypt will never allow the Palestinians of Gaza to become refugees in the Sinai. In the 2008-09 campaign, when some Palestinians attempted to flee into Egypt, the Egyptian military just shot them. So the Palestinians of Gaza are Israel's problem, now and in the future. Gaza faces increasingly dire water problems, a recipe for severe future conflict. Israel eventually will face not 4.3 million stateless Palestinians but twice that.

As the living conditions in Gaza deteriorate, and people begin to thirst to death, the international outcry will grow louder. The boycott, divestment, and sanctions movement will grow, at first mainly in civil society and the business world, but ultimately it will be adopted by governments in the face of an absolutely unacceptable ongoing humanitarian catastrophe.

Ironically, the very mechanisms of economic sanction engineered by Israeli and pro-Israel lobbies against Iran and Syria are likely increasingly to be applied to Israel itself. The Israeli economy is fragile and highly dependent on outside trade and on European technology transfer, which could be sanctioned.

All it would take would be for the economy to be hurt enough to make it attractive for more Israelis to emigrate every year than immigrate for a reverse snowball effect ultimately to doom Israel, slowly and over decades. The Israeli right wing will likely fail in its attempt to subject Gaza and uproot radicalism there since the radicalism grows out of the conditions that Israel imposes on the Palestinians. It is incurring increasing ill will with its episodic lawn-mowing since the outside world is unwilling to accept that it was necessary to kill all those women and children and soccer spectators with aerial and naval bombardment.

As in the 1993 Bill Murray science fiction vehicle *Groundhog Day,* the Israelis, the Palestinians, and the world are doomed to relive these periodic slaughters over and over again until slowly, inexorably, they further corrupt the Israeli soul and make the Zionist enterprise so unlovely in the eyes of the world that it loses crucial support, and the snowball rolls uphill, getting smaller and smaller.[2]

Notes

[1] Creepy Israeli Planning for Palestinian "Food Insecurity" in Gaza Revealed - https://www.juancole.com/2012/10/creepy-israeli-planning-for-palestinian-food-insecurity-in-gaza-revealed.html

[2] For Operation Protective Edge see now Finkelstein, *Gaza*, 292-325 and and Baconi, *Hamas Contained*, 263-276.

18.   Israel Bombs Gaza back to Stone Age: Razes only Power Plant and Plunges Strip into Darkness

July 30, 2014

Israel launched a 7-hour campaign of intensive bombing of Gaza on July 29, 2014, destroying its only power plant. Gaza can no longer generate its own electricity.[1] Without electricity, the water purification plants cannot operate, and the drinking water ends up being mixed with sewage or saltwater. Without electricity, patients on life support in the hospitals just die, even if Israel does not bomb the hospital, as it has in some instances. The power plant will take the good part of a year to rebuild even after the war ends. Gaza gets some electricity from Israel and Egypt, but many of those lines have been damaged in the fighting. AJ+ explains: "90 percent of people in Gaza now have no electricity."[2]

Many Palestinians in Gaza have been reduced to living by candlelight after sunset. This dearth of electricity also has implications for what the outside world can know about the condition of Palestinian families there.

Israel has completely reduced to rubble some 5,000 homes and damaged 26,000.[3] If you figure that Palestinians in Gaza live on average five in a dwelling, there would be roughly 340,000 domiciles in Gaza. Israel has therefore destroyed or damaged about ten percent of the housing stock. This is on top of past campaigns of indiscriminate and wanton bombing campaigns. Since Israel keeps

Gaza under blockade, it won't receive the necessary materials to rebuild. The Israelis, having bald-facedly stolen the homes and farms of the people of Gaza, won't be satisfied until they are forced to sleep in open fields.

Israel has forced some 200,000 Palestinians to flee their homes. But since the Gaza Strip is so small, they have no place to go. Israel will not let them leave the Strip but is intensively bombarding it. Some of the places they have taken shelter, including schools and U.N. refugee shelters, have themselves been bombed by the Israelis. Channel 4 reported from inside Gaza on "shock and awe."[4]

While one can argue about whether this mortar fire or that aerial bombing was justified, the destruction of the power plant and therefore of civilian water purification is certainly a war crime. Babies in particular are vulnerable to dirty water, and often take revenge on their parents for the inability to give them clean water by dying. Israel is, as Rashid Khalidi argues, collectively punishing the entire Palestinian population of Gaza for being insufficiently cowed and for refusing to accept having been ethnically cleansed from what is now Israel.[5]

Notes

[1] "Gaza's only power plant destroyed in Israel's most intense air strike yet," *The Guardian*, 29 July 2014.
https://www.theguardian.com/world/2014/jul/29/gaza-power-plant-destroyed-israeli-airstrike-100-palestinians-dead

[2] AJ+: "90% Of People In Gaza Now Have No Electricity."
http://youtu.be/kpekJnM7Zpg?list=UUV3Nm3T-XAgVhKH9jT0ViRg

[3] "Israel has completely reduced to rubble some 5,000 homes in Gaza, Maan News, July 30, 2014.

[4] Channel 4 News: "Reports from inside Gaza on 'shock and awe'."
http://youtu.be/eH7gRFKTZ8g?list=UUTrQ7HXWRRxr7OsOtodr2_w
[5] Rashid Khalidi in *The New Yorker*: "Collective Punishment in Gaza."
http://www.newyorker.com/news/news-desk/collective-punishment-gaza

19. Boycott of Israel Spreads in Europe over Gaza War

August 6, 2014

The ill-considered and remarkably brutal Gaza war likely will give further impetus to the Boycott, Sanction and Divestment (BDS) movement by Western civil society to pressure Israel on its illegal actions toward the Palestinians. A thoroughgoing such European set of sanctions could cost Israel as much as $5 bn a year and more. Roughly a third of Israeli trade is with Europe, and the EU is Israel's largest single trading partner.

Unite, the largest British trade union, has now resolved to campaign for adoption of Boycott, Divestment and Sanctions (BDS) against Israel.[1] The Sinn Fein mayor of Newry in Northern Ireland is also calling on retailers in the town to boycott Israel.[2] Although the Irish government has declined to slap sanctions on Israel over the latest Gaza War, Irish civil society is generally disgusted with actions like the Gaza campaign, with its ruthless disregard for the well-being of noncombatants: "Many businesses, notably The Exchequer bar in Dublin, and the whole town of Kinvara have pledged to boycott Israeli products. The trade union of retail workers, Mandate, has called on shops not to sell Israeli goods and last night Irish rugby legend Gordon D'Arcy tweeted his support for the boycott campaign."[3] Exchequer won't carry Israeli alcohol products.[4] Some Israeli wines are produced on the Occupied Golan Heights and so are illegal enterprises. Note that these Irish businesses, towns and activists are going beyond boycotting squatter firms on the Occupied West Bank to boycotting Israel per se.

The idea of entire towns and cities boycotting Israeli goods is growing. Kinvara in Ireland is one. But several Spanish cities, especially those that lean left, are considering a similar policy.[5] Many in the Spanish Left also want to pressure the European Union as a whole to take more forceful action to sanction Israel for Apartheid policies and war crimes.

BDS applied to Israelis in the West Bank is more common, still, in Europe. After the Israelis deep-sixed John Kerry's peace negotiations last April, 17 European governments cautioned their businesses against doing business with Israeli squatter firms based in the Occupied West Bank, according to *The Economist*.[6] Under European Union law, these companies could be sued by Palestinians in European courts, claiming a tort over theft of their resources by the squatters and their European partners.

The Economist writes of the growing movement to boycott the West Bank squatters that the British Tesco supermarket chain has "axed fruit from Israel," specifying squatter-settler harvests from the occupied West Bank. It continued, "A Dutch pension-fund manager, PGGM, and Denmark's largest bank, Danske Bank, have sold stakes in Israeli banks that finance settlement construction. The Netherlands' largest public water-supplier, Vitens, cut ties to Israel's water company, Mekorot, which takes water from the West Bank and then sells it back to Palestinians."[7]

The Soros Fund has sold off its shares in Sodastream, which has a factory in the West Bank (that no longer employs any Palestinians).[8] So too has Norway's Sovereign Wealth Fund. The Bill and Melinda Gates Foundation also seems to be divesting from West Bank squatter companies. Also in Norway, "the leader of Norway's largest trade union confederation LO call[ed] for a boycott of products from Israeli-occupied land and clearer marking of Israeli goods."[9]

BDS in Europe is clearly growing as a movement. It could have a severe impact on the squatter settlements on the West Bank. But insofar as Israel proper is increasingly intertwined with the squatter enterprises, it seems inevitable that the boycott will spread to Israel itself. This is more especially likely if Israel goes on brutalizing the occupied Palestinians.

Notes

[1] UK's largest trade union, Unite, resolves to support BDS against Israel - http://www.redressonline.com/2014/07/uks-largest-trade-union-resolves-to-boycott-israel/

[2] Sinn Fein mayor in Newry, Northern Ireland urges local retailers to boycott Israeli goods - http://www.belfasttelegraph.co.uk/news/politics/fury-at-sinn-fein-boycott-israel-call-30466049.html

[3] Irish civil society's disgust with the Gaza war translated into local boycott actions against Israeli products - http://www.irishtimes.com/news/ireland/irish-news/some-2-000-dublin-marchers-call-for-an-end-to-gaza-violence-1.1886227

[4] Dublin's Exchequer bar boycotts Israeli alcohol products, including those from the Occupied Golan Heights - http://www.herald.ie/news/gordons-bar-first-to-boycott-israeli-goods-30478373.html

[5] Spanish cities, with a left-leaning inclination, consider boycotting Israeli goods akin to Kinvara in Ireland - https://latamnews.lat/20140725/Colectivos-y-partidos-en-Espaa-piden-un-boicot-a-Israel-160956866.html

[6] "Us and them," *The Economist*, July 30, 2014 - https://www.economist.com/briefing/2014/07/31/us-and-them

[7] Ibid.

[8] The Soros Fund, along with other significant funds and foundations, divests from Israel's Sodastream due to its West Bank operations. http://www.thenational.ae/business/industry-insights/economics/soros-fund-drops-shares-in-israels-sodastream

[9] The leader of Norway's largest trade union confederation calls for a boycott of products from Israeli-occupied territories.

http://www.newsinenglish.no/2014/07/26/jewish-museums-remain-closed/

20.   Top Five Ways the U.S. is Israel's Accomplice in War Crimes in Gaza

August 4, 2014

The U.S. State Department became a little testy with Israel on Sunday over the 6th school shelling by the Israeli military, which killed 10, saying "The United States is appalled by today's disgraceful shelling outside an UNRWA school in Rafah sheltering some 3,000 displaced persons, in which ten more Palestinian civilians were tragically killed." State Department spokesperson Jen Psaki added, "We once again stress that Israel do more to meet its own standards and avoid civilian casualties."[1]

As for the standard Israeli military pretext for such war crimes, that Hamas was hiding out in the school or firing from the school, no reporter on the ground has seen any evidence of any such activity by Hamas in schools where there are people. Then the Israeli military obfuscates things by saying that Hamas was "in the area." Since Gaza is so small, I suppose they are in the area of almost everything. But the State Department didn't let Tel Aviv off the hook this time: "The suspicion that militants are operating nearby does not justify strikes that put at risk the lives of so many innocent civilians."

Despite this bold criticism, the State Department and the U.S. government won't actually do anything about Israel's lawlessness in Gaza. That is because the U.S. is a full ally of the Likud government in its war on Gaza, which is configured as a fight to destroy or attrite the capabilities of the Hamas party-militia, a Muslim fundamentalist movement that has foresworn any attack on U.S. facilities or interests. As the head of U.S. military intelligence recently testified, however, if Hamas were destroyed something worse would almost certainly take its place. That is because you cannot expect people to live the way Israel makes them live in Gaza without their forming a resistance movement. Since they are kept poor and on the edge of hunger, the resistance movements they throw up are lean and hungry, and as ruthless as the Israeli army.

Here are the ways that the U.S. is actively helping Israel in its war on Gaza:

1.   The U.S. shares its raw signals intelligence directly with Israeli intelligence, enhancing Israeli eavesdropping and surveillance capabilities, as Glenn Greenwald shows in a new article for Firstlook.[2] Israel somewhat ungratefully repaid the favor by spying on John Kerry during his failed peace negotiations.[3]

2.   The U.S. continually replenishes Israel's ammunition.[4] If Washington were actually so distressed about the U.N.RWA school shelling, it could just stop sending the shells for a while. It did this to Egypt after the massacre at Rabi`a al-Adawiya last summer.

3.   The U.S. State Department actively helps Israel to economically blockade the civilians of Gaza. It even pressures Egypt to uphold the blockade (which is why it is silly to say that Egypt is also responsible for the siege of Gaza; Egypt doesn't have a choice in this policy that is made from Tel Aviv and promulgated from Washington).[5]

4.   Amnesty International shows that "Since 2012, the U.S.A has exported $276 million worth of basic weapons and munitions to Israel, a figure that excludes exports of military transport equipment and high technologies."[6]

5.   The U.S. actively opposed the granting by the U.N. to Palestine of the status of nonmember observer state.[7] It is this status that Palestine could use to go to the International Criminal Court and get a judgment against Israel for its illegal

squatting on Palestinian land in the West Bank. That the U.S. opposed Palestine having the standing to apply to the ICC shows how hand in glove Washington is with Israel.

The U.S. cannot serve as honest broker in Israel-Palestine negotiations because its government is overwhelmingly committed to and identified with Israel, including in this war. That is why President Obama keeps mouthing propaganda like that Israel has a right to defend itself (it doesn't enjoy an absolute right of that sort-- its defense has to be proportionate and within international law). The U.S. political system is the most corrupt[8] in the industrialized world, and our representatives have simply been bought and paid for by Israel fanatics like Sheldon Adelson or Haim Saban (the latter has also taken over Middle East analysis at Brookings, which used to have an independent editorial line).[9] It is scary since the Likud took over, since it is just as though a Serbian Lobby in the 1990s had bribed Congress to support Slobodan Milosevic.

Notes

1 "As Israeli Forces pull back, another U.N. Shelter Hit," *Sacramento Bee*, August 3, 2014. https://www.sacbee.com/news/nation-world/article2605735.html

[2] Glenn Greenwald article on U.S. sharing signals intelligence with Israel. https://theintercept.com/2014/08/04/cash-weapons-surveillance/

[3] "Israel Eavesdropped on John Kerry in Mideast Talks," *Der Spiegel*, August 3, 2014. https://www.spiegel.de/international/world/israel-intelligence-eavesdropped-on-phone-calls-by-john-kerry-a-984246.html. NB I have slightly revised this passage for print publication to ensure that the allegation is clear and uncontroversial.

[4] U.S. continues to supply ammunition to Israel despite shelling of a U.N. school. https://abcnews.go.com/blogs/politics/2014/07/u-s-has-sold-ammunition-to-israel-since-start-of-gaza-conflict/

[5] U.S. pressures Egypt to uphold the blockade on Gaza. http://electronicintifada.net/content/egypt-aid-conditioned-enforcing-gaza-siege/7272

[6] Amnesty International report on U.S. arms transfers to Israel. https://www.amnesty.org/en/latest/news/2014/07/usa-stop-arms-transfers-israel-amid-growing-evidence-war-crimes-gaza/

[7] U.S. opposition to Palestine's status of nonmember observer state at the U.N. https://press.un.org/en/2012/ga11317.doc.htm

[8] Juan Cole discusses the corruption of the U.S. political system. https://www.juancole.com/2013/12/corrupt-country-world.html

[9] John Mearsheimer and Stephen Walt, *The Israel Lobby and U.S. Foreign Policy* (New York: Farrar, Straus and Giroux, 2007).

21. Open-Ended Ceasefire between Israel and Gaza: But how Long will it Last?

August 27, 2014

As of August 27, 2014, Israel on the one side and Hamas and Islamic Jihad on the other have announced an open-ended cease-fire brokered by Egypt.[1] Its terms are similar to those of 2012.[2] Mass celebrations broke out among war-weary Palestinians in the Gaza Strip.

The Palestinians could argue that they have won some concessions. New checkpoints will be open and restrictions on imports into Gaza by Israel will be eased. The zone of the Mediterranean allowed for Palestinian fishing will start at 6 nautical miles and extend to 12 by the end of the year. (Current Israeli restrictions on fishing have meant a huge loss in protein for the population, and it is difficult to see what their purpose is beyond imposing a caloric restriction on the people of Gaza. The U.S. and Israel will drop their objections to Palestinian government officials in Gaza being paid. In further negotiations, Israel will press for Gaza to be a demilitarized zone (sort of on the model of Austria in the Cold War) and Hamas will press for the strip to be allowed an airport and seaport. Egypt will oversee these further talks and will police the agreements just made.

The Israeli side can claim to have inflicted substantial attrition on Hamas military capabilities, having destroyed many tunnels, rockets, and armaments stockpiled by the party-militia that has ruled Gaza since it won the 2006 elections. Moreover, because the current Egyptian government abhors the Muslim Brotherhood and movements of political Islam like Hamas, it is unclear that Hamas can restock its rockets and other weapons via the Sinai, as in the past.

Still, what the Israeli military was going for was a result similar to its 2006 war on Hezbollah in Lebanon; since that conflict, Hezbollah has not fired any rockets into Israel or Israeli-occupied territories like the Shebaa Farms (which belong to Lebanese farmers). It is not at all clear that the war produced any such similar cessation of hostilities between Gaza and Israel. There are undisciplined small groups in Gaza perfectly able and willing to construct some flying pipe bombs and send them over to Beersheba and Sderot (former Palestinian cities, from which Gaza refugees hail, that are now Israeli cities). One drawback of Israel reducing Hamas's capabilities is that it also reduced its ability to police the Strip. Hamas itself has in the past honored cease-fires as long as Israel has observed their terms. In part, that 70 percent of Palestinians in Gaza are refugee families from what is now Israel and that 40 percent still live in squalid refugee camps means that they are very unlike the Shiites of southern Lebanon, who are farmers with their own land.

If the Palestinian side really does get the things it is asking for —an end to the illegal and creepy Israeli blockade of the civilians in its Occupied Territory—then the struggle will have been a big win for them.

The good thing about peace, however, is that it need not be a zero sum game. Both sides can gain from it.

Obviously, this open-ended cease-fire is fragile. Some of the goals of the two sides will be very hard to attain. And, at root, the Israel-Gaza war won't really be over until there is a comprehensive peace settlement with either a two-state or a one-state solution to Palestinian statelessness. Israeli propagandists say that Gaza could be "Singapore" if it chose peace, but in fact, 1.8 million stateless people do not have the kind of rights, including rights over property and trading routes, that would allow them to prosper.

Israel's Likud government has the doctrine of the Iron Wall, of hitting its enemies hard and consistently until they comply. It has failed to secure the acquiescence of Palestinians in their dispossession because being stateless is intolerable. Israel is put forward by Zionists (Jewish nationalists) as a solution to the statelessness of European Jews under the fascists during the 1930s and 1940s. But they have a blind spot when it comes to the statelessness of Palestinians, figuring that that does not need a solution. Until Israelis come to terms with the Catastrophe (Nakba) that they have inflicted on generations of Palestinians, who have been left more or less homeless and in a kind of vast concentration camp, they cannot really make peace. And each episode of the Iron Wall with its Iron Fist degrades Israel a little more. Perhaps it can survive being an international pariah. But Israelis will one day look in the mirror and not like what they see, one little bit.

Notes

[1] Announcement of an open-ended cease-fire between Israel and Hamas and Islamic Jihad, brokered by Egypt - https://www.aljazeera.com/news/2014/8/27/palestinian-joy-as-israel-agrees-gaza-truce.

[2] The terms of the cease-fire agreement between Israel and Palestinian groups in Gaza being similar to those established in 2012. http://www.theguardian.com/world/2014/aug/26/gaza-ceasefire-israel-palestinians-halt-fighting.

22. What would Happen if the International Criminal Court Indicted Israel's Netanyahu?

January 2, 2015

[*On the occasion of Palestine's accession to the ICC and signing of the Rome Statute*].

If the International Criminal Court takes up Israeli government actions in the occupied Palestinian territories, it could well find specific officials guilty of breaches of the Rome Statute of 2002.[1] Article 7 forbids "Crimes against Humanity," which are systematically repeated war crimes. Among these offenses is murder, forcible deportation or transfer of members of a group, torture, persecution of Palestinians (an "identifiable group") and "the crime of Apartheid."

The Israeli government murdered Palestinian political leaders (not just guerrillas) and have routinely illegally expelled Palestinians from the West Bank or from parts of the West Bank illegally incorporated into Israel. They deploy torture against imprisoned Palestinians. Their policies on the West Bank, of building squatter settlements on Palestinian land from which Palestinians are excluded, is only one example of Apartheid policies. Getting a conviction on Article VII should be child's play for the prosecutor. And there are other articles which Israel is guilty of contravening.

If Israeli government officials or leaders of the squatters in the Palestinian West Bank were convicted by the ICC, would there be any hope of enforcement? Israeli firms doing business in the West Bank would be exposed to billions of dollars of legal actions in European courts and would be unable to sell their goods in Europe, if they were declared fruits of crimes against humanity and apartheid. If the legal actions were brought by Palestine, Israel would be ordered to pay it massive reparations.

The ICC can only work through member states. But it could authorize those states to capture and imprison Prime Minister Benjamin Netanyahu, for instance. While it is unlikely that this could happen, Israel's leadership might not be able to visit most of Europe, which would isolate them and much reduce their influence. The European institutions in Brussels would take an ICC conviction seriously.

The African Union and the Arab world decided to protect Sudanese President Omar al-Bashir from the ICC verdict against him. According to the African Union, he can freely visit African countries. But he cannot visit Europe or large numbers of other countries without risking arrest. And even in Africa, al-Bashir in 2013 had to abruptly leave the Nigerian capital of Abuja after only 24 hours because a Nigerian international law association filed a court case to have him arrested.[2]

Over a third of Israeli trade is with Europe, and technology transfers from Europe are crucial to Israel. It could be kicked out of European scientific and technological organizations, where it presently has courtesy memberships. And Israeli leaders could end up being afraid to visit European capitals lest they be arrested, as Chilean dictator Augusto Pinochet was arrested in 1998 after being indicted in Spain. Even if governments ran interference for them, they could not be sure to escape lawsuits by citizen groups and could not be insulated from activist judges.

The world wouldn't end for Israeli leaders if they were convicted, as it hasn't ended for al-Bashir. But the consequences would be real and unpleasant, and over time could have a substantial impact.

-Informed Comment

Notes

[1] The Rome Statute of 2002, the treaty that established the International Criminal Court (ICC), detailing crimes that come under ICC jurisdiction such as genocide, war crimes, and crimes against humanity. http://www.icc-cpi.int/nr/rdonlyres/ea9aeff7-5752-4f84-be94-0a655eb30e16/0/rome_statute_english.pdf

[2] Elise Keppler, "Dispatches: Bashir's hasty departure – Did he feel the heat?" *Human Rights Watch*, July 22, 2013. https://www.hrw.org/news/2013/07/22/dispatches-bashirs-hasty-departure-did-he-feel-heat. [Revised note.]

23. How Israel became a Typical Middle Eastern Dictatorship

April 2, 2018

The Israeli army snipers who were ordered to shoot unarmed Palestinian protesters last Friday at the Gaza border, killing 17 outright and wounding hundreds of others, were acting according to the contemporary script of Middle Eastern dictators. The Palestinians of Gaza were engaged in demonstrations for the "Great March of Return," underlining that 70 percent of them are from families expelled from what is now southern Israel by Zionist gangs in 1948, and that they want finally to go home.

The Israeli army initially admitted in a tweet that the tactic was premeditated and precise, but then deleted the tweet, as the Israeli peace group B'tselem pointed out.[1]

Sociologists who study how people mobilize to challenge an oppressive situation have noted that one possible response of any regime under pressure from below is to raise the cost to dissidents of their social action.

Imposing the death penalty is of course the ultimate in raising such costs. But randomly shooting into crowds is more than just threatening people with death. It is a means of terrorizing the dissidents. Simply taking hundreds of people out and executing them has dangers as a course of action for oppressive rulers, as well, inasmuch as it threatens to create large numbers of martyrs and impel reprisals. Moreover, large massacres can impose costs on the regime in the form of boycotts from other states or civil society actors. Randomly shooting into a crowd, killing a few people but wounding many others, has the advantage for the regime of creating uncertainty and fear.

This tactic was deployed during the youth protests of 2011. Secret police in Tunisia shot into peaceful rallies in provincial towns in late December 2010 and early January 2011 and then denied it and ordered the state press not to cover it. Blogger Lina Ben Mhenni took her smartphone to the hospitals down there and got pictures of and interviews with the victims and put them up at her blog (very bravely, since the regime could have direly punished her; but it fell before it could do so). See my book, *The New Arabs*).[2]

In Sana'a, Yemen, during the demonstrations at Change Square, dictator Ali Abdullah Saleh had his troops occasionally fire into the crowd. In one such incident one night, 350 people were injured.[3] Over time a couple thousand people were killed in this way (that is, being sniped at by professional soldiers while peacefully protesting-- I am not talking about clashes among fighters).

In Syria in 2011, the regime would station snipers on rooftops above town squares around the country. In each town a few people would be killed at each demonstration this way by army live ammunition. The regime was trying to discourage rallies by raising their cost, and indiscriminate such fire is a force multiplier, since the uncertainty of where the bullet will come from and whom it will strike is excruciating. Syria's brave protesters never were cowed by this cowardly tactic, and even today would protest if they were allowed to.

One downside of sniping unarmed noncombatants is a negative reaction from other countries. Israel's current far right-wing leadership does not worry about that. They think that the U.S. and the UK are the only countries that matter. Like Putin, they have tried to shape the U.S. political scene to suit them, targeting uncooperative congressmen and senators for reprisals. This is not only a matter of campaign donations by the Israel lobbies but of government covert ops. They also do this in the UK.[4]

Of 535 members of Congress, exactly one, Bernie Sanders, has condemned the massacre.

The Likud Party can also rely on an American television news blackout. Palestine is almost never reported on the airwaves and when it is, it is replete with propaganda. There are even problems with print news.

Robert Mackey, @robertmackey, observed, on Twitter, "By my count, there are currently 163 stories on the @nytimes home page and 116 on @washingtonpost but not 1 is about the Israeli massacre in Gaza, which was featured in print by both. There is also no mention among 126 stories on @CNN's U.S. home page, or in 100 stories on @latimes."

Academics in communications departments should look into this remarkable phenomenon. How it is arranged?

Be careful, though— even professors can be fired.[5]

It may be objected that Israel is not a dictatorship like that of Yemen or Syria. But for Palestinians in the Occupied Territories, that is precisely what it is. The Israeli military controls the Palestinian West Bank, though it farms out some duties to the PLO. The Israeli military encircles and blockades little Gaza with its 1.8 million concentration camp inmates. Stateless Palestinians experience Israeli military rule as a foreign military dictatorship. Palestinians are probably a majority of the people ruled by the Israeli government.

Moreover, dictators such as Egypt's Hosni Mubarak, had no bigger boosters than the Likud government in Israel.

So it is not really surprising that the Israeli military would adopt the same tactics as its peers, with which it often collaborates in maintaining the rotten status quo.

\-   *Informed Comment*

Notes

[1] B'tselem's Twitter post: https://twitter.com/mjplitnick/status/980307521545138177?s=21

[2] Juan Cole, *The New Arabs* (New York: Simon & Schuster, 2014).

³ *The Guardian* article on the incident in Yemen:
https://www.theguardian.com/world/2011/sep/19/yemens-bloodiest-day-yet
⁴ Juan Cole's article about Israeli influence in the UK:
https://www.juancole.com/2017/01/outraged-israeli-parliament.html
⁵ Juan Cole on professors being fired:
https://www.juancole.com/2014/08/nationalism-political-salaita.html

24. Palestine takes Israel to International Criminal Court over Gaza Massacre

May 23, 2018

Palestine has submitted a formal referral to the International Criminal Court in the Hague[1] over Israeli sniping with live fire at peaceful Gaza protesters this spring, which killed some 60 persons and literally wounded thousands.[2]

Palestine, which is a cautious and timid government, had earlier declined to go to the ICC, in hopes instead of reaching a negotiated settlement. The decision by President Donald J. Trump to recognize Jerusalem as Israel's capital, however, forestalled a negotiated settlement on that issue. Israel's illegal flooding of its citizens onto Palestinian property in the West Bank and refusal to negotiate any freeze in squatter settlements has also convinced Palestine that the U.S.-Israeli "peace process" is a cover for slow genocide. Ironically, it was Trump's lack of diplomatic grace that in large part impelled this step.

Palestine (or the Palestine Authority) was established in 1994 as a result of the Oslo peace accords signed by Palestine Liberation Organization chairman Yasser Arafat and Israeli prime minister Yitzhak Rabin. It held elections in 1996 and 2006. The PA was recognized as having authority over Gaza and Areas A and B of the West Bank, and the Israelis had promised at Oslo in 1993 to turn over all of the West Bank and Gaza to Palestine by 1998. Instead, they flooded hundreds of thousands of Israeli squatters into the Palestinian West Bank and ultimately reneged entirely on their Oslo commitments. In 2013 the PA began styling itself the State of Palestine after U.N. recognition.

This spring, activists rallied near the fence erected by the Israelis to cage Palestinians into Gaza, but none of them appears actually to have crossed the fence into what Israel considers its territory (Israel and Palestine have no formal recognized borders with one another, only armistice lines that Israelis have seldom honored). Palestinians in refugee camps demanded to be allowed to return to their confiscated homes in what is now Israel.

Shooting down unarmed people on their own territory when they posed no immediate physical danger to any Israeli is a war crime in international law. In fact, a war crime pursued so systematically after a while becomes a crime against humanity.

The International Criminal Court began functioning in 2002, when the Rome Statute came into effect.[3] The Statute is an international treaty now ratified by 123 countries, which attempts to strengthen the prosecution of war crimes where local courts cannot or will not do so.

So how could a Palestinian referral work? In the law, issues of standing and jurisdiction have to be settled before there is even a court case. The Israelis are denying that the ICC has jurisdiction and that the Palestinians have standing. They are wrong, and here is why.

In 2012, the United Nations General Assembly bestowed on Palestine (as created by virtue of the Oslo Accords, which Israel signed onto), recognition as a "non-member observer state."[4] This is the same status enjoyed by the Vatican. The vote made Palestine a U.N. observer and recognized it as a sovereign state. That vote in turn gave Palestine the standing to join the International Criminal Court, which it did in 2015.[5] Israel has refused to sign the ICC or recognize the body's jurisdiction over Israeli territory. So, Palestine is a member of the ICC and has been recognized as a state by the UNGA, and it certainly has standing to take this issue to the court.

How about jurisdiction? The Israelis are correct that the ICC does not have jurisdiction over crimes committed on Israeli territory, since Israel is not a signatory. The only way for the ICC to pursue a case in Israel proper would be for the United Nations Security Council to refer it to the court on the grounds that the issue was a threat to world order. The UNSC took this step with regard to Libya, and Moammar Gaddafi and his son Saif were found guilty at the court of crimes against humanity, which helped the Libyan people in their quest to overthrow the brutal and erratic regime.

The ICC does, however, have jurisdiction over war crimes and crimes against humanity committed in Gaza and the West Bank. So, the shooting dead of Palestinian protesters on Gaza soil by Israeli army snipers certainly would lie within its jurisdiction.

In short, Israel doesn't have a legal leg to stand on here. In the past, Prime Minister Binyamin Netanyahu has threatened to simply destroy the ICC if it dares move against any Israeli official. Israel certainly has levers it can pull against the funding of the court and it can target individual justices in various ways (Netanyahu invented many techniques later made famous by Trump). Whether this simple bullying can succeed is unclear.

The ICC does not charge governments with crimes, only individuals. If specific Israeli army snipers can be identified who shot dead unarmed civilians in Gaza, they could be tried, even in absentia. Further, the Israeli chief of staff and the prime minister, who have vocally supported the Gaza massacre, could be charged, as the responsible authorities. If they were convicted, they would experience difficulty traveling internationally, though obviously it would be difficult for the court itself to have them arrested. Their political enemies in Israel would certainly be emboldened against them, however.

In the past, the Israelis have also threatened tit for tat, saying that if Palestine brought charges against Israeli officials of war crimes, Israel would initiate similar charges against old PLO guerrillas guilty of past attacks on civilians. This threat could be carried out by Israeli courts, but, ironically enough, not at the ICC. Since Israel is not a signatory it cannot refer cases. And, if the attacks occurred in Israel proper, the ICC would not have jurisdiction over them. Moreover, by now few State of Palestine officials could be so charged.

The most significant implication of these developments, however, had to do not with the Gaza Massacre of 2018, but with Israeli squatter settlements on the West Bank. They constitute a violation of the Geneva Accords of 1949 on the treatment of populations in militarily occupied territories, and are so arranged as to fall under the crime of Apartheid as defined in the Rome Statute. If the ICC takes up that issue, it could reach decisions with far-reaching implications for Israeli policy. Again, even if the decision would be difficult to implement, it would certainly result in growing sanctions on Israel internationally.

- *Informed Comment*

Notes

[1] Palestine has submitted a formal referral to the International Criminal Court - https://www.aljazeera.com/news/2018/05/palestine-submits-icc-referral-open-probe-israel-crimes-180522101121093.html

[2] TRT World - "Palestine to submit a referral to ICC: Interview with Dr. Anis Qasim." https://youtu.be/EhdQ8tHpfVY

[3] Rome Statute of the International Criminal Court. http://legal.un.org/icc/statute/99_corr/cstatute.htm

[4] United Nations General Assembly recognition of Palestine as a "non-member observer state." https://www.un.org/press/en/2012/ga11317.doc.htm

[5] Palestine formally joins the International Criminal Court - https://www.aljazeera.com/news/2015/04/palestine-formally-joins-international-criminal-court-150401073619618.html

PART 4

Formal Apartheid and Israeli Extremism

In 2018 through summer of 2023, Israeli politics swung further than ever to the right. In 2018, the Knesset passed a law investing Israeli sovereignty solely in the country's Jews, some 79 percent of the population, formally making Israelis of Palestinian Christian, Druze and Sunni Muslim heritage —a fifth of the population — second class citizens. It was a harbinger of an Israeli turn to virulent ethnonationalism. The blockade on Gaza produced more misery, including dirty water that contributed to a quarter of maladies in the Strip and some twelve percent of infant mortality. The Trump administration's Middle East envoy, Donald Trump's son-in-law Jared Kushner, put together the Abraham Accords, in which the United Arab Emirates, Bahrain and Morocco were persuaded to recognize Israel. Each received a quid pro quo. The UAE, a fabulously wealthy postage stamp oil state, gained access to Israeli high tech and found a new field for investment. Bahrain's Sunni monarchy, perennially worried about its Shiite majority and Iranian ambitions, gained another geopolitical ally against Tehran. Morocco's claims to the Western Sahara, a former Spanish colony claimed by Rabat, were recognized by the United States. This set of somewhat seedy deals had the effect of throwing the Palestinian cause under the bus and announcing the irrelevance of the Palestinians. The despair this produced in the latter had a radicalizing effect. If the Arabs were going to abandon them, many young Palestinians appear to have felt, then they would have to take matters into their own hands.

Even as some Arab regimes forsook the Palestinians to make a separate peace with Tel Aviv and Washington, the International Criminal Court took their plight ever more seriously, with its justices deciding in 2021 that the court had jurisdiction over war crimes committed in the Palestinian Territories by both Israel and Palestinian actors, because of the Palestine Authority's signing of the Rome Statute. We now know that the court reached this decision despite a covert campaign of harassment and threats by the Israeli government from which the Dutch government did not protect its judges.[1] The Trump administration also engaged in thuggish tactics against the ICC, sanctioning its judges and even targeting their families.

Through 2021, a series of human rights organizations began announcing that they had concluded that Israel was guilty of the crime of Apartheid under the Rome Statute. They included B'Tselem in Israel itself as well as Amnesty International and Human Rights Watch. They reached this conclusion in part because of the inexorable expansion of Israeli squatter-settlements, promoted by the Israeli government, in the Palestinian West Bank on Palestinian land. This expansion was increasingly accompanied by squatter violence against the indigenous population, which the Israeli army often either ignored or even abetted. At the same time, militant far right Israelis increasingly pressured Palestinians in East Jerusalem, which Israel had illegally annexed from the occupied West Bank but where the some 400,000 Palestinians declined Israeli citizenship. The Israeli bombing campaign against Gaza in spring 2021 brought Palestinians out to protest in the West Bank, East Jerusalem, and towns in Israel itself with large Palestinian-Israeli populations, creating a political and spiritual unity among the four major Palestinian populations between the Jordan River and the Mediterranean Sea for the first time in decades.

In spring In 2022 and again in 2023, Israeli authorities put unreasonable restrictions on the worship by Palestinians at the sacred al-Aqsa mosque complex, resulting in clashes. Nothing was better calculated to create virulent Jewish-Muslim tensions than attacks by Israeli security forces on worshippers during the sacred month of Ramadan at Islam's third-holiest shrine, from where Muslims believed the Prophet Muhammad had ascended to the outskirts of heaven. Israeli fanatics on the extreme right, members of

Kahanaist groups that dreamed of entirely ethnically cleansing the Palestinians, increasingly stormed the al-Aqsa complex and began laying claim on it as the site of the Jewish Second Temple, which the Romans had destroyed in 70 A.D. Neither the rabbinate nor archeologists agreed that the Muslim holy buildings were situated over remains of the Second Temple, but the Israeli extremists continued nevertheless to press their claim. I was reminded by this conflict over sacred space of the attack on the Shiite Golden Shrine of Samarra by al-Qaeda in Iraq in February 2006, which plunged that country into a Sunni-Shiite civil war for a year and a half.

In late 2022, Israelis went to the polls, electing the most far right government in the country's history. Benjamin Netanyahu had been in the political wilderness for over a year, and was only able to put together a 64-seat majority in the 120-seat Knesset by bringing aboard the Kahanaist extremists of Religious Zionism and Jewish Power. Through spring and summer, these far-right ministers encouraged vigilante attacks on Palestinian hamlets by Israeli squatters in the West Bank, at one point passing out guns to them. The frequent storming of the sacred al-Aqsa complex, the squatter-led pogroms in the West Bank, the increasing repression of Palestinians in East Jerusalem (and the eviction of some of them from their family homes in favor of Israeli squatters) took tensions to a fever pitch. At the same time, the Abraham Accords sidelined the Palestinians and allowed Israelis access to Arab capital and investment even as the Palestinians were driven into ever greater poverty and insecurity. It was a perfect storm of despair and anger.

Notes

[1] Harry Davies, "Revealed: Israeli spy chief 'threatened' ICC prosecutor over war crimes inquiry," 28 May 2024. https://www.theguardian.com/world/article/2024/may/28/israeli-spy-chief-icc-prosecutor-war-crimes-inquiry.

25. In 2018, Israel announced Apartheid and Shot Thousands of Civilians

December 26, 2018

The year 2018 was in many ways a turning point for the position of Israel in the system of Western, liberal, capitalist democracies. It had long sat uneasily among France, Britain, and the United States, inasmuch as it was founded on a formal racial supremacist principle that Jews must rule the state. Racism is important in the other democracies, as well, but it is not typically enshrined in the constitution. The French Rights of Man mentioned nothing about race.

After 1967, Israel acquired substantial colonial possessions in the form of the Palestinian West Bank and Gaza, in which its leaders began implementing a classic settler colonial regime reminiscent of Apartheid South Africa. The Israeli leadership egregiously violated international law by flooding their own citizens into a militarily occupied territory, and by extensively altering the lifeways of the occupied population. I would argue that the occupation has lasted so long and witnessed so many severe violations of the Geneva Convention of 1949 that it is now illegal. Palestinians living under the Israeli jackboot do not have secure rights of property or control over their natural resources and, being kept stateless, lack even the right to have rights.

Somewhat astonishingly, the assemblage of far-right Israeli parties that rules Israel has managed to worsen its wretched human rights record in 2018 and to depart from liberal capitalist democracy almost entirely. Not only is Israel not the only democracy in the Middle East (that distinction belonged in 2018 to Tunisia), it isn't a democracy at all in the sense of a state of equal citizens able to vote for the government that rules them.

Informed Comment reported that on July 19, the Likud-led government passed a new Nationality Law formally vesting "sovereignty" solely in the hands of Jews.[1] About 21 percent of Israelis are of Arab Palestinian heritage and another 300,000 or so persons are not recognized as Jews by the Grand Rabbi and so would not participate in sovereignty; these are mostly immigrants whose mothers were not Jewish.

I wrote at the time, "It would be as though the U.S. passed a law designating America as a state for white Christians, excluding African-Americans and Latinos, and making English the only official language." I also pointed out that Apartheid is considered a crime against humanity in the Rome Statute signed by most countries in the world, which governs the judgments of the International Criminal Court.

Having formally turned non-Jews into second-class citizens inside Israel, the Likud government accelerated its colonization program in the Occupied Palestinian West Bank. The pace of building squatter settlements on stolen Palestinian land has doubled under the Trump administration in 2018.[2]

You may say it can't get any worse.

It got worse.

The Likud has a boycott on Gaza. This Israeli party roundly denounces boycotts of Israel, but is eager to place boycotts on others. Many key materials are not allowed into Gaza by the Israelis, and although food is not interdicted, in fact medical treatment is being de facto denied to most of those patients who can't be treated at Gaza's own rundown and relatively primitive medical facilities.

Some 70 percent of the people in Gaza are refugees violently displaced there by militant Zionist militias from their homes in what is now Israel. Most of them are still living close enough to their old homes that they could walk to them if they were allowed to. Again, Israel is in violation of international law in having expelled people from Israel and made them refugees, and then refused to allow them ever to return. Now it has placed them under blockade in their place of exile on the grounds that they haven't meekly accepted the loss of their property and lives at the hands of Poles, Russians, Ukrainians, French and Germans.

The horrible conditions of civilian siege under which people in Gaza labor has become intolerable, and this year they began conducting marches demanding the right to return.

These marches could have been a public relations disaster for Israel if the Western press actually did its job when it comes to Israel and Palestine. It does not, viewing the situation through a racialized and colonial lens rather as it used to view South Africa in the 1970s and 1980s.

I do not believe any of the U.S. news networks so much as mentioned the weekly protests in Gaza after the initial two or three.

Prime Minister Binyamin Netanyahu and his officer corps decided to deal with these marches by shooting the demonstrators down in cold blood on the Gaza side of the border. The American press, which despises the Palestinians with a passion for the crime of having been victimized by an American ally, invented entirely imaginary headlines claiming that the Palestinians had been killed or injured in "clashes." But there were no clashes. They with perhaps one exception never reached the Israeli border or actually encountered Israeli soldiers. They were shot down well inside Gaza even though they posed no danger to any Israeli military personnel.

They were sniped at by professional snipers. They were murdered. It is a measure of how ineffective and pusillanimous the mechanisms of international law and order are that no Israelis have been indicted for these murders.

The U.S. Senate passed a resolution naming Saudi Crown Prince Mohammed Bin Salman as the murderer of dissident journalist Jamal Khashoggi.

It did not pass a resolution about Netanyahu and his generals murdering unarmed, peaceful Palestinian demonstrators (not to mention journalists, medical personnel, and random children).

As of October 2018, Amnesty International reported that 150 Palestinians had been killed, 10,000 had been injured, "including 1,849 children, 424 women, 115 paramedics and 115 journalists. Of those injured, 5,814 were hit by live ammunition." The death toll rose by early December to 175 and by the end of the year to an alleged 220, and those shot in the legs are by now at least 6,392.[3]

One Israeli soldier has been killed and one injured.

The rallies are still being held every Friday and almost no one reports on them despite the creepy casualty tolls. The Israeli snipers appear to have deliberately aimed to cripple the Palestinians they shot in the lower limbs.

I haven't even gone into the rising tide of violence and sabotage conducted by Israeli squatters on Palestinian land against the Palestinians from whom they stole.[4] There is of course some Palestinian violence against the squatters, as well, but the Palestinians are so penetrated by Israeli intelligence and so regimented by the Israeli military and the armed settlers that there isn't as much of that sort of violence as one might expect given what is being done to the Palestinians.

The Israeli police have urged that Netanyahu be indicted for blackmailing and bribing the Israeli press to cover him positively. That is another way in which it is no longer possible to speak of Israeli democracy. American casino mogul Sheldon Adelson started a free newspaper to praise Netanyahu, which was hurting the business of the real newspapers, and Netanyahu offered them lower Adelson print runs if they would make nice with him in their stories on the prime minister. Press freedom under Netanyahu in Israel has been significantly eroded.

So, to avoid being indicted, Netanyahu has announced early elections for April. He put the attorney general in a difficult position. If he indicts Netanyahu now, he could be accused of forestalling a decision that should belong to the voters. If Netanyahu wins the election, he will argue he should not be indicted because the people have spoken.

Israel rules over about five million stateless Palestinians in the Occupied Territories. They will not have the right to vote in this election, even though the next Prime Minister of Israel will decide their long-term fate.

So, there you have it. Israel at the end of 2018 is now unambiguously an Apartheid state, admired only in the U.S. Deep South among those who are nostalgic for their own Jim Crow. Its leaders deprived a fifth of Israeli citizens of any share in national sovereignty. They sped up the colonization program in the Palestinian West Bank and coddled armed, violent squatters (who are often secretly subsidized by the Israeli state).

But worst of all, the Israeli elite decided just to shoot down unarmed protesters in the thousands, a clear war crime.

A systematic pattern of war crimes amounts to crimes against humanity, which Israel is certainly guilty of this year, even if the international institutions are too cowardly to indict the Netanyahus and the Liebermans, and even if the even more cowardly (or just frankly neocolonial) American press has been largely afraid to say these things out loud. There are significant exceptions here, and the print press has been better than television for the most part.

2018 was the year Israel finally went completely rogue and ensured that it can no longer be considered to be in the club of liberal capitalist democracies. It is now formally an Apartheid state even inside the Green Line. It is also the year when the Israeli elite consciously decided to shoot down with live ammunition unarmed, peaceful demonstrators in the thousands. These authoritarian policing methods most resemble those of fascist states of the interwar period.[5]

- *Informed Comment*

Notes

[1] Nationality Law: "The Nationality Law formally vesting sovereignty solely in the hands of the Jewish population."
https://www.juancole.com/2018/07/nationality-apartheid-supremacy.html

[2] "The pace of building Israeli settlements on Palestinian land has doubled under the Trump administration in 2018."
https://www.juancole.com/2018/09/construction-settlements-palestine.html

[3] At least 6,392 shot in the legs: "Details on the large number of Palestinians shot in the lower limbs by Israeli snipers" – *The National* (UAE), https://www.thenational.ae/world/mena/gaza-s-walking-wounded-israeli-snipers-have-shot-6-392-protesters-in-lower-limbs-this-year-1.800691

[4] Rising tide of violence and sabotage: "Assessment of violence and acts of sabotage by Israeli settlers against Palestinians" – B'Tselem. https://www.btselem.org/topic/settler_violence

[5] For the Great March of Return see now Craig Jones, "Gaza and the Great March of Return: Enduring violence and spaces of wounding," *Transactions of the Institute of British Geographers*, 48, 2 (June 2023): 249-262; see also Roy, *Unsilencing Gaza*, 312-317; United Nations Human Rights Council, "Report of the independent international commission of inquiry on the protests in the Occupied Palestinian Territory – A/HRC/40/74," February 25, 2019. https://www.ohchr.org/sites/default/files/Documents/HRBodies/HRCouncil/CoIOPT/A_HRC_40_74.pdf

26. Israeli Blockade of Gaza Causing Contaminated Water, Infant Deaths

December 17, 2019

Abeer Butmeh writes at *Al Jazeera* that because of the Israeli blockade on Gaza, equipment for water purification has not been imported and 97 percent of the Strip's water is now polluted.[1] Gaza has a population of about 2 million, equivalent to that of the entire state of Nebraska. Only it is Nebraska behind barbed wire, a large concentration camp imposed by Israel.

Most of the problems come from the Israeli blockade. But in a one-two punch, rising Mediterranean sea levels from the climate emergency are contributing to a salinization of the Strip's aquifer, its only local source of drinking water. These problems could be addressed with infrastructure improvements, but the Israeli blockade stops the importation of the needed equipment.

A quarter of illnesses are now because of bad water, and by 2014, 12 percent of children's deaths were attributed to unhealthy drinking water, with the likelihood is that that percentage is now much higher. *Haaretz* notes that Palestinians in Gaza spend 33 percent of their meager income on water, compared to 0.7 percent in the rest of the world. Over half of Palestinians in Gaza are unemployed because of Israel's blockade.[2]

This blockade is strongly supported by Trump, Pompeo at State, Esper at Defense, and by almost all the 535 people in Congress– that is, they support war crimes.

Rates of diarrhea in children have spiked in the past couple of years, and there is an increase in not only gastrointestinal disease but also diseases of the kidneys.[3] Cases of blue baby syndrome have also increased. Among the material Israel has refused to allow in are water pumps and their components, along with the components for water purification.

Shira Efron, Jordan R. Fischbach, Ilana Blum, Rouslan I. Karimov, and Melinda Moore write of Gaza at *Rand Quarterly* at the website of the National Institute of Health:

> Its dual water crisis combines a shortage of potable water for drinking, cooking, and hygiene with a lack of wastewater sanitation. As a result, over 108,000 cubic meters of untreated sewage flow daily from Gaza into the Mediterranean Sea, creating extreme public health hazards in Gaza, Israel, and Egypt.[4]

They add that "The main source of water—its aquifer—is being depleted and its quality diminished by seawater intrusion, wastewater seepage, and agricultural runoff."

Bad water accounts for one in four people who fall ill in the Strip, and given that wastewater is going into the aquifer, the major source of drinking water, the authors warn that major disease outbreaks are imminent and should be prepared for.

-       *Informed Comment*

Notes

[1] See Abeer Butmeh's most recent article on the Israeli blockade's effect on water purification in Gaza: https://www.aljazeera.com/news/2021/10/12/gaza-undrinkable-water-slowly-poisoning-people

[2] Study linking children's deaths and water quality in Gaza: https://www.haaretz.com/middle-east-news/palestinians/2018-10-16/ty-article-magazine/.premium/polluted-water-a-leading-cause-of-gazan-child-mortality-says-rand-corp-study/0000017f-e847-dc7e-adff-f8ef68c50000

[3] Increase of children's illnesses in Gaza related to water quality: https://www.aljazeera.com/indepth/features/gaza-drinking-water-

spurs-blue-baby-syndrome-illnesses-181029110434881.html
[4] Shira Efron et al. article on Gaza's dual water crisis: https://www.ncbi.nlm.nih.gov/pmc/articles/PMC6557038/

27. Abraham Accords: The War Pact Among Jim Crow States of the Middle East

September 16, 2020

The Middle Eastern parties to the "Abraham Accords," Bahrain, the United Arab Emirates, and Israel, did not make peace by signing them.[1] The small Arab Gulf principalities have long had behind-the-scenes relations with Israel and Israeli firms. They weren't at war with the Israelis. As members of the Arab League, they did in public observe some elements of that organization's embargo, such that they did not have diplomatic relations with Tel Aviv (that is where their embassies will be). But Egypt is a member of the Arab League (after having been expelled for a few years after 1979) despite having a peace treaty with Israel, and so is Jordan. So, adherence to the embargo is not anyway universal or a requirement for membership.

The state-owned Dubai Ports company admitted as far back as 2006 that it dealt with Israeli firms.[2]

The accords are in fact a war agreement among three heavily armed Middle East states characterized by a version of Jim Crow society.

The Israeli government is militarily Occupying five million stateless Palestinians, who are without basic rights, in the West Bank and Gaza. The government of PM Binyamin Netanyahu is determined forever to keep them stateless, and every day encroaches further on their land, property and human rights.

The Emirates is a tiny country of about a million citizens and 8 million guest workers with no political rights. It is run as seven absolute monarchies with oil-rich Abu Dhabi primus inter pares, with its crown prince Mohammed Bin Zayed al-Nahayan in charge. Bin Zayed has developed ambitions of regional hegemony. He pursued a brutal and ruinous war in Yemen, where his campaigns and those of his Saudi and other allies displaced millions of poor Yemenis and driven much of the country to food insecurity and the brink of starvation. The United Nations has accused the UAE of war crimes in Yemen.[3] The UAE also has wider ambitions throughout the Arabian Sea and Red Sea regions, in Eritrea even as far away as Libya.[4]

I wrote in August 2020[5] about the AP report that Trump brought up the sale of Lockheed Martin F-35 Lightning II Stealth fighter jets to the Emirates, suggesting that such a transaction would reward Abu Dhabi for contributing to peace in the Middle East.[6] I added that BBC Monitoring translated a report in the Israeli newspaper *Yediot Aharonot* that alleged that a high UAE official told its correspondent that the aircraft are part of the deal.

Despite all the talk about allying against Iran, the ambitions of the UAE are for military expansionism to the west and south. It already has a U.S. security umbrella against Iran. Mohammed Bin Zayed, by the way, did not come for the signing, possibly because the FBI wants to question him about his suspected role in campaign interference on behalf of Trump in 2016 and his secret visit to Trump Tower in December of that year when Obama was still president.[7]

Bahrain is also a small country, a set of islands, with a population of about 1.5 million. Roughly two-thirds are Shiites. The Sunni monarchy of Bahrain thus rules over a Shiite majority that is systematically discriminated against and deprived of basic human rights.[8] The government crushed the democracy movement of 2011 ruthlessly, and Saudi Arabia and the United Arab Emirates sent in small troop contingents to help. The major vehicle of majority Shiite political aspiration, the Wefaq Party, has been dissolved and its leader sentenced to life imprisonment for thought crimes.

Bahrain practices torture of political prisoners, something its secret police were trained in by the notorious British colonial official Ian Henderson,[9] the "Butcher of Bahrain," who had cut his teeth repressing the Mau Mau[10] movement in Kenya, and then was posted to Bahrain, where stayed on after independence to impart the Empire's specialized and exquisite knowledge of vulnerable anatomy.

Human Rights Watch wrote of its record last year,[11] "Bahrain's human rights record worsened in 2019, as the government carried out executions, convicted critics for peaceful expression, and threatened social media activists, Human Rights Watch said today in its World Report 2020 . . ."[12]

Ordinarily in diplomatic affairs some countries are afraid to get too close to Israel for fear of being tainted by its Jim Crow policies toward Palestinians. But in this case, it is surely Israel that has taken the hit in its reputation for cozying up to these ruthless regimes.

Notes

[1] Mahjoob Zweiri, "The UAE-Israel Normalisation: "If you can't convince them, confuse them," Qatar University, Center for Gulf Studies, *Gulf Insight*s, no. 35 (August 2020): 2-7. https://qspace.qu.edu.qa/bitstream/handle/10576/15890/Gulf%20Insights%2035.pdf

[2] Dubai Ports company deals with Israeli firms, Fox News article. https://www.foxnews.com/story/dp-world-says-it-works-with-israeli-firms

[3] U.N. accuses the UAE of war crimes in Yemen, *The New York Times*. https://www.nytimes.com/2018/08/28/world/middleeast/un-yemen-war-crimes.html ; Juan Cole, "Terraforming Yemen: Geoeconomic imperialism, the UAE and the southern secessionists," *Journal of Gulf Studies*, 1, 1 (Jan 2024):59 - 79

[4] UAE's ambitions extending to Eritrea, *The Middle East Observer* https://www.middleeastobserver.org/2016/09/20/___trashed-4

[5] Details on the F-35 deal within the Abraham Accords context, Commentary by Juan Cole. https://www.juancole.com/2020/08/stealth-israel-netanyahu.html

[6] Matthew Lee, "Trump weighs F-35 jet sales to UAE over Israeli objections," AP, Aug. 19, 2020. https://apnews.com/article/middle-east-e510c9e183b24299633b75d886f561b0

[7] Mohammed Bin Zayed's suspected role in campaign interference and visit to Trump Tower: see Juan Cole. https://www.juancole.com/2018/05/collusion-afraid-uae.html

[8] Marc Owen Jones, *Political Repression in Bahrain* (Cambridge: Cambridge University Press, 2020).

[9] Ian Henderson and his legacy of repression in Bahrain, IPS News article. http://www.ipsnews.net/2013/04/op-ed-ian-henderson-and-repression-in-bahrain-a-forty-year-legacy/

[10] Ian Henderson's involvement in repressing the Mau Mau movement in Kenya – *The Guardian*: https://www.theguardian.com/commentisfree/2011/apr/14/torture-mau-mau-camps-kenya

[11] Bahrain's human rights record in 2019, Human Rights Watch article: https://www.hrw.org/news/2020/01/14/1aaretz-worsening-rights-record

[12] Human Rights Watch's World Report 2020 on Bahrain, Human Rights Watch publication. https://www.hrw.org/world-report/2020

28. In Game Changer, International Criminal Court will take up Israeli War Crimes in Palestine

February 6, 2021

On February 5, 2021, the International Criminal Court found that it had jurisdiction to consider war crimes and crimes against humanity and the crime of Apartheid in the Palestinian territories.[1] Israeli politician Abba Eban once quipped that Palestinians never lost the opportunity to lose an opportunity. But Palestinians have carefully, methodically created this opportunity to be heard in an international tribunal. It is the ruling Israeli right wing about which one can now quip about missing opportunities.

It has been impossible for anyone to stop Israel's repeated and serious crimes against the Palestinians because the United States backs them to the hilt and is deeply implicated itself in keeping Palestinians stateless. The "two-state solution" long since became geographically impossible, and invoking it and an alleged "peace process," as the Biden administration does, is just a way of keeping the Palestinians from enjoying any human rights.

Israeli prime minister Binyamin Netanyahu cynically called the ruling "anti-Semitic," in the ultimate debasement of a term that has otherwise been central to human rights struggles.

The Palestinian Information Center quotes Rami Abdu, head of the Euro-Mediterranean Human Rights Monitor, as saying that the International Criminal Court announcement that it has jurisdiction over the Palestinian Territories represents a victory, won by many sacrifices, for justice, freedom and ethical values in the world.[2] It is, he said, the fruit of a Palestinian struggle that has lasted decades to win recognition of the right of the Palestinian people to self-determination.

As a result, he said, Palestinian victims of Israeli war crimes from various generations will gain the right to seek justice after decades of occupation and to see the perpetrators tried in the Hague. He cautioned, however, that "The decision does not mean the end of the road, and the task will not be easy. The hope is that the Biden administration will adopt a different course from its predecessor and will refrain from putting any pressure on the court."

In spring of 2020, Trump declared a national emergency as a pretext for being able to target justices and staff of the International Criminal Court with sanctions because they were looking into alleged crimes by U.S. military personnel in Afghanistan.[3] These outrageous and ineffectual sanctions have been lifted by the Biden administration.

The International Criminal Court was established by the Rome Statute circulated to U.N. member states in the late 1990s and finalized in 2002.[4] The United States and Israel refused to sign or to recognize the court's jurisdiction. In 2021 some 123 countries have, however, ratified the treaty and so incorporated it into their national law.

The court can take up cases of war crimes, crimes against humanity, genocide and Apartheid committed by officials in the signatory states. It can apply sanctions to individuals in those governments after trying them. It does not sanction states but individuals. So far, its cases have been entirely from Africa. But the court's hands are usually tied with regard to non-signatory governments. It cannot move against their officials unless the United Nations Security Council forwards a case to them.

The State of Palestine led by Mahmoud Abbas had little hope of the U.N. Security Council asking the ICC to look into Israeli war crimes in the West Bank and Gaza since the United States almost always uses its veto to protect Israeli officials from sanctions for their illegal occupation policies in the Palestinian Territories that they grabbed beginning in 1967.

The Palestinian David very carefully and with foresight therefore moved to join the International Criminal Court. The first obstacle they faced is that court members have to be members of the United Nations. Since the assassination of Yitzhak Rabin and the eclipse of Labor in favor of the far, far right Likud and its offshoots, Israel's policy against the Palestinian people has been predicated on preventing Palestinians from ever having a state. They are to be kept stateless and deprived of the basic human rights that come with citizenship in a state.

So, Palestine sought the same status at the U.N. as is enjoyed by the Vatican, of permanent observer state. The General Assembly can grant this status, and did so for Palestine in 2012.[5] Permanent observer states cannot vote, but they are not voiceless and can attend sessions. Palestine's prerogatives were expanded in 2019 when the Group of 77 at the U.N. elected it their chairman that year.[6]

In 2015, the state of Palestine (as the U.N. calls it) acceded to the International Criminal Court and recognized its jurisdiction in the Palestinian Territories, including East Jerusalem.[7]

This is like three-dimensional chess on the part of the Palestinians. Because they now have what is called in the law "standing." They are a permanent observer state at the U.N. and they are signatories to the Rome Statute.

Now just one step was left, which was to take to the ICC those Israeli officials operating in the Palestinian Territories in such a way as to violate the Rome Statute. Palestine did not hurry to do so, hoping that the government of Binyamin Netanyahu would see the legal peril and become more reasonable. But Netanyahu kept stealing their land and urging U.S. President Donald Trump to cut their funding (which he did), and by 2019 the Palestinians concluded that they had nothing left to lose by filing a claim.

The ICC prosecutor, Fatou Bensouda, declared a delay while she sought reassurances that the court had jurisdiction over Gaza, the West Bank and East Jerusalem.[8] A little over a year later, she has been assured that it does, given the recognition of the Palestine Authority as the government of those regions in the Oslo Accords.

As Mr. Abdu said, this step is more the beginning of something rather than its end. Netanyahu will attempt to obstruct the workings of the court. But this is a great day for the international rule of law, and all believers in human rights should rejoice.

Notes

[1] *The Guardian* reports the International Criminal Court's ruling on jurisdiction over Palestinian territories: https://www.theguardian.com/law/2021/feb/05/icc-rules-it-can-investigate-war-crimes-in-palestine-despite-israeli-objections

[2] `Abdu quoted at https://palinfo.com/news/2021/02/06/187809/

[3] Brookings writes about the Trump administration's sanctions on ICC justices and staff: https://www.brookings.edu/blog/order-from-chaos/2020/06/11/the-danger-of-trumps-new-sanctions-on-the-international-criminal-court-and-human-rights-defenders/

[4] "The Rome Statute establishing the International Criminal Court." https://www.icc-cpi.int/resource-library/documents/rs-eng.pdf

[5] "The United Nations grants Palestine non-member observer state status in 2012." https://www.un.org/unispal/document/auto-insert-187149/

[6] "Expansion of Palestine's prerogatives at the U.N. in 2019 by the Group of 77." https://www.un.org/press/en/2018/ga12078.doc.htm

[7] "The State of Palestine accedes to the International Criminal Court." https://www.icc-cpi.int/news/state-palestine-accedes-rome-statute

[8] "ICC prosecutor Fatou Bensouda's delay on jurisdiction in Palestinian territories." https://www.icc-cpi.int/Pages/item.aspx?name=20191220-otp-statement-palestine

29. Israel is an Apartheid State seeking Systemic Domination of Palestinians: Human Rights Watch

April 28, 2021

Human Rights Watch has issued a 214-page report concluding that between the Jordan River and the Mediterranean there are 6.8 million Jews and 6.8 million Palestinians, and that the Israeli state systematically privileges the Jews, wherever they are, and disadvantages the Palestinians, on the basis of race.[1]

HRW, like other human rights organizations, had avoided using this language about Israel-Palestine because its officials had considered the Israeli occupation to be temporary, and that the "peace process" would eventually lead to a Palestinian state. Over fifty years are not temporary, however, and there is no end in sight. Israeli officials are increasingly bold in insisting that no Palestinian state will ever be allowed and that the Israeli Occupation of Palestinian territories must remain permanent. It is the permanency of the situation that warrants the change in nomenclature, HRW says. "Israeli policies toward the Occupied Palestinians also resemble those of American whites toward African-Americans in the Jim Crow era, being based on systematic racism."

The Israeli human rights organization, B'tselem, came to the same conclusion about Israeli Apartheid this winter.[2]

The argument for Israel being an Apartheid state rests primarily on its 50-year-long occupation of the Palestinian West Bank, East Jerusalem and the Gaza Strip, the land, water, and airspace of which Israel controls. Israel has determinedly sponsored Jewish colonies on West Bank land owned by Palestinians and has universally excluded Palestinians from living in these squatter settlements. In about 40 percent of the West Bank, Israel has a junior partner in the rump Palestine Authority, but the latter ultimately is under Israel's thumb. Occupied Palestinians under Israeli military rule suffer from a deficit of civil rights.[3]

Even within Israel proper, however, the Israeli parliament in 2018 passed a law investing sovereignty solely in Israeli Jews and excluding the 20 percent of the population that is of Palestinian heritage. Although there are a handful of Palestinian-Israelis in Parliament, they are systematically excluded from cabinet positions or playing any part in forming governments, a role reserved for Jewish Israelis. Some Palestinian-Israelis, locally called "Arab-Israelis" still live in unrecognized villages such that they are not permitted by the Israeli state to build or to repair or improve their buildings. They were, of course, living there before there was any Israel, but have been retrospectively demoted to people without basic rights.

Some observers have complained that Israel is not exactly like South Africa under Apartheid. This is true but it is beside the point. For one thing, the current South African government and media see a firm parallel, as that country's SABC News affirmed.[4] For another, the Rome Statute that established the International Criminal Court adopted a universalized definition of Apartheid practices unconstrained by the South African historical model, which is intended to be applied to other societies in the world.

As HRW notes, the Rome Statute defines Apartheid as "inhumane acts… committed in the context of an institutionalized regime of systematic oppression and domination by one racial group over any other racial group or groups and committed with the intention of maintaining that regime." That language clearly does describe Israeli activities in the West Bank and Gaza.

HRW continues:

> The crime of apartheid under the Apartheid
> Convention and Rome Statute consists of three

primary elements: an intent to maintain a system of domination by one racial group over another; systematic oppression by one racial group over another; and one or more inhumane acts, as defined, carried out on a widespread or systematic basis pursuant to those policies. Among the inhumane acts identified in either the Convention or the Rome Statute are 'forcible transfer,' 'expropriation of landed property,' 'creation of separate reserves and ghettos,' and denial of the 'the right to leave and to return to their country, [and] the right to a nationality.'

The problem now is Israeli intentionality. The government means to do these things. HWR points out, "The Knesset in 2018 passed a law with constitutional status affirming Israel as the 'nation-state of the Jewish people,' declaring that within that territory, the right to self-determination 'is unique to the Jewish people,' and establishing 'Jewish settlement' as a national value." It isn't just a matter of the rush of events anymore. Apartheid has been enshrined in Israeli law.

Moreover, it is not just a matter of privileging Israelis. There is a policy of keeping the Palestinians down, as HRW notes:

To sustain Jewish Israeli control, Israeli authorities have adopted policies aimed at mitigating what they have openly described as a demographic 'threat' that Palestinians pose. Those policies include limiting the population and political power of Palestinians, granting the right to vote only to Palestinians who live within the borders of Israel as they existed from 1948 to June 1967, and limiting the ability of Palestinians to move to Israel from the OPT and from anywhere else to Israel or the OPT. Other steps are taken to ensure Jewish domination, including a state policy of 'separation' of Palestinians between the West Bank and Gaza, which prevents the movement of people and goods within the OPT, and 'Judaization' of areas with significant Palestinian populations, including

Jerusalem as well as the Galilee and the Negev in Israel.

As Turkey's *TRT World* reminds us, the Palestinians living in occupied East Jerusalem face eviction.[5]

Nor it is only a matter of limiting the population and power of the Palestinians. There is the systemic cruelty and inhumanity of Israeli policy in the Occupied territories:

Those include sweeping restrictions on the movement of 4.7 million Palestinians there; the confiscation of much of their land; the imposition of harsh conditions, including categorical denial of building permits in large parts of the West Bank, which has led thousands of Palestinians to leave their homes under conditions that amount to forcible transfer; the denial of residency rights to hundreds of thousands of Palestinians and their relatives, largely for being abroad when the occupation began in 1967, or for long periods during the first few decades of the occupation, or as a result of the effective freeze on family reunification over the last two decades; and the suspension of basic civil rights, such as freedom of assembly and association, depriving Palestinians of the opportunity to have a voice in a wide range of affairs that most affect their daily lives and futures.

HRW dismisses Israeli special pleading that these inhumane measures are necessary for Israeli security. In many instances, this is demonstrably not the case. In others, absolute Israeli security would have to be measured against the harm inflicted on the Palestinians. The HRW report and its new categorization of Israeli policy as consisting of Apartheid and crimes against humanity has predictably drawn the ire of the Israeli officials who are committing Apartheid and crimes against humanity.

Notes

[1] "Human Rights Watch issues a 214-page report concluding systemic privileging of Jews over Palestinians." https://www.hrw.org/report/2021/04/27/threshold-crossed/israeli-authorities-and-crimes-apartheid-and-persecution

[2] "Israeli human rights group B'tselem's conclusion about Israeli Apartheid." https://www.juancole.com/2021/01/president-respected-apartheid.html

[3] "HRW video on Civil Rights for Palestinians." https://youtu.be/yuSXuTSKOFM

[4] "SABC News discusses Human Rights Watch report on Israeli apartheid crimes." https://youtu.be/hFpbkCR6r8c

[5] "TRT World video about Palestinians in occupied East Jerusalem facing eviction." https://youtu.be/4NBXzb1NpyY

30. Israel's Pyrrhic Victory

It Razed some buildings, but Reinforced Palestinian National Identity

May 21, 2021

Regarding Israel's bombing campaign against Gaza in May, 2021, Israel and Hamas agreed on an unconditional ceasefire to begin at 2 am on Friday morning, which both sides put into effect, according to the *Washington Post*.[1] Palestinians throughout the Occupied territories celebrated what they saw as a victory, according to *Al Jazeera*.[2] One man in Gaza told the network that he took pride in the Hamas fighters who had allowed him to hold his head up high in the face of the enemy. Palestinians have an ideology of *sumud* or steadfastness in the face of a militarily superior enemy.

In the Occupied West Bank, people also celebrated, in part because the ceasefire came after only 11 days of heavy bombardment of Gaza. In 2008-2009, it went on for several weeks. People also were jubilant in Israeli-annexed Sheikh Jarrah, one of the flashpoints that provoked the recent round of Israeli bombardment of Gaza. Some of them told *Al Jazeera* that this time, it was different, that Palestinians across the board had been united in spirit.

There is a severe division between Hamas in Gaza and its rival, the Palestine Liberation Organization, with the latter controlling some of the West Bank. But in this conflict, Israeli harshness toward Palestinians in the East Jerusalem neighborhood of Sheikh Jarrah and the al-Aqsa Mosque in Jerusalem were rallying cries that united Palestinians across political factions and geography.

Aside from uniting the Palestinians as perhaps never before, the Israelis had no particular success. Gaza has been made even more of a humanitarian catastrophe than it already was, but Israel accomplished nothing of significance militarily. The Israeli military dreams of decapitating the pro-Islam party-militia Hamas, and we saw Ariel Sharon's assassination campaign against its leaders (one in a wheelchair) in 2004. Hamas didn't collapse then and it won't now. The 2004 assassinations in Gaza helped kick off demonstrations and attacks on U.S. mercenaries in Falluja in occupied Iraq, since Fallujans identified with Palestinians in Gaza and had formed a local branch of Hamas. Americans died in all that.

The Israeli military maintains that it destroyed arms depots and rocket manufactures. Maybe Hamas's ability to make the handful of long-distance rockets they stocked has been harmed. But most little Gaza rockets could be put together by a science class of eighth-graders, and they haven't lost the ability to construct them. Most of the rockets are useless militarily anyway—they are just a means for Hamas to wage psychological warfare with the Israelis who have had Gaza under blockade since 2007. While the rockets are a big nothing and almost all of them land uselessly in the desert or are intercepted, a tiny few get through and force Israelis to go to shelters. Israelis would like to forget the 5 million Palestinians they keep stateless and without basic rights just over the Green Line. The Palestinians are mostly weak and helpless, but they occasionally remind the Israelis that they are there. Some 70 percent of Gaza families were expelled by Israel from its southern cities, and they remember where they used to live. Israelis had hoped they would forget. They haven't. They won't.

Gaza has been left without much electricity. Water purification and sewage has broken down, raising the specter of cholera. There is still a COVID-19 pandemic in Gaza, since the Israeli government has ignored its obligations to the people it occupies under international law and refused to vaccinate them. Thousands of families have been made homeless. The major bookstore was bombed. The life of Palestinians under Israeli occupation will go on being hell.

Israel's Occupation and slow ethnic cleansing of the Palestinians flourish in the dark. By attacking worshipers in the al-Aqsa Mosque, Israel threw an enormous spotlight on its actions in

Sheikh Jarrah. These actions had the effect of uniting Palestinians across all four of their major administrative categories—Gaza, the West Bank, Jerusalem, and Israel proper. Israel imagines that it has defeated Palestinian aspirations to statehood. But what it has done since mid-May is to contribute further, and powerfully, to the ethnogenesis of the Palestinian people, and to uniting them across the board.

-    *Informed Comment*

Notes

[1] *Washington Post* article on Israel and Hamas agreeing to an unconditional ceasefire.
https://www.washingtonpost.com/world/2021/05/20/israel-gaza-conflict-latest-updates/
[2] *Al Jazeera* report on Palestinians celebrating the ceasefire as a victory. https://tinyurl.com/3wjazz4c

31.   How Israel Occupied Itself

August 10, 2023

On July 24th, 2023, the Israeli Knesset passed a measure[1] forbidding the country's High Court of Justice from in any way checking the power of the government, whether in making cabinet decisions or appointments, based on what's known as the "reasonability" standard. In the Israeli context, this was an extreme act, since right-wing parliamentarians were defying massive crowds that had, for months on end, demonstrated with remarkable determination against such radical legislation. And that measure was only one part of a wide-ranging redesign of the court system unveiled by Prime Minister Benjamin Netanyahu in January, which deeply alarmed his critics.

As exemplified by prominent world historian Yuval Noah Harari[2], such protestors warned that limiting the functions of the highest court, in a land with a parliamentary system largely lacking other checks and balances, represented a big stride toward a future autocracy. After all, dangers abound in a nation with a one-chamber legislature, lacking the equivalent of a Senate, that elects the prime minister as the instrument of its will.

The central motivation for that legislation, however, lay not in domestic politics but in the desire of extremists in the cabinet to ensure that the courts won't be able to interfere with their plans to vastly increase the number of Israeli squatter-settlements on Palestinian land on the West Bank and perhaps someday soon simply annex that occupied territory. Under such circumstances, members of the far-right Religious Zionist Party were recently excoriated[3] by Tamir Pardo, a former head of Israeli intelligence, as Israel's "Ku Klux Klan."

Reasonability, Fraud, and Occupation

The Israeli supreme court had invoked what's called "the reasonableness doctrine," rooted[4] in British common law, to strike down[5] Netanyahu's January appointment of Aryeh Makhlouf Deri as Minister of Health and the Interior in his ever more extreme cabinet. Deri, a Moroccan-Israeli, leads the ultra-Orthodox Shas Party, largely comprised of Mizrahim, or Jews of Middle Eastern ancestry, like himself. Deri has often been in trouble with the law. He was given a three-year jail sentence[6] in 1999 for fraud and bribery. In 2022, he was facing a possible conviction for tax fraud by the High Court of Justice, which could have resulted in jail time and a seven-year ban on political activity. According to the justices of that court, Deri promised to retire from politics to avoid being sentenced, a vow on which he later reneged.

Netanyahu managed to keep Shas in his current coalition despite its loss of that important cabinet seat. Indeed, he still needs its support to stay in power. Over time, the Shas Party has swung far to the right on the Israeli political spectrum, while taking an ever-harder line in favor of expanding Jewish settlements in the Palestinian West Bank, which Israel seized in 1967. It is now inhabited by some three million stateless Palestinians whose land continues to be usurped. The Shas leadership has shifted to ever stronger support for Jewish settlements on the West Bank in large part because of the increasing proportion of Israeli squatters there who hail from the Haredim[7] or Ultra-Orthodox religious tradition. They had already become about a third[8] of all West Bank settlers by 2017.

In the Israeli system, the Ultra-Orthodox pay little in taxes, are subsidized to study the Bible, and are exempted from military service. Moreover, as a group, thanks to their tendency to have large families, they have grown to about 13 percent of the Israeli population.[9] They place a substantial burden on the state, which, in recent years, has responded by giving them inexpensive housing on Palestinian land.

At the left-leaning +972 Magazine, journalist Ben Reiff recently pointed out that Minister of Justice Yariv Levin, a long-time factotum in Netanyahu's Likud Party and a driving force behind the recent attack on the judiciary, justified his actions primarily in terms of the Palestine issue.[10] He singled out High Court decisions that prevented the blackballing of individuals who supported[11] the Boycott, Divestment, and Sanctions (BDS) on Israel movement for the country's apartheid-style policies toward the Palestinians or who backed[12] "refuseniks," Israeli soldiers who decline to serve as part of an occupation force in the Palestinian West Bank. Levin also complained bitterly about court rulings requiring that Palestinians be treated in accord with the Geneva Conventions.[13] One conclusion from Reiff's reporting is that there will be ever more blackballing of critics of the occupation by the present government.[14]

The High Court (Sometimes) Recognizes the Rights of Palestinians

Another step Netanyahu has said he would like to implement is to allow a simple majority in the Knesset to overrule any High Court rulings striking down legislation as inconsistent with the country's basic laws on human rights, passed in the 1990s. Among the grievances of the particularly extremist Greater Israel faction in the cabinet is that court's dependence on international law in some of its rulings against "illegal settlements" — those established by militant vigilantes on West Bank land owned by Palestinian families for centuries.

Over the years, the High Court has, in fact, ruled in favor of numerous settlements, while drawing on aspects of Ottoman, British, and international law to do so. Ottoman law, for instance, permitted the state to assume ownership[15] of fallow land. On that basis, the court has, in the past, allowed the Israeli state to declare swathes of the Palestinian West Bank "state land." It mattered little that an occupying state settling its citizens on such territory gravely breached the

Geneva Convention IV[16] and the 2002 Rome Statute that acts as a charter for the International Criminal Court.[17]

In other words, all such settlements should be illegal. Palestinians often protest, to no avail, that land designated by authorities in Tel Aviv as ownerless and fallow is, in fact, private property and has even been recently cultivated. Once it officially becomes state land, however, the court has indeed permitted Israeli citizens to build on it, which is how most Israeli settlements on the West Bank came to be. The court considers such Jewish-only housing projects "legal" under Israeli law.

Although those settlements on the West Bank are often depicted as a volunteer and private activity, the Israeli government has long provided subsidies[18] and other incentives to people moving into such remarkably low-rent settlements and continues[19] to do so to this day. Because so many Ultra-Orthodox men, with their limited educations (and incomes), are unemployed, they are especially open to such obvious opportunities.

Although once upon a time many illegal Israeli settlements were swiftly dismantled[20] by the Israeli army, some survived and began lobbying the government for recognition. In 2017, the Knesset took a radical step, passing a law that allowed the Israeli state to expropriate Palestinian land at will and used that power to legalize sixteen previously illegal squatter-settlements. In 2020, the High Court shocked Knesset right-wingers by striking down[21] that very law and explicitly stating that Israeli sovereignty simply didn't apply to West Bank Palestinians who were under occupation and must be treated in the context of international law on military occupations. The Court even cited Article 27 of the Fourth Geneva Convention, which guarantees occupied persons respect for their dignity and family rights.

"Sovereignty and Settlement"

That ruling, with its explicit denial of Israeli sovereignty over the Occupied Territories, proved a genuine shock to the political right and underlies its ongoing Knesset campaign to neuter the courts. Extremist Bezalel Smotrich, now both minister of finance and responsible for the Palestinian West Bank, was deeply angered[22] by that High Court ruling. He insisted that the only acceptable response would be "passing the bill allowing the Knesset to override the courts immediately." As it happens, his own home[23] was built on private Palestinian land just outside the municipal limits of the "legal" settlement of Kedumim. The left-leaning Israeli newspaper Haaretz also reported[24] in June 2020 that then-speaker of the Israeli parliament, Yariv Levin, lashed out, claiming the High Court had "once again today trampled, as is its unacceptable tradition, Israeli democracy and the basic human rights of many Israeli citizens." As for Netanyahu, at the time he suggested that the problem of illegal settlements would best be resolved by a formal Israeli annexation of a large area of the Palestinian West Bank.

The way the high Court held that Israel has no sovereignty over the West Bank deeply offended the members of the extremist Religious Zionism bloc led by Smotrich, including its coalition partner, the Jewish Power Party led by extremist Itamar Ben-Gvir (who is now Israel's minister of national security). Under the circumstances, you undoubtedly won't be surprised to learn that their platform[25] for the November 2022 parliamentary election centered on "sovereignty and settlement" — that is, sovereignty over and settlement of the Palestinian West Bank. Indeed, they claimed that Palestinian agricultural and building projects in their own villages were "expansionist" and vowed to act quickly to curtail them.

Having joined Netanyahu's ruling coalition since that election, they have now acquired substantial power to pursue the goal of halting Palestinian economic life. Smotrich even called for a Palestinian village to be wiped off[26] the map of the West Bank. Though he later backpedaled under pressure, the lawless extremism that he and a significant part of Netanyahu's coalition today represent should be all too obvious.

Given that the High Court stands in the way of such lawlessness, despite its own frequent betrayal[27] of Palestinian rights, the extremists are determined to gut it. Significant numbers of those who responded to the recent mass demonstrations against Netanyahu's court decision with counterdemonstrations were bussed[28] in from the squatter-settlements, many of them Haredim.

The Imperiled Rights of Women, LGBTQ+, and Minorities in Israel

Although the right wing's primary motivation for eviscerating the authority of the courts had to do with the urge to take fuller control of the Occupied Palestinian Territories, the changes already implemented and still contemplated by Prime Minister Netanyahu and crew have dire implications for all too many Israeli citizens as well. As a start, more than 20 percent of them are persons of Palestinian heritage. Think of them as Palestinian-Israelis (on the model of "Italian-Americans"), though they are called "Arab Israelis" in Hebrew. Some 60 laws[29] and administrative decrees have already ensured that they remain second-class citizens. In 2018, in fact, the Knesset explicitly deprived[30] them of "sovereignty," reserving it for Jewish Israelis alone (while stripping Arabic of its previous designation as an "official language").

Admittedly, on occasion, the High Court has ruled[31] in favor of equal rights for Israelis of Palestinian heritage. It did, for instance, allow government funding of their religious communities and school administration. In most other instances, however, it repeatedly rebuffed their demands for equal treatment under the law, which helps explain why they have largely been absent from the enormous demonstrations that have shaken the country every week since January. Still, Palestinian-Israeli community activists are alarmed[32] that the Knesset's removal of court oversight when it comes to the reasonableness of administrative appointments could prove a carte blanche for far more active discrimination against Muslim and Christian Palestinian-Israelis.

Despite a distinct lack of concern for Palestinian rights, centrist and secular Jewish Israelis are in no doubt about the serious impact the Netanyahu government's gutting of the judiciary could have on their lives. That explains why a quarter of the country has participated in those huge, ongoing demonstrations and 58 percent of all Israelis want the government to stop trying to curtail the power of the courts.[33]

Haaretz[34] reports that women fear such power could lead the present right-wing government to put authority over alimony and child support in the hands of all-male rabbinical courts, block the government from signing onto the Istanbul Convention for the Prevention of Violence against Women, and increase gender segregation at beaches, parks, and the Wailing Wall. It might even move to reduce any commitment to their very presence on governmental bodies.

Similarly, LGBTQ+ Israelis, who had, through their activism, secured ever more rights[35] in Israel since the repeal of the country's "sodomy laws" in 1988, feared that their freedoms might be reversed by the most homophobic government in the country's history. That self-described "proud homophobe" Bezalel Smotrich typically supports[36] a law that would exempt religious people from being charged with discrimination if they decline to provide a service on the basis of their religious beliefs.

Corruption

Although the rights of women, the LGBTQ+ community, and minorities are obviously on the line, another pressing concern for those protesting the limits being imposed on judicial authority is the growth of government corruption, which could have a striking impact on the country's future. Netanyahu is already on trial for accepting bribes (a trial he's tried to legislate away).[37] He also wanted to make the notoriously corrupt Aryeh Makhlouf Deri his deputy prime minister and may now proceed with that plan.

A Netanyahu government unconstrained by the courts could engage in favoritism in contracts, licenses, and legislation of all sorts. The fear of such things has led 28 percent percent of Israelis, including a surprising number of young married professionals, to admit that they are at least considering leaving the country.[38] Many claim they fear that "the government is going to take their money."[39] Although 600,000 to a million Israelis are typically out of the country at any time, studying or working elsewhere, they usually do come home sooner or later. Now, however, relocation agencies report that such returns are plummeting. There has also been a 20 percent drop[40] in immigration to Israel this year and that shortfall would undoubtedly be even more serious were it not for the Russian Jews fleeing their ever more unstable, war-embroiled country. Reuters[41] reports that investors in the usually vibrant Israeli high-tech sector that accounts for about 14 percent of the country's $500 billion gross domestic product are now keeping about 80 percent of their new start-ups abroad. Many tech companies have also moved both their bank accounts and some of their assets out of the country.

Meanwhile, the protests — with hundreds of thousands of people in the streets every Saturday evening — continue, with demonstrators experiencing increasing police brutality. Masked[42] cops are arbitrarily beating them up and aiming water cannons at their heads, sometimes using "skunk water" — a putrid chemical that sticks to your clothing and skin — to disperse them.

Once upon a time, such tactics were honed to a kind of grim perfection to repress Palestinians on the West Bank. Now, the Israeli opposition is discovering that such brutalization of indigenous West Bank villagers has boomeranged and the government has begun to deal with them as it once did with stateless Palestinian demonstrators. Consider this the new Israeli reality: the 56-year-long brutal occupation of the Palestinian Territories has come home to roost and Israel is now occupying itself.

- *Tomdispatch*

Notes

[1] Stanford Law School's Allen Weiner Discusses Israel's Contentious Judicial Overhaul Legislation. https://law.stanford.edu/2023/07/26/slss-allen-weiner-discusses-israels-contentious-judicial-overhaul-legislation/

[2] Yuval Noah Harari on the Dangers of Israel's Judicial Changes. https://www.ft.com/content/b027a525-05b1-45fc-a2c2-f131d341bc6b

[3] Ex-Mossad Chief Compares Israeli Right to the KKK. https://www.haaretz.com/israel-news/2023-07-27/ty-article/.premium/ex-mossad-chief-compares-israeli-right-to-the-kkk/00000189-96cf-d1ae-a38b-f7ef6b960000

[4] Israel Unpopular Judicial Reform and Its Roots in British Colonial Rule. https://theconversation.com/israel-unpopular-judicial-reform-involves-repeal-of-law-set-up-under-british-colonial-rule-in-palestine-heres-what-that-tells-us-210401

[5] How Netanyahu's Cabinet Picks Challenge Israel's Judicial System. https://www.juancole.com/2023/01/1aaretz1u-crumbles-considers.html

[6] Aryeh Makhlouf Deri's 1999 Jail Sentence for Fraud and Bribery. http://www.cnn.com/WORLD/meast/9903/17/israel.deri/

[7] Special Privileges for Ultra-Orthodox in Israel Coming to an End?" https://worldcrunch.com/culture-society/why-israel039s-special-privileges-for-ultra-orthodox-must-end

[8] 30 percent of West Bank Settlers are Now Haredim. https://www.timesofisrael.com/black-is-the-new-orange-30-of-settlers-are-now-haredim/

[9] Israel's Ultra-Orthodox Jewish Population Growth. https://www.i24news.tv/en/news/israel/society/1682505239-israel-ultra-orthodox-jewish-population-grew-by-509-since-1979

[10] +972 Magazine Article on Israeli Judicial Overhaul. https://www.972mag.com/judicial-coup-reasonableness-yariv-levin/

[11] High Court Ruling on Israel Prize to Professor Accused of BDS Support. https://www.timesofisrael.com/high-court-rules-israel-prize-must-be-given-to-professor-accused-of-bds-support/

[12] High Court Decision on Academic's Appointment in Israel. https://www.timesofisrael.com/high-court-tells-minister-his-nixing-of-academics-appointment-unreasonable/

[13] Ajuri v. IDF Commander Case Study. https://casebook.icrc.org/case-study/israel-ajuri-v-idf-commander

[14] Israeli protesters concerned freedoms could be limited – *Al Jazeera English*. https://youtu.be/ynxgGnw2HS8

[15] How Israel Confiscates Palestinian Lands. https://www.aljazeera.com/news/2021/7/8/how-israel-backs-settlers-to-confiscate-palestinian-lands

[16] The Fourth Geneva Convention – Article 49. https://ihl-databases.icrc.org/en/ihl-treaties/gciv-1949/article-49

[17] Rome Statute of the International Criminal Court. https://legal.un.org/icc/statute/99_corr/2.htm.

[18] Israeli Settlers Lured by Subsidies. https://www.aljazeera.com/features/2012/8/23/1aaretz-settlers-lured-by-subsidies

[19] Housing Crisis Plan Turns More Israelis into Settlers. https://www.haaretz.com/israel-news/2023-02-15/ty-article-magazine/.premium/go-west-bank-israels-housing-crisis-plan-turns-even-more-israelis-into-settlers/00000186-545c-de95-a1fe-f65f212f0000

[20] Israeli West Bank Settlements Evacuation. https://www.theguardian.com/world/2009/jul/21/israel-west-bank-settlements-evacuation

[21] Adalah's Challenge to Israel's West Bank Land Appropriation Law. https://www.adalah.org/en/content/view/10035

[22] Israeli High Court's West Bank Land Grab Law As Unconstitutional. https://www.haaretz.com/israel-news/2020-06-09/ty-article/.premium/israels-high-court-strikes-down-west-bank-land-grab-law-as-unconstitutional/0000017f-e5d9-d62c-a1ff-fdfbdd720000

[23] West Bank Home of Israeli Lawmaker Built Illegally. https://www.haaretz.com/israel-news/2017-03-01/ty-article/.premium/west-bank-home-of-israeli-lawmaker-who-

championed-land-grab-law-built-illegally/0000017f-e2b1-d804-ad7f-f3fbdc170000

24 Haaretz Report on Speaker's Lash Out at High Court. https://www.haaretz.com/israel-news/2020-06-09/ty-article/.premium/israels-high-court-strikes

25 Religious Zionism's Platform on Sovereignty and Settlement. https://www.haaretz.com/israel-news/2022-11-06/ty-article/.premium/religious-zionism-will-seek-portfolios-with-most-control-over-west-bank/00000184-4988-d176-ab95-698817db0000

26 Call to Wipe Palestinian Village Off the Map. https://www.aljazeera.com/news/2023/3/1/israel-arrests-settlers-after-anti-palestinian-pogrom

27 U.N. Experts Alarmed by Israel High Court Ruling. https://www.ohchr.org/en/press-releases/2022/05/un-experts-alarmed-israel-high-court-ruling-masafer-yatta-and-risk-imminent

28 Haredim Bussed in for Counterdemonstrations. https://twitter.com/yadindudai/status/1683181536001048577

29 60 Laws Ensuring Second-Class Citizenship for Palestinian-Israelis. https://www.aljazeera.com/news/2021/1/12/this-is-apartheid-rights-group-slam-israeli-rule

30 Knesset Deprives Palestinian-Israelis of 'Sovereignty'. https://www.aljazeera.com/news/2018/7/19/israel-passes-controversial-jewish-nation-state-law

31 High Court Rulings in Favor of Palestinian-Israeli Rights. https://www.mei.edu/publications/judicial-reform-will-make-things-worse-israels-supreme-court-has-long-failed

32 Palestinian-Israeli Community Activists Alarmed by Judicial Reforms. https://www.aljazeera.com/news/2023/7/24/passage-of-israels-judicial-reform-entrenches-jewish-supremacy.

33 Majority of Israelis Oppose Government Curtailing Power of Courts. https://www.jpost.com/israel-news/politics-and-diplomacy/article-750301

34 *Haaretz*: Israeli Women's Rights Under Threat. https://www.haaretz.com/israel-news/2023-07-25/ty-article-

magazine/.premium/israels-government-frightening-steps-against-women-explained/00000189-8d4c-d95c-a7ab-fd7dec9e0000

[35] Struggle for LGBTQ+ Rights in Israel. https://theconversation.com/israeli-protesters-fear-for-the-future-of-their-countrys-precarious-lgbtq-rights-revolution-205915

[36] Smotrich, a Proud Homophobe, Supports Discrimination Exemption Law. https://www.timesofisrael.com/smotrich-my-voters-dont-care-im-a-homophobic-fascist-but-my-word-is-my-word/

[37] Netanyahu Attempts to Legislate Away His Bribery Trial. https://www.aljazeera.com/news/2023/8/3/challenge-to-israeli-law-protecting-pm-from-removal-goes-to-supreme-court

[38] 28 percent of Israelis Considering Leaving the Country. https://www.haaretz.com/israel-news/2023-07-27/ty-article-magazine/.highlight/exodus-the-israelis-planning-their-escape-from-netanyahus-judicial-coup/00000189-97c2-d00f-a7db-b7db7c0c0000

[39] Israelis Claim Fears of Government Seizing Their Assets. https://www.haaretz.com/israel-news/2023-07-27/ty-article-magazine/.premium/exodus-the-israelis-planning-their-escape-from-netanyahus-judicial-coup/00000189-97c2-d00f-a7db-b7db7c0c0000

[40] Drop in Immigration to Israel Amid Judicial Overhaul Concerns. https://www.haaretz.com/israel-news/2023-07-17/ty-article/.premium/the-judicial-overhaul-effect-aliyah-down-nearly-20-percent-in-first-half-of-2023/00000189-6487-de4e-adeb-ffa7dd1f0000

[41] Economic Risks Surface as Netanyahu Moves Judicial Changes Forward. https://www.reuters.com/world/middle-east/netanyahu-judicial-move-spawns-economic-political-risks-2023-07-25/

[42] Israeli Police Use of Skunk Water Against Protestors. https://www.haaretz.com/israel-news/2023-07-30/ty-article-magazine/.premium/masked-unidentifiable-cops-beat-israeli-civilians-with-impunity-how-long-can-it-go-on/00000189-a835-d00f-a7db-b9bfb10c0000

PART 5

October 7 and Colonial Revenge Genocide

The history of modern Gaza can now be divided into the era before Hamas' terrorist attack of October 7, 2023, and the period after it. The assault was launched broke through the militarized border with Gaza on Shabbat, the last day of the Jewish holiday of Sukkot. In the aftermath, the Israelis would turn the Strip into a Mad Max post-apocalyptic nightmare, even altering its physical geography, and likely setting in train the death of at least ten percent of the population of 2.2 million. The al-Qassam Brigades, Hamas' paramilitary, and its allies such as the Palestinian Islamic Jihad, was found by the United Nations Independent International Commission of Inquiry on the Occupied Palestinian Territory and Israel on May, 2024, to have committed grave war crimes.[1]

The Commission reviewed the horrific statistics for that day, quoting from Israeli sources, saying that upwards of 1,200 individuals were directly killed by members of various Palestinian militant factions and by rockets and mortars fired from the Gaza Strip. Among these casualties, at least 809 were civilian noncombatants, including a minimum of 280 women and 68 foreign nationals. Some 314 Israeli military personnel were killed. The deceased also included 40 children (at least 23 boys and 15 girls) and 25 individuals aged 80 and above. Additionally, 14,970 people sustained injuries and were transported to hospitals for medical care.

The assault chased 150,000 Israelis from their homes, most of who had not been able to return nearly a year later. The Commission reviewed the militants' onslaught on kibbutzim, the old-time Israeli agricultural cooperatives dedicated to communal living and labor socialist principles, inhabited by a dwindling breed of Israeli peaceniks. The authors explained that they targeted a minimum of 24 localities, including civilian objectives, public areas, and outdoor gatherings. At these locations, they wrote, militants systematically moved from house to house igniting homes, firing into both private and public shelters, and forcibly removing individuals from their hiding spots, resulting in deaths, injuries, and abductions to Gaza.

The Commission scrutinized six distinct attacks in Kibbutz Be'eri and eight assaults in Nir Oz, each involving multiple casualties, predominantly from the same households. The authors wrote that in Be'eri, 105 civilians were killed (63 men and 42 women) by members of Hamas's military wing, the Palestinian Islamic Jihad (PIJ), and armed civilians from Gaza. Furthermore, 31 civilians (13 men and 18 women) were kidnapped and taken to the Gaza Strip. The kibbutz attackers opened fire on residents, vehicles, pets, and homes, causing fatalities and injuries, and also committed arson.

Then there was the monstrous attack on the Nova music festival in Re'im, where the Commission says that of the 3,000 attendees, 364 participants (including 215 men and 136 women) were killed by members of Hamas's military wing and other Palestinian militant groups, with around 40 others being kidnapped to Gaza. The victims, the authors write, were slain at the main festival site while trying to hide under the stage, in portable toilets, inside parked cars, and in garbage bins.

The Commission concluded that although Hamas fighters degraded the bodies of women, leaving them unclothed after their murder and parading them when taken as hostages in Gaza, it could not independently corroborate allegations of rape. It is crucial to note that the Commission deemed the allegations plausible based on the condition and positioning of some deceased bodies. However, its investigation was hindered by Israel's refusal to cooperate, preventing a definitive conclusion. Clear evidence of sexual violence was found.

The United Nations charter and subsequent U.N. instruments and treaties give a national liberation movement the right to wage a war against foreign occupiers.[2] Certainly, the cruel and grossly illegal

Israeli treatment of the Palestinians of Gaza, detailed above, constituted a plausible casus belli, inasmuch as the effort was made to prevent them from attaining self-determination as a people. That right to pursue a war of liberation (which was after all how the United States came to be), however, is not a blank check to commit war crimes, and peaceful farmers and attendees at a rave are not legitimate targets. Such a guerrilla war is not something I wish on either my Israeli or Palestinian friends, and I wish the conflict could have been settled by mature diplomacy instead. I argue below that, moreover, fighters for national liberation have a responsibility only to mount such a campaign when the geographical and other contexts are favorable; otherwise, as even Mao Zedong observed, they become mere roving bandits who do more harm to their people than good. The Hamas attack was, of course, also directed at military objectives, where the militants even managed to take over an Israeli base, and in the course of which they killed 314 Israeli soldiers. The Commission concluded, however, that the militants killed unarmed and wounded soldiers who were no longer in combat and should not have been killed according to the laws of war. Even in the minority of cases where their targets were military, the militants acted lawlessly and in a cowardly fashion. The Commission determined that Hamas, Palestinian Islamic Jihad, and other factions were culpable of significant breaches of the laws of war as detailed in International Humanitarian Law and International Human Rights Law.

Having traveled in Israel, and having Israeli friends, I was as horrified by these events as anyone else. I later wrote to colleagues in an email, "The niece of a Jewish American friend of mine was kidnapped by Hamas with her family, and although she and her children were released at the pause, her husband was killed. When I heard about the massacre at Kibbutz Be'eri it was like a gut punch. I remembered my own stay at a kibbutz near Beersheba when at a conference once at Ben Gurion University. I have written about how it seems to me that Qassam Brigades commanders like Mohammed Deif and its cadres appear to have adopted the ISIL doctrine of *tawahhush* or beastliness." (For more on the possible influence of the so-called Islamic State group — ISIS or ISIL — see below.)

It must also be acknowledged that on that day, the Israeli high command invoked the "Hannibal Directive," issuing an order in a communique at 11:22 am that said, "Not a single vehicle can return to Gaza."[3] The order was for the Israeli military to destroy those vehicles rather than let Hamas and its allies take hostages back to the Strip. That is, some of the 1,139 deaths were owing to Israeli fire on vehicles carrying hostages. It is not clear how many Israelis perished at the hands of their own troops in this way, but it should be underlined that most of the killing was committed by Hamas and its allies.

We all expected that the Israeli government would reply vigorously to the attack, most of all to reassure skittish Israelis about the future of their country. Some 12,300 of them fled abroad in the month after the assault and did not return. Moreover, returnees from the large Israeli expatriate population of several hundred thousand fell by 21 percent between November and March.[4] What I think few expected was that the extremist character of Netanyahu's cabinet would lead the government into more than the typical reprisal, of killing ten Palestinians for every Israeli, that we had seen in the previous two decades. Rather, Netanyahu announced the application of the Amalek doctrine of total war, citing 1 Samuel 15:7-8, "Saul defeated the Amalekites, from Havilah as far as Shur, which is east of Egypt. He took King Agag of the Amalekites alive but utterly destroyed all the people with the edge of the sword."[5] The Israeli government announced that it would immediately cut off Gaza from food and water deliveries, the only way most people there could live. The U.N. Commission cited above quoted Israeli Minister of Defense Yoav Galant as saying, "Gaza will never return to be what it was," and "I have released all restraints, we use everything." The Commission authors noted that they often could not find any evidence of a military target when they looked at the intensive Israeli bombardment of several residential neighborhoods with 2,000-pound bombs. By mid-December, U.S. satellite imagery showed 500 craters created by these massive bombs, which kill everyone within a 1,000-foot radius.[6] Since I have many Palestinian friends, this unfolding atrocity has been a daily horror for me, invading my dreams and turning them into nightmares.

Notes

[1] Report of the Independent International Commission of Inquiry on the Occupied Palestinian Territory, including East Jerusalem, and Israel, 27 May, 2024. Link via https://www.ohchr.org/en/press-releases/2024/06/israeli-authorities-palestinian-armed-groups-are-responsible-war-crimes

[2] Noelle Higgins, "The Regulation of Armed Non-State Actors: Promoting the Application of the Laws of War to Conflicts Involving National Liberation Movements," *Human Rights Brief* 17, 1 (2009): 12-18. https://digitalcommons.wcl.american.edu/cgi/viewcontent.cgi?article=1101&context=hrbrief

[3] Yaniv Kubovich, "IDF Ordered Hannibal Directive on October 7 to Prevent Hamas Taking Soldiers Captive," *Haaretz*, July 7, 2024. https://www.haaretz.com/israel-news/2024-07-07/ty-article-magazine/.premium/idf-ordered-hannibal-directive-on-october-7-to-prevent-hamas-taking-soldiers-captive/00000190-89a2-d776-a3b1-fdbe45520000

[4] "Data shows post-Oct. 7 emigration surge from Israel, which has since stabilized," *Times of Israel*, July 19, 2024. https://www.timesofisrael.com/data-shows-post-oct-7-emigration-surge-from-israel-which-has-since-stabilized/

[5] Juan Cole, "Netanyahu declares a Holy War of Annihilation on Civilians of Gaza, Citing the Bible," *Informed Comment*, October 29, 2023. https://www.juancole.com/2023/10/netanyahu-annihilation-civilians.html

[6] Tamara Qiblawi et al., "'Not seen since Vietnam': Israel dropped hundreds of 2,000-pound bombs on Gaza, analysis shows," CNN,

December 22, 2023. https://www.cnn.com/gaza-israel-big-bombs/index.html

32. Can Hamas Survive the Stupidity of its "Wild Beast" Tactics?

October 10, 2023

Hamas leaders have said they were driven to their attack on Israel on October 7, 2023 by two major considerations, the danger posed by right wing religious Zionism to the al-Aqsa mosque complex, the third holiest shrine for 2 billion Muslims, and a wave of Israeli squatter attacks on Palestinian hamlets in the Palestinian West Bank. Ibrahim Ibrash, writing for the London-based pan-Arab daily, *al-Arab* is puzzled by these announced goals because, being based in Gaza, Hamas does not have the capability of intervening in East Jerusalem or the Palestinian West Bank.[1]

These articulated objectives, if we take them seriously, suggest to me that Hamas's Operation al-Aqsa Storm may have been intended in part to allow it to displace the Palestine Authority from the West Bank. Palestinians are furious at Mahmoud Abbas and the PA for helping Israel crack down on "Lion's Den" militant young men in Nablus, and at their helplessness before the repeated storming of the al-Aqsa complex by Jewish Power and Religious Zionism fanatics, who are vowing to partition the complex and to establish a Jewish place of worship there. (This plan is denounced by all the rabbis, who say that Jews should not go atop the Temple Mount lest they commit blasphemy. Archeologists say that the al-Aqsa complex is not on the site of the Second Temple, which the Romans destroyed in 70 AD.)

Ironically, Israeli intelligence backed Hamas beginning in the late 1980s in hopes of offsetting the power of the PLO, led by Yasser Arafat.[2] They do not seem to have stopped to consider that secular forces like the PLO are typically more pragmatic than messianic religious movements.

Israeli Prime Minister Benjamin Netanyahu has accused Hamas of being identical to ISIL, the so-called "Islamic state" group that terrorized Iraq and Syria with killings of civilians and mass violence in 2014-2018.

It is not an exact parallel, but Hamas is deploying some of the techniques of ISIL, of mass violence as a spectacle and object lesson, and for the same purpose. ISIL wanted to mobilize Muslim activists behind it, and to demonstrate that its direct action made it most suited to lead the Muslim world. The purpose of the violence deployed against the West was to make Muslims choose between ISIL and the North Atlantic states, to polarize them and remove any "gray zone" where allegiances were unclear.[3]

My guess is that Hamas's terrorism against Israelis was meant to announce that its leaders could get the job done, of throwing off Israeli hegemony and halting the march toward Israeli appropriation of Palestinian holy sites, land and resources. In such a situation, staying loyal to the Palestine Authority becomes tantamount to siding with Israel against the active Resistance.

It seems likely that if there were fair elections, Hamas would win a majority of votes in the West Bank, even before its recent attack on Israel. Now, it will be wildly popular in the West Bank, not because it slaughtered Israeli concertgoers but because it demonstrated that Palestinians could still go on the offensive. For people worried about Israeli squatters shooting up their communities and stealing their water and other resources, the prospect of having a group among them who would defend them and fight back, as Fateh and other West Bank-based groups have not, would be attractive.

Hamas does not, however, appear to have learned anything from ISIL's catastrophic failures. ISIL's use of "beastly" [*tawahhush*] violence alienated everyone from it and left it with no allies at all.[4] With the Shiites of Iraq, the Kurds, the Iraqi and Syrian governments, the U.S., NATO, Iran, and the Russian Federation all determined to destroy it, it was doomed to be rolled up. Of course, the beastly tactics of mass murder, enslavement, beheadings, and so forth are objectionable on human rights grounds. But they also were pursued in a particularly moronic fashion. It was for that reason that I shocked some people in 2014 by calling ISIL a flash in the pan.

ISIL deployed the tactics of guerrilla war without having a covert base to which it could retreat. It had a return address, at its headquarters in Raqqa, Syria. The point of guerrilla tactics, including terrorist attacks on noncombatants, is to offset the enemy's conventional military might and to spread fear in their ranks. But that only works if you can retreat to hills or caves or swamps, to some place that the conventional military of the enemy can't easily get at you.

I read somewhere that Mao Zedong said that a guerrilla army without a covert base to which to retreat is like a man without an ass. He has to keep running around until he becomes exhausted because he has nowhere to sit. More formally, in his writing about guerrilla war, Mao emphasized the importance of the "establishment of base areas." He predicted, "in order to safeguard his gains in the occupied areas, the enemy is bound to step up his anti-guerrilla measures... and to embark on relentless suppression of the guerrillas. With ruthlessness added to protractedness, it will be impossible to sustain guerrilla warfare behind the enemy lines without base areas."[5]

Mao cautioned, "Without such strategic bases, there will be nothing to depend on in carrying out any of our strategic tasks or achieving the aim of the war... guerrilla warfare could not last long or grow without base areas. The base areas, indeed, are its rear."

He was caustic about the idea of guerrillas trying to operate without an inaccessible base or a clear long-term strategy: "History knows many peasant wars of the roving rebel type, but none of them ever succeeded. In the present age of advanced communications and technology, it would be all the more groundless to imagine one can win victory by fighting in the manner of the roving rebels. However, this roving rebel idea still exists among impoverished peasants, and in the minds of guerrilla commanders it becomes the view that base areas are neither necessary nor important."

He identified three types of base areas to which guerrillas could retreat and where they could hide: "the mountains, those on the plains and those in the river-lake-estuary regions." Mountains, he said, are best. Rivers and swamps are the next best bases. Plains are useful only as temporary bases, which are not fixed, when the enemy is harried and unable to concentrate on them. When it can mass forces against vulnerable bases in the plains, the guerrillas "will gradually have to move up into the mountains."[6]

In essence, ISIL attempted to fight an international insurgency from Raqqa and Mosul, its fixed capitals on the plains, without an inaccessible base to which to retreat. These were not what Mao thought of as guerrilla bases at all, and as he predicted, they were overrun when the enemy concentrated its full firepower on them.

Hamas likewise has a return address, in Gaza City. It has no mountains or swamps, only a vulnerable plain. Fighting a guerrilla war and deploying tactics of terrorism when the enemy knows exactly where to find you is just plain stupid. Ask the ISIL caliphate. Oh, that's right, you can't. They're dead.

Nor is the West Bank a promising site for waging a guerrilla struggle. The Israelis have heavily penetrated it and control it militarily.

The hopes of the extremist Israeli government that it can destroy Hamas may therefore not be completely unrealistic, though it will have to expect high Israeli casualties in the effort. And it will commit a form of genocide in Gaza during this attempt to extirpate Hamas that will simply give rise to future hatred and violence.

The problem is that as long as the harsh Israeli occupation of the Palestinians continues, they will just throw up other militant organizations to continue the struggle. In the late 1960s and the 1970s that was groups like the Popular Front for the Liberation of Palestine (PFLP) and Fateh. Hamas, despite what pundits are now saying, has vacillated between militancy and pragmatism. At one point they were talking about a long-term truce with Israel. The 16-year blockade of Gaza and the increasing violence toward the West Bank Palestinians and toward the al-Aqsa Mosque complex have re-radicalized Hamas in the past couple of years. Whoever succeeds them will be radicalized by the same things. You can't expect a people to suffer under Apartheid without putting up resistance.

- *Informed Comment*
(Slightly revised with addition of a few phrases, and Mao quotations, along with book citations).

Notes

[1] Ibrahim Ibrash's analysis of Hamas's announced goals and their implications on the conflict in East Jerusalem and the Palestinian West Bank, as published in *al-Arab*: https://tinyurl.com/394hvav8

[2] Richard Sales, "Analysis: Hamas history tied to Israel ," UPI, June 18, 2002   https://www.upi.com/Defense-News/2002/06/18/Analysis-Hamas-history-tied-to-Israel/82721024445587/

[3] Juan Cole, "Sharpening Contradictions: Why al-Qaeda attacked Satirists in Paris," *Informed Comment*, January 7, 2015. https://www.juancole.com/2015/01/sharpening-contradictions-satirists.html

4 Ufuk Ulutaş, *The State of Savagery: ISIS in Syria* (Istanbul: Seta, 2016); Jack McCants, *The ISIS Apocalypse: The History, Strategy, and Doomsday Vision of the Islamic State* (New York: St. Martin, 2015).

[5] Mao Tse-Tung, *Selected Military Writings of Mao Tse-Tung* (Peking: Foreign Languages Press, 1963), pp.165-168.) [Quotes added 6/20/24.]

[6] Ibid.

33.   Israel's Colonial Revenge Genocide in Gaza

October 14, 2023

The Palestinian civilians in Gaza are bearing the brunt of a colonial revenge genocide. Half of Gaza consists of children, most born after 2006 when Hamas came to power in the Strip through elections insisted upon by George W. Bush. Large numbers of these children are set to be killed, and several hundred already have been, by Israeli aerial, tank, and artillery bombardment. Although the stated military objective is to destroy the Hamas guerrillas, that objective is being pursued with obvious reckless disregard for the welfare of civilian noncombatants. There is talk of the decapitation of babies. You know, when a child is struck by a bomb from above, it is frequently decapitated, inasmuch as its body is torn apart. Movies do people a disservice by showing bodies in the aftermath of a bombing as whole, if bloodied. That's not what they look like. Parts, including heads, are strewn around.

Hamas viciously attacked Israel and committed unspeakable war crimes, and it is legitimate for the Israeli armed forces to go after it in a determined way.[1] It is not legitimate to ethnically cleanse civilians in Gaza or to blow them to smithereens in pursuit of ethno-national revenge.[2] Anyone who thinks the latter is not happening doesn't have eyes in their head, and the reason for which Israel has cut off the internet in Gaza (not a legitimate move since it endangers noncombatants) is to ensure that no real-time record can emerge of the coming massacre.

Gaza has been in a condition of Israeli coloniality since 1967 when Tel Aviv illegally seized it and militarily occupied it, and the Israeli elite has gone on to compound these actions by actively harming the civilian population for decades despite its duties to the people it occupied as laid out in the Geneva Conventions and the Rome Statute.[3] No international body ever awarded Gaza to Israel. It was not even part of ancient Israel, not that that should be relevant.

Such vendettas against civilian populations have been routinely pursued by colonial militaries in the wake of a forceful challenge to their control. We must be clear-eyed and recognize that such revolts have sometimes been characterized by the deployment of the most ghastly terrorism against the settler population by the indigenous resistance. The main characteristic of the phenomenon, however, is the disproportionate response by the settlers and their colonial military so that the number of indigenous people killed is orders of magnitude higher than the casualties among the settlers. Another frequent trope is the patriarchal justification of subsequent massacres by pointing to settler women and children killed. This rhetoric drove London's repression of the first Indian Great Rebellion against British rule in 1857-1858.

These slogans and raw emotions have typically been reinforced by racism, which is why rape of white settlers by brown or black indigenes has played such an outsized role in colonial revenge narratives. Racism — calling people "animals" or "insects" or "demons" — allows for a conscience-free killing field since the extermination of dangerous animals or pests that have attacked women and children is perfectly natural and understandable. Colonial feelings of racial superiority have led to expressions of astonishment that the black or brown natives should rise up with such fierceness after all the benefits of civilization had been graciously bestowed on them by a wise metropole.

In the early 1950s in Kenya, militant members of the Kikuyu tribe, joined by some others, hived away from the staid Kenya African Union and began attacking white settler farms. From 1952 to 1960, the "Mau Mau" forces killed 32 white settlers.

The British colonial authorities in Kenya brought in troops to repress the Kenyan militants, killing between 11,000 and 25,000 mostly Kikuyu Kenyans, of whom a little over 1,000 were hanged. A later Kenyan truth-finding commission found that the British killed, tortured, or maimed 90,000 persons, and imprisoned 160,000 in subhuman conditions. The BBC quotes Oxford's David Anderson as saying, "Everything that could happen did happen. Allegations about beatings and violence were widespread. Basically, you could get away with murder. It was systematic."[4] Needless to say, 11,000 people had not been involved in murdering the 32 white people, much less 25,000. They were killed in revenge for the deaths of the whites because they were perceived as being of a common "race" with the perpetrators.

I call it a genocide not because of the numbers of Kenyans the British killed but because the Kikuyu activists were targeted in part for their ethnicity, which is the textbook definition of genocide.

One of the features of the colonial revenge genocide is that the number killed among the indigenous must be grotesquely disproportionate to those killed among the settlers. Another feature is that the settlers hold all members of an ethnicity responsible for the actions of the militants among them. By 1960, the British campaign against the militants had come to an end. By late 1963, the British had to withdraw from Kenya and recognize it as an independent country. The London authorities and later archivists actively covered up the atrocities that British troops committed and the truth only came out decades later because of a lawsuit.

Likewise, regarding the National Front for Liberation (Front de libération nationale or FLN) in French Algeria from 1954, L. Carl Browne and Salah Zaimeche write at Britannica, "A decisive turn in the war took place in August 1955 when a widespread armed outbreak in Skikda, north of the Constantine region, led to the killing of nearly 100 Europeans and Muslim officials. Countermeasures by both the French army and settlers claimed the lives of somewhere between 1,200 (according to French sources) and 12,000 (according to Algerian sources) Algerians."[5]

Between 1954 and 1962, FLN attacks on French settlers left 5,000 to 6,000 dead. The French put in thousands of troops, of whom some 27,000 were killed by the guerrillas. French historians estimate that French forces and settlers (who staged their own uprising in 1961) killed 300,000 to 500,000 Algerians. The independent Algerian government puts Algerian lives lost at closer to 1.5 million, in a total population of 11 million. Again, note the disproportion between the number of French killed and the number of Algerians.

Although the orgy of mass violence in Algeria is not usually called a genocide, it certainly was by the contemporary definition of genocide in international law.

You can't kill half a million or a million people if you are merely confronting guerrilla forces. You have to be demonstrating an intent to kill civilians or a reckless disregard for their lives, both of which are war crimes. The French massacred villages that provided help and cover to the FLN, in order to deprive that group f their aid. Nevertheless, in 1962 Algeria became independent.

There were lots of colonial revenge genocides. The Germans in Namibia carried out the Herero and Namaqua genocide in 1904-1908, blockading the populations from food and water and using machine guns against civilians in revenge for the killing of 100 German settlers. The Germans slaughtered between 24,000 and 100,000 Hereros and 10,000 Namaqua.[6]

The U.S. State Department has forbidden its diplomats from calling for de-escalation in Gaza and the Biden administration has rebuked Democrats who want to forestall the massacre, showing that the power elite in the United States now is embroiled in white supremacist revenge fantasies. This bloodthirstiness is not new — Washington sacrificed hundreds of thousands of Iraqi lives in revenge for 9/11. They did not care then that Iraqis had nothing to do with it, just as they do not care now that most people In Gaza had nothing to do with October 7.

Notes

[1] Hamas viciously attacked Israel and committed unspeakable war crimes, and it is legitimate for the Israeli armed forces to go after it in a determined way. https://www.juancole.com/2023/10/survive-stupidity-tactics.html

[2] It is not legitimate to ethnically cleanse civilians in Gaza or to blow them to smithereens in pursuit of ethno-national revenge. https://www.juancole.com/2023/10/palestinian-revenge-satisfying.html

[3] Geneva Conventions and the Rome Statute. https://www.juancole.com/2023/10/tribalism-international-palestinian.html

[4] The British colonial authorities in Kenya brought in troops to repress the Kenyan militants. https://www.bbc.com/news/uk-12997138

[5] Britannica: "A decisive turn in the war took place in August 1955 when a widespread armed outbreak in Skikda, north of the Constantine region, led to the killing of nearly 100 Europeans and Muslim officials." https://www.britannica.com/place/Algeria/The-Algerian-War-of-Independence

[6] Dominik J. Schaller, *Genocide in Colonial South-West Africa: The German War against the Herero and Nama, 1904–1907* (London: Routledge, 2011).

34. A Tale of Two Sets of Dead Babies: The Preemies of Gaza and Imaginary Beheadings

November 12, 2023

Israel's repeated shelling in the vicinity of hospitals and clinics in Gaza has led 20 of 38 hospitals to close their doors to patients, since they lacked the electricity, medicine and functioning equipment they needed to treat patients.[1] The Israeli government's cut-off of electricity has killed premature babies in incubators, diabetes patients on dialysis, and other people with health crises. The al-Shifa medical complex in the northern Rimal neighborhood of Gaza City had valiantly attempted to continue to function, having had stores of fuel for its generators, and even though its gate was shelled by the Israelis on Friday and there was bombing all around it as Israeli troops advanced on it as though it were Hamburger Hill in an old Vietnam war movie. Attacking hospitals and ambulances is strictly forbidden in international law even if enemy combatants are sited there. It is a war crime. The commanders of the Serbian militiamen who cut off water and electricity to Sarajevo and bombarded it for 3 years in the 1990s ended up on trial at the Hague.

Staffers at Al-Nasr Pediatric hospital came under such heavy Israeli fire that they were forced to flee the premises, according to the *Washington Post*, leaving five premature babies in incubators behind.[2]

The U.N. Office for the Coordination of Humanitarian Affairs reports, that Israeli bombardment repeatedly hit hospitals on

Saturday.[3] The Israelis say they were only bombing in the vicinity of hospitals. But why in God's name were they doing that? OCHA says, "Israeli shelling and ground attacks intensified around hospitals in Gaza city and northern Gaza on 11 November, with several being directly hit. According to media reports, civilians, patients, and staff were shot at while attempting to flee the Shifa hospital in Gaza city."

It isn't only hospitals. OCHA reports, "On 10 November, at about 17:00, an Israeli airstrike hit Al Buraq school in Gaza city, which was being used as a shelter for IDPs, killing 50 people. The Israeli military stated that the airstrike targeted a Palestinian commander hiding in the school." IDPs are "internally displaced people."

On Saturday morning (November 11), we learned that al-Shifa had collapsed as a medical center when the complex's generator stopped working. No electricity, no lights, no machines, no medical care. OCHA says, "On 11 November, power at the Shifa and the Indonesian hospital (northern Gaza) was reportedly cut off after fuel for generators ran out; generators at Al Quds hospital (Gaza city) failed and could not be repaired due to the bombardment and fighting. At Shifa, two babies died when their life support stopped working and 37 babies in incubators are at imminent risk of death, according to the Ministry of Health in Ramallah."

Some 39 of the hospital's patients, then, could not hit the road for south Gaza as the Israeli military insisted. They were premature babies in incubators. Preemies need to be kept warm and provided with extra oxygen. The incubators that do that work do not function without electricity.

As OCHA reported, two of the babies died on Saturday, killed by the Israeli army as surely as though they had been propped up against a wall and shot.[4]

The other 37 are in urgent danger of dying.

These brown, Muslim premature babies haven't made the headlines, in contrast to their fictional Israeli counterparts.

A few days after the sanguinary October 7 Hamas attack on Israel, President Joe Biden came out for a news conference and said, "I never really thought that I would see, have confirmed, pictures of terrorists beheading children."[5] President Biden had not in fact seen such pictures of the decapitated babies of Kfar Aza kibbutz, since they do not exist.

The incorrect allegation was first floated as a trial balloon by a journalist on the Israeli i24 channel. Then Prime Minister Binyamin Netanyahu's picked up the report, saying that it had confirmed the information. Sarah Snider of CNN, who like several thousand other Western journalists had flown to Israel to cover events from an Israeli point of view, heard the accusation from the prime minister's press office and repeated it on screen. But then the next day someone with some common sense in the Israeli government shot down the entire talking point, saying that the report could not be confirmed. Snider and CNN apologized. Biden never did, though his staff issued "clarifications" the way Reagan's staff used to when he said things like trees cause air pollution.

Why was it necessary to float this horror story about beheaded babies or children? Hamas committed plenty of brutal crimes on October 7, including mowing 260 people down at a music festival and firing unguided rockets at civilian neighborhoods.[6] Hamas even killed Israelis of Palestinian heritage. Amnesty International reports that indiscriminate rocket fire killed and wounded many people and that these "unlawful attacks killed both Israelis and Palestinians. They also hit Palestinian villages in the Negev region, killing at least six civilians, five of them children."[6]

That's right. Hamas killed at least 5 Palestinian children on October 7. Plus they killed Jewish Israeli children, and kidnapped others as hostages. The Israeli government has revised down the death toll of that gut-wrenching day to 1,200, about a thousand of them innocent non-combatants. This atrocity was a series of horrific Hamas war crimes, one after another.

So, we can agree that Hamas killed children. But it didn't behead any babies. Beheading babies was such compelling war propaganda because anyone who would do such a thing is a savage, not a civilized person. It is essential to put the Palestinians under the sign of the savage, because the lives of such people do not matter. The civilized can subject savages to genocide without repercussions.

Back in the nineteenth century in North America, it was the American Indians who were branded savages by immigrant Europeans. The European whites constantly encroached on Indian lands and resources, and if they fought back, as the Cree did in attacking Fort Mims in 1814, white Tennessee militiamen massacred them.[7] That nice Mr. Davy Crockett said of the bloodbath, "We shot them like dogs!" Whom a people would destroy, they first make animals, make them less than human. Mr. Crockett was later killed at the Alamo by Mexican troops defending their territory from a land grab by white slavers. Mexico had completely abolished slavery in 1837.

So just as the European settler-colonists genocided the indigenous population, leaving less than 238,000 American Indians alive by 1900, so the Israeli settler-colonists are now wreaking a revenge genocide on the Palestinians.[8] That the current brutal attack on densely populated Gaza has killed 11,000 people, only a handful of them Hamas fighters, shows that revenge and mass murder are the point of the exercise. I mean, I started out with my historian and journalist hats on, speaking of "reckless disregard" for civilian life. But that diction is by now ludicrous. You can't polish off the entire population of Half Moon Bay, California, in a fit of absent-mindedness.

As for the babies, we won't know the full story of how the Israeli army was responsible for their deaths, since the Gaza Ministry of Health can no longer gather statistics from the collapsed hospital system. No U.S. president will speak out against the unnecessary deaths of the preemies denied warmth and oxygen, which they needed to live. I guess those are savage preemies, doomed to expire before the unholy might of the civilized.

Notes

[1] Israel's repeated shelling in the vicinity of hospitals and clinics in Gaza has led 20 of 38 hospitals to close their doors to patients, since they lacked the electricity, medicine and functioning equipment they needed to treat patients. https://www.juancole.com/2023/11/israels-hospitals-patients.html

[2] Staffers at Al-Nasr Pediatric hospital came under such heavy Israeli fire that they were forced to flee the premises. https://www.washingtonpost.com/world/2023/11/11/gaza-israel-hamas-war/

[3] The U.N. Office for the Coordination of Humanitarian Affairs reports, that Israeli bombardment repeatedly hit hospitals on Saturday. https://reliefweb.int/report/occupied-palestinian-territory/hostilities-gaza-strip-and-israel-flash-update-36-enarhe

[4] As *Al Jazeera* reported, two of the babies died on Saturday. https://www.aljazeera.com/news/2023/11/11/37-babies-at-risk-of-dying-in-gaza-hospital-israel-says-to-aid-evacuation

[5] President Joe Biden came out for a news conference and said, "I never really thought that I would see, have confirmed, pictures of terrorists beheading children." https://www.aljazeera.com/news/2023/10/12/white-house-walks-back-bidens-claim-he-saw-children-beheaded-by-hamas

[6] Hamas committed plenty of brutal crimes on October 7. https://www.amnesty.org/en/latest/news/2023/10/israel-palestinian-armed-groups-must-be-held-accountable-for-deliberate-civilian-killings-abductions-and-indiscriminate-attacks/

[7] The European whites constantly encroached on Indian lands and resources, and if they fought back, as the Cree did in attacking Fort Mims in 1814, white Tennessee militiamen massacred them. https://www.history.com/news/native-americans-genocide-united-states

[8] So just as the European settler-colonists genocided the indigenous population, leaving less than 238,000 American Indians alive by 1900, so the Israeli settler-colonists are now wreaking a revenge genocide

on the Palestinians. https://www.juancole.com/2023/10/colonial-genocide-massacres.html

35. The Plague as Life

December 15, 2023

In Albert Camus' novel *The Plague*, a character at one point asks, *"But what does it mean, the plague? It's life, that's all."*

The plague has come to Gaza.

What happens when you force 2.2 million people into a postage-stamp-sized territory and destroy or damage half of their dwelling places, breaking the water pipes with 2000-pound bombs? You create homeless people sleeping rough, with few toilets. Many people are forced to urinate and defecate in the streets.

The U.N. explains,

> Due to the lack or limited capacity of latrines especially in IDP shelters, people are adopting unhealthy coping mechanisms, such as open defecation. In shelters, people wait for hours to access toilets, and in some other locations where IDPs [internally displaced people] are located, no toilets are available at all. Children reportedly defecate in the open, while adults resort to buckets and dispose of the waste in improvised areas or solid waste dumps. In many locations, solid waste is piling up with no effective waste management mechanism for collection or disposal. Reportedly, rats and insects, including mosquitos, congregate in these areas, contributing to the risk of spreading disease.[1]

Human waste carries bacteria and viruses. The winter rains come and spread around the urine and feces and bacteria and viruses.

Since many water pipes have been broken by the bombardment and anyway there is no fuel to pump the water through them, there is almost no potable water. People are drinking from puddles, which are contaminated. Most have no means of boiling the water collected from such puddles, so there is no way to make it safe.

"Well, personally, I've seen enough of people who die for an idea. I don't believe in heroism; I know it's easy and I've learned that it can kill. What interests me is living and dying for what we love." - Raymond Rambert, journalist, *The Plague.*

The Palestinian Ministry of Health provided the following information, conveyed by the U.N.: "There have been significant increases or increased risk of outbreak in some communicable diseases and conditions such as diarrhea, influenza, chicken pox, meningitis, jaundice, impetigo acute respiratory infections, skin infections and hygiene-related conditions like lice and scabies. The heavy rains and flooding which affected large parts of Gaza on 13 December compounded human misery and added to the risk of waterborne diseases."[2]

Chicken pox and meningitis sound dangerous. Cholera is also being reported. Ironically, it is possible that these diseases will spread back into Israel through its soldiers.

Some of these diseases are especially dangerous to the little ones because, as Ministry of Health spokesman Ashraf Al-Qudra reported Thursday, the hospitals have completely run out of vaccines for children.[3]

James Elder of UNICEF, just back from Gaza, explains that 100,000 children have diarrhea and 150,000 suffer from respiratory diseases. One physician on the ground told him that he expects the same number of children to die of disease as have been killed by Israeli bombing. Currently the latter are estimated at over 7,000, though that does not count the little bodies under the rubble.[4]

"I have no idea what's waiting for me, or what will happen when this all ends. For the time being, there are sick people and they

must be cured." — Dr. Rieux, *The Plague*

Elder calls this campaign a "war on children" because the proportion of children killed by Israeli actions has been twice that of other conflicts. He insists that Israelis are bombing indiscriminately, and frequently with dumb bombs rather than precision munitions. Indiscriminate fire that recklessly endangers the lives of noncombatants is a war crime. President Biden also complained this week about indiscriminate Israeli fire.[5]

In the south of Gaza where a handful of hospitals are still trying to operate, often without medicines or functioning equipment, a Ministry of Health spokesman said that displaced individuals huddling in shelters had fallen ill and come for treatment. Among them, some 327,000 were diagnosed with infectious diseases. Apparently the doctors have run out of antibiotics to give them, according to Ministry of Health spokesman Ashraf Al-Qudra.[6]

"Yes, I realized that I still felt ashamed that we are all living with plague, and I lost my peace. I'm still looking for it today, trying to understand them all and avoid being anyone's mortal enemy." — Jean Tarrou, idealist, *The Plague.*

Notes

Quotes from Albert Camus, *The Plague*, translated by Laura Marris (New York: Alfred A. Knopf, 2021); quotes in order: pp. 329; 174; 135; 270.

[1] U.N. report on latrine capacity and unhealthy coping mechanisms. https://reliefweb.int/report/occupied-palestinian-territory/hostilities-gaza-strip-and-israel-flash-update-69

[2] Information from the Palestinian Ministry of Health on disease outbreaks and risks. https://reliefweb.int/report/occupied-palestinian-territory/hostilities-gaza-strip-and-israel-flash-update-69

[3] Ministry of Health spokesman Ashraf Al-Qudra on the lack of vaccines for children. https://www.middleeastmonitor.com/20231214-gaza-327000-cases-of-infectious-diseases-detected-in-shelters/

[4] James Elder of UNICEF on child health crises in Gaza. https://www.channel4.com/news/this-is-a-war-on-children-says-unicef-spokesperson-james-elder-who-recently-returned-from-gaza

[5] President Biden's complaint about indiscriminate Israeli fire. https://www.juancole.com/2023/12/suddenly-accuse-israel.html

[6] Ministry of Health spokesman Ashraf Al-Qudra on the diagnosis of infectious diseases in displaced individuals. https://www.middleeastmonitor.com/20231214-gaza-327000-cases-of-infectious-diseases-detected-in-shelters/

36. Netanyahu Advocates Ethnically Cleansing Palestinians of Gaza

December 26, 2023

The extremist and arguably fascist government of Benjamin Netanyahu continues to press its monstrous, illegal and most of all completely implausible plan to push the 2.2 million Palestinians of Gaza out of the Strip into Egypt's Sinai Peninsula or into other Arab countries. Netanyahu also pledged to continue the high-intensity military campaign against the people of Gaza.[1]

This blatant project of ethnic cleansing recalls the ways in which the dictators of the 1930s and 1940s moved around entire ethnic groups. Stalin displaced the Soviet Koreans to Uzbekistan or Siberia.[2] I met some of their descendants in Tashkent in the mid-1990s. The Soviet exile of the Crimean Tartars is recognized by Ukraine as a war crime. Hundreds of thousands died in these paroxysms of ethnic cleansing. Hitler ethnically cleansed millions, as well, and at the end of the war there were 11 million displaced persons in Europe, 8 million in Germany.[3]

After the end of WW II, world authorities attempted to forestall such atrocities, creating or strengthening International Humanitarian Law. In the Rome Statute, which went into effect in 2002 and has been signed by 124 countries, one of the offenses constituting "Crimes Against Humanity" is: "Deportation or forcible transfer of population" (Rome Statute Art. 7 d).[4]

The heinous character of these plans of the Israeli far right is not masked by the phrase "voluntary" transfer. Helpless Palestinians made homeless and denied food and water by the Israeli authorities can no more assent to exile from their homeland of millennia than an enslaved woman can assent to sex with her master.

On Monday, Netanyahu held a meeting of his Likud bloc and told the other far right politicians there that he was still working on the "voluntary" immigration of Gaza's inhabitants to other countries. He said the only problem is finding countries willing to absorb them. A Likud member of parliament concurred, saying that such plans were already accepted by the Canadian immigration minister and by U.S. presidential candidate Nikki Haley.[5]

For its part, the Palestinian Foreign Ministry was scathing about Netanyahu's remarks, saying they were "a slap in the face to all the countries that supported Israel in its war against our people, and still do, under the pretext of self-defense, especially since it reveals a malicious conspiracy hatched by the ruling Israeli right against our people with the aim of liquidating their cause and existence."[6]

That Netanyahu is talking in this desperate way, the ministry said, is a clear sign that Israel has failed in its stated war aims. That is, the Palestine Authority correctly recognized that Netanyahu is using revenge on Hamas as a cover story, and that the actual purpose of his total war on the civilians of Gaza is to ethnically cleanse them. The Foreign Ministry called on other countries roundly to condemn Netanyahu's grotesque remarks.

No one is going to take the Palestinians off the Israeli prime minister's hands. Egypt roundly rebuffed any such suggestion.[7] In fact, the Egyptians have warned of a severe rupture in ties with Cairo if Israel tries to push the Palestinians south into the Sinai.[8]

Meanwhile *Al-`Arabi al-Jadid* (The New Arab) reported on December 25, 2023, that the Egyptian military is bulking up the number of troops it has stationed near the Rafah Crossing from Gaza into the Sinai.[9] It is also building more barriers and watchtowers. This activity reflects Egyptian anxieties as the Israeli military campaign against the Palestinians in Gaza stretches south to Rafah, raising the specter of mass displacement. Apparently, an unusual number of Palestinians are approaching Egyptian border authorities pleading for asylum.

The government of President Abdel Fattah al-Sisi has spent a decade attempting to wipe out the Muslim Brotherhood from Egypt and has also repeatedly fought heavy battles to assert Cairo's authority in the Sinai Peninsula, the people of which often feel badly treated by the government. The prospect of having 2.2 million hungry and desperate Palestinians, many of whom Cairo would view as essentially Muslim Brothers, plopped into a place famed for its lawless smuggling and terrorism networks is a horror show for the Egyptian authorities. Egypt is a country of over 100 million people and its military is ranked 14 out of 145 countries in the global firepower review.[10] If its officer corps doesn't want that influx of Palestinians, it won't happen.

Netanyahu's plans to ethnically cleanse the Palestinians of Gaza, which have been echoed by many other Israeli politicians, including cabinet members, aren't just plans to commit crimes against humanity. They are also highly implausible fantasies. The hard line, fascist government that Netanyahu has cobbled together dreams big, but just isn't that powerful in the real world, and nor does the Biden administration want to see the Palestinians ethnically cleansed. Though, if it somehow did happen, no doubt Washington would put lipstick on that pig for Israel's sake, as well.

- *Informed Comment* (slightly revised June 22, 2024).

Notes

[1] Netanyahu's pledge to continue the high-intensity campaign against Gaza. Source: https://www.youtube.com/watch?v=TVY_gFwOmyA

[2] Stalin's displacement of Soviet Koreans. Source: https://www.unhcr.org/us/publications/unhcr-publication-cis-conference-displacement-cis-punished-peoples-mass-deportations

[3] The displacement of millions in Europe after WW II. Source: https://www.nationalww2museum.org/war/articles/last-million-eastern-european-displaced-persons-postwar-germany

[4] Rome Statute's definition of "Crimes Against Humanity". Source: https://www.icc-cpi.int/sites/default/files/RS-Eng.pdf

[5] *Al-Ghad* report on Netanyahu's meeting.
https://tinyurl.com/bddaxwt4; *Yisrael Ha-Yom* report on Netanyahu's meeting.
https://www.israelhayom.co.il/news/geopolitics/article/15002089

[6] Ibid.

[7] Egypt's rebuff of Netanyahu's suggestion to absorb Gaza refugees. Source: https://www.timesofisrael.com/report-netanyahu-sought-us-pressure-on-egypt-to-absorb-gaza-refugees-was-rebuffed/

[8] Egyptian television anchor's report on rebuff of Gaza refugees. Source: https://www.facebook.com/watch/?v=628944052579771

[9] Egyptian military's increased presence near Rafah Crossing. Source: https://tinyurl.com/y2j6wjux

[10] Egypt's military ranking. Source: https://www.globalfirepower.com/country-military-strength-detail.php?country_id=egypt

37. How Biden inherited the War with an Iraqi Shiite Militia from Bush, Trump and Netanyahu

January 29, 2024

The "Party of God Brigades" (*Kata'ib Hezbollah*) of Iraq struck the Tower 22 U.S. military base in the far north of Jordan on the border with Syria on Sunday, killing three U.S. military personnel and wounding dozens more. The Shiite militia said that it was part of its continued attempt to force U.S. "occupation" troops out of Iraq and the region, and in sympathy with the Israeli attacks on the Palestinians of Gaza, in which the Party of God Brigades [PGB] consider the U.S. to be co-belligerent, since they re-arm the Israelis by airlift daily.

The Party of God Brigades were founded by Abu Mehdi al-Muhandis. The organization is not related to the Hezbollah in Lebanon, though the two have a collegial relationship. Al-Muhandis was assassinated by President Donald Trump on January 3, 2020 along with the Iranian general, Qasem Soleimani. Ever since, the Brigades have sought to force out of Iraq the remaining 2500 U.S. troops there and to force out of Syria the remaining 900 U.S. troops stationed in that country. U.S. troops were put into those two countries by the Obama administration during the fight against the ISIL (ISIS, Daesh) terrorist organization, 2014-2018. In those years, the U.S. was often de facto allied with Shiite militias such as the PGB and with their sponsor, the Iranian Revolutionary Guards Corps. In 2018, Trump destroyed the Iran nuclear deal of 2015 and placed a "maximum pressure" economic siege on the Iranian economy. That and his assassination of Soleimani and al-Muhandis set Iran and its allies, the Shiite militias of the Middle East, on an increasingly belligerent footing.

The Party of God Brigades and other Iraqi Shiite militias have launched around 150 attacks on bases housing U.S. troops since the Gaza conflict broke out on October 7. *Al-Zaman* (The Times of Baghdad) printed the communique it received from the God's Party Brigades:

In the Name of God, the Merciful, the Compassionate.

"Leave is given to those who fight because they were wronged — surely God is able to help them ." [Qur'an 22:39].

Continuing our path of resisting the American occupation forces in Iraq and the region, and in response to the massacres of the Zionist entity against our people in Gaza, at dawn today, Sunday 1/28/2024, the fighters of the Islamic Resistance in Iraq attacked four enemy bases with unmanned aerial vehicles — three of them in Syria and they are Al-Shaddadi, al-Rukban and al-Tanf bases, and the fourth inside our occupied Palestinian lands, and it is the U.S. Marines' Zafulun Facility. The Islamic Resistance affirms that it will continue to destroy enemy compounds.

"Victory is only from God. God is Almighty, All-Wise." [Qur'an 8:10].

The Islamic Resistance in Iraq Sunday 16 Rajab 1445.[1]

Apparently the obscure "Zafulun" is their term for the place that Tower 22 stands. It is interesting that the group views the Hashemite Kingdom of Jordan as part of occupied Palestine. Palestine and the Transjordan were conquered by the British army during World War I and Britain subsequently ruled the West Bank and the rest of Palestine as a League of Nations Mandate, while giving charge of the Transjordan to the family of the Sharif Hussain, the Naqib or leading noble of Mecca, who claimed descent from the Prophet Muhammad and his clan, the Banu Hashem. Hussain and his sons had supported the British against the Ottomans during WW I because the British lied to them and promised them an independent Arab state after the war.

In any case, this Shiite militia appears to view the Hashemite Dynasty (King Abdullah II is a descendant of Sharif Hussain) as illegitimate.

In return, the highly capable and effective Jordanian General Intelligence Directorate, or GID, is even as we speak making plans to help track down and kill the PGB cadres behind this attack on Jordanian soil. Jordan will also have some harsh words for Iraqi Prime Minister Mohammed Shia' Al Sudani, who came to power with the support of the Shiite militias and is thought to be close to them.

The *Ma`refa* site says that al-Muhandis was born in 1954 or 1955 in Basra, originally named Jamal Jaafar Muhammad Ali Al Ibrahim.[2] He married an Iranian woman. In 1973 he was in Baghdad, where he entered the Technological University in the Engineering School, being graduated with an engineering degree in 1977. While working as an engineer he did further degrees in political science. He also took off some time to study at a Shiite seminary in Basra that was part of the establishment of Ayatollah Muhsin al-Hakim, the clerical leader of Iraq's Shiites in the 1960s.

Right from the time he was in high school in the early 1970s, he joined the Dawa Party. Some say that Dawa, or "the Call," was founded by clerics and lay Shiites in 1958 to compete with the Communists and Baathists, who were appealing to Shiite youths. Baathism is a mixture of socialism and Arab nationalism with a strong secularist cast, and it instituted an authoritarian Stalinist-style one-party state in Iraq from 1968. The Dawa party, in contrast, theorized a Shiite state as a believers' paradise in opposition to the Communists' workers paradise. Its leaders made room for consultative government.[3]

In 1979, the Islamic Revolution of Ayatollah Khomeini in Iran began radicalizing Iraqi Shiites. Saddam Hussein came to power in an internal Baath Party putsch in 1979. In 1980 he outlawed the Dawa Party, executed its clerical leader Muhammad Baqir al-Sadr, and made belonging to it a capital crime. For the past twenty years the post-Baath government has been finding mass graves in the Shiite south of Iraq, where the Baath secret police shot down suspected Dawa members.

Al-Muhandis, his nom de guerre, which means "the engineer," was forced to flee to Kuwait. There, he was part of a Dawa cell that turned radical and committed acts of terrorism against the U.S. and French embassies, given the hostility of those countries to the Islamic Republic. He then appears to have gone to Iran, where he left the Dawa Party for the Supreme Council for Islamic Revolution in Iraq (SCIRI), an even more radical organization founded by Iraqi expatriates in Tehran in 1982 at the suggestion of Khomeini. Muhammad Baqir al-Hakim, the son of Muhsin al-Hakim, became the head of it in 1984. Thousands of Iraqi Shiites defected to Iran during the 1980s, and SCIRI organized them. Those who remained loyal to the Da`wa Party, who mostly rejected Khomeini's vision of a clerically ruled Muslim state, tended to make their way to London instead. The Supreme Council developed a paramilitary branch, the Badr Corps, which was trained and funded by the Iranian Revolutionary Guards Corps, and which carried out operations against Baath installations in Iraq. Al-Muhandis Joined the Badr Corps and rose to become one of its commanders.

In 2003, the U.S. invaded Iraq.[4] The independent Shiite site *al-Khanadeq* in Lebanon says that the Party of God Brigades was founded by al-Muhandis the same year with the aim of forcing the occupiers back out.[5] He appears to have broken with the Badr Corps at that point and formed his own militia, primarily out of armed groups based in the Shiite holy city of Karbala (the Ali Akbar Brigades, the Karbala Brigades and the Abu al-Fadl Abbas Brigades).[6] By 2007, they had begun jointly calling themselves the Party of God Brigades. They mounted some attacks on U.S. bases.

The organization became prominent in 2014 when Grand Ayatollah Ali Sistani called on Iraqi young men to rise up to defend the country from ISIL, which had taken Mosul, at a time when the Iraqi Army built by the Bush administration had collapsed. The Party of God Brigades and other Shiite militias armed themselves and went to fight, with training and support from the Iranian Revolutionary Guards Corps and Genera Qasem Soleimani, against ISIL in Amerli and later in Tikrit and Fallujah. They helped ensure that ISIL was defeated. The militias developed political parties which got a fair-sized bloc of seats in parliament. In 2018 parliament recognized the Shiite militias or "Popular Mobilization Forces" as a formal part of the Iraqi military — a sort of national guard.

After 2018, when ISIL was rolled up, the U.S. kept several thousand troops in Iraq for mop-up operations and to continue to train the new Iraqi army.

Israel is accused of committing covert ops against Iraqi Shiite militias inside Iraq, blowing up a weapons depot in 2019.[7]

In Syria, the government of Bashar al-Assad initially faced a rebellion by civil society groups in 2011, but attacked the demonstrators militarily and turned the struggle into a civil war. It took on sectarian tones, since most rebels were Sunnis, while the elite of the government were Alawi Shiites. Lebanon's Hezbollah came in on the side of Damascus, as did the Iranian Revolutionary Guards Corps. The Party of God Brigades came up from Iraq along with some other Shiite militias. With help from the Russian air force, the Shiite militias defeated the Sunni rebels and drove their remnant into the far north Idlib province.

In the east of Syria, the U.S. enlisted Syrian Kurdish militia, the People's Defense Units (YPG) as ground troops to defeat ISIL in Raqqa and Deir al-Zor provinces, with U.S. air support. The U.S. put in a small number of its own troops, embedded with the YPG. After ISIL was defeated, the U.S. maintained a small military presence in Syria's southeast. Again, they aimed to mop up ISIL and prevent it from reconstituting itself, and to lend continued support to the YPG in these largely Arab provinces. It is alleged that they also attempt to block Iranian activities, including shipments of weapons to Lebanon's Hezbollah, on behalf of Israel. Further, they may be helping the Kurds siphon off oil from fields in the southeast, denying the petroleum wealth to Damascus. If this latter charge is true, it is a war crime.

On January 3, 2020, Trump blew away al-Muhandis and Soleimani at Baghdad International Airport. Soleimani had just come on a civilian airliner with a diplomatic passport to negotiate better relations with Saudi Arabia via the good offices of then Iraqi Prime Minister Adil Abdul Mahdi.

The Party of God Brigades went to war with the U.S. troops in the country, subjecting the Iraqi bases that housed them to rocket and drone strikes. The Iraqi parliament demanded that Abdul Mahdi find a way to kick U.S. troops out of Iraq (he never did).

Since October 7, the Party of God Brigades' secretary-general, Ahmad al-Hamidawi, has branded the U.S. an equal partner in the Israeli war on Gaza and it and other Shiite militias have launched dozens of attacks on U.S. bases. None had resulted in a fatality until Sunday.

In a historical irony, one of the reasons some Neoconservatives around George W. Bush wanted to invade Iraq was to stop it from being a danger to Israel. Over two decades later, the PGB hit a school in Eilat with a drone, and the U.S., having destroyed the secular Baath Party, is at war with political Shiism in Iraq, Syria and Yemen. Maybe the problem is U.S. policy in the region, and maybe no number of wars and conquests are going to reshape the Middle East in ways really favorable to that policy?

Notes

[1] *Al-Zaman* (The Times of Baghdad) reports on the communique from the Party of God Brigades about their attacks on U.S. and allied forces. https://www.azzaman-iraq.com/content.php?id=86514

[2] *Ma`refa* provides a biographical account of Abu Mehdi al-Muhandis, his background, education, and involvement in Iraqi politics and militant activism. https://tinyurl.com/2ptyksmk

[3] Da`wa Party's history and role in shaping the vision of political Shiism in Iraq. https://www.bostonreview.net/articles/juan-cole-iraqi-shiites/

[4] Juan Cole, "The United States and Shi'ite Religious Factions in Post-Ba'thist Iraq," *The Middle East Journal*, 57, no. 4 (Autumn 2003): 543-566.

[5] *Al-Khanadeq* offers information on the foundation of the Party of God Brigades by al-Muhandis and their activities since the U.S.

invasion of Iraq. https://tinyurl.com/d7zuw5ac

[6] Juan Cole, "Shia Militias in Iraqi Politics." In Markus Bouillon, David M. Malone and Ben Rowswell, eds., *Iraq: Preventing a New Generation of Conflict* (Boulder, Co.: Lynne Rienner, 2007), 109-123.

[7] *The Times of Israel* examines instances where Israeli covert operations have targeted Iraqi Shiite militias on Iraqi soil. https://www.timesofisrael.com/iraqi-official-blames-israel-for-blast-in-iran-backed-militia-weapons-depot/

38. Water Crisis and untreated Sewage could kill more Gaza Palestinians than Bombs: Threat of Infant Mortality

February 16, 2024

Al-Arabi al-Jadid (The New Arab) reports, "The streets of the Gaza Strip are witnessing a catastrophic environmental crisis due to the mixing of rainwater with sewage water, which is now flooding various roads as a result of a continuous overflow, resulting from the targeting of infrastructure by the Israeli military, and the inability to drain the necessary quantities of wastewater due to the depletion of fuel, and the complete outage of electricity."[1]

Some 70 percent of people in Gaza are forced to drink contaminated water or water with too much salt in it, which is a health hazard, according to Doctors without Borders (MSF).[2] Although each person needs about 3 liters (about 4/5s of a gallon) a day of drinking water, and needs four times that for hygiene and other purposes, entire families are getting only 3 liters a day, according to MSF. There is an estimated one toilet for every 500 people. There is a severe risk of a massive spike in infant mortality from dirty water, not to mention malnutrition from insufficient food being allowed into the Strip.[3]

The U.N. Office for the Coordination of Humanitarian Affairs reports on a seldom-considered issue concerning the Israeli assault on the civilians of Gaza, which is the water and sanitation catastrophe.[4] The Israeli government of Prime Minister Binyamin Netanyahu forced over a million Palestinians of Gaza into the far south of the Strip, Rafah, which is only 20 percent of its land area.

Although the Israelis said that this zone would be safe for noncombatants, they have been bombing it in recent days and say they will invade it. Some two-thirds of the Palestinians so far ethnically cleansed from their homes in the north and center of the Strip have congregated in Rafah.

Although most press reporting has considered mainly the deaths of Palestinian civilians from Israeli bombardment, which have risen to over 27,000 in February, 2024, some 70 percent of them women and children, the deaths from malnutrition and dirty water, i.e. from poor sanitation, have not been reported with the same clarity. Israel has destroyed the Gaza hospital system on the phony pretext that medical complexes are "power centers" and sites of militant Hamas activity. There is no compelling evidence that this narrative is true, and in some instances it has been debunked by U.S. newspapers of record.[5]

Hosny Muhannad, spokesman for the Gaza Municipality, explained to *al-Arabi al-Jadid* that "the scorched earth policy followed by the [Israeli] occupation [government] during its aggression against the Gaza Strip led to the cessation of many basic service sectors, including the work of municipalities, including repairing main and secondary roads, rainwater drainage, and wastewater drainage from the streets."

The ground water in Gaza is heavily polluted with sewage and industrial waste. Because of climate change and the rising Mediterranean, salt water has leaked into the aquifer. Only 4 percent of ground water in Gaza is believed by international health experts to be potable.

Clean water came from three desalinization plants, but the Israelis closed them after October 7 and only restored their production after severe pressure from the Biden administration. However, they deliver water through pipelines. Many of the pipelines do not work because there is not enough fuel to operate their pumps. Other pipelines have been broken by intensive Israeli bombing.

Neither the some 150,000 remaining Palestinians in North Gaza nor the 1.4 million crowded into Gaza have clean water and sanitation. All 2.25 million Palestinians in Gaza need assistance in these areas.

The U.N. reports, "Currently only 5.7 percent of water is being produced from all the water sources in Gaza, compared to pre-war production levels. Safe drinking water and water for domestic use, including personal hygiene, remains very limited."

There had been 284 groundwater wells. As noted, the water they yielded was problematic. It has a high salt content, which can cause dehydration, and it is often polluted. In ordinary times people could boil it, but people living in tents and shelters without sufficient fuel cannot reliably boil their water. Only 17 percent of the wells are operating. Some 39 were destroyed by Israeli bombing, and 93 have been damaged.

Needless to say, Gaza City, Rafah and other municipalities cannot run wastewater treatment centers in the midst of this war, in which Israeli pilots and tank commanders have deliberately targeted civilian buildings and infrastructure. None of the wastewater treatment systems are operative. They have either been damaged by bombing, or do not have enough fuel. There isn't enough power for solid waste management.

Muhannad told *Al-Arabi al-Jadid*, "the repeated Israeli targeting of streets and intersections, and the repeated attacks on the already exhausted infrastructure, which caused great destruction in it and hindered its ability to deal with weather depressions and rainwater, which have become traffic obstacles for private vehicles, ambulances, and civil defense"

The bombed-out streets are pockmarked so rain water and sewage is standing in these holes.

Gaza is afloat in piss and shit. That is a cholera and hepatitis epidemic waiting to happen.

Infants and toddlers are extremely vulnerable to dehydration from diarrhea, and there is almost certainly an epidemic of dead babies as a result of these unsanitary conditions. Although bombing has killed perhaps 8,000 children (probably many more), the lack of water and lack of clean water will potentially kill many thousands more.

It should be remembered that one reason given by al-Qaeda for the 9/11 attacks was that U.S. policy in Iraq in the 1990s was to deny the country chlorine imports for water purification, resulting in thousands of deaths of infants.

OCHA notes, "Two out of three desalination plans are partially operating: the Middle Area plant produces an average of 750 cubic metres per day and is distributed via water trucking and the South Gaza desalination plant produces 1,700 cubic metres per day; around 600 cubic metres are distributed via water trucking and 1,100 cubic metres via the water network. The UAE's small desalination plant located on the Egyptian side of Rafah, operates at full capacity, providing 2,400 cubic metres per day, following the construction of a 3-kilometre transmission line."

That is 4,850 cubic meters of water per day, or 4,850,000 liters. Each individual needs on the order of 12 liters per day of water for drinking, food, hygiene and cooking purposes, according to the World Health Organization.[5] The 2.2 million Palestinians therefore need about 26.4 million liters a day of water. They are only getting 18 percent of that from the desalinization plants, assuming it can be distributed to them, which is the only really potable water to be had.

The groundwater is dirty. Some refugees are reduced to cupping their hands amidst the sewage in the streets and drinking from it.

The reason I question whether the water from the remaining desalinization plants is even being reliably distributed is that OCHA says this: "Mekorot Connections: Two of the three water pipelines are not functioning (the Mentar pipeline since the beginning of the conflict, and the Bani Suhaila pipeline since 18 December. The Bani Saeed pipeline is functioning, but is currently producing 6,000 cubic metres per day, which is only 42 percent of its full capacity. Plans are in place to repair the Bani Suheila pipeline, but there are challenges for safe access, communication, and coordination of repair activities."

OCHA notes anecdotal reports from aid workers and medical personnel of a rise of hepatitis A cases in Gaza. Since the building materials for constructing toilets and repairing the sewage system are considered dual-use by the Israeli authorities (i.e., they could be used by Hamas for its own infrastructure), they are not being let in at the requisite rate. UNICEF tried to construct 80 family latrines this week. But, OCHA says, "the sanitation coverage remains very low. WASH partners continue to construct family latrines, but the lack of cement, wood and other construction materials slows down the progress."

Finally, OCHA warns, "The crisis is exacerbated by a fuel shortage, hindering sewage station operation and leading to environmental and public health concerns. The situation is worsened by continuous restricted access to essential sanitation supplies and services in Gaza."

Notes

[1] *Al-Arabi al-Jadid* reports on the environmental crisis in the Gaza Strip caused by rainwater mixing with sewage and flooding the streets. https://tinyurl.com/yvnme62k

[2] Doctors without Borders (MSF) on the health hazards due to contaminated drinking water in Gaza. https://slguardian.org/infections-on-the-rise-in-gaza-as-israel-impedes-delivery-of-water-food/

[3] A report on the risk of a spike in infant mortality from dirty water and malnutrition in Gaza. https://maktoobmedia.com/world/20000-babies-born-into-gaza-war-135000-minors-at-severe-risk-of-malnutrition-unicef/

[4] The U.N. Office for the Coordination of Humanitarian Affairs discusses the water and sanitation crisis in Gaza. https://reliefweb.int/report/occupied-palestinian-territory/hostilities-gaza-strip-and-israel-flash-update-119-enarhe

[5] Louisa Loveluck, Evan Hill, Jonathan Baran, Jarrett Ley and Ellen Nakashima, "The case of al-Shifa: Investigating the assault on Gaza's largest hospital," *The Washington Post*, December 21, 2023 https://www.washingtonpost.com/world/2023/12/21/al-shifa-hospital-gaza-hamas-israel/

[6] The World Health Organization on the necessary daily water requirement for individuals. https://cdn.who.int/media/docs/default-

248

source/wash-documents/who-tn-09-how-much-water-is-needed.pdf

39. Black Thursday: Israel's Great Flour Massacre in Gaza

March 1, 2024

The U.N. Office for the Coordination of Humanitarian Affairs reports on the Great Flour Massacre committed by the Israeli army on Black Thursday, February 29, 2024, at the Dawar al-Nabulsi in the south of occupied Gaza City.[1]

OCHA says that the Gaza Ministry of Health reported that 104 Palestinians have been killed and 760 were injured in the early morning hours of 29 February on Al Rashid Road southwest of Gaza city, warning that the actual death toll is likely to be higher as medical teams are struggling to handle the situation with limited critical care resources. The incident occurred as thousands of Palestinians reportedly gathered around trucks carrying supplies when they were allegedly hit by artillery shells and gunfire, according to initial media reports. The Israeli military, cited by the media, has reportedly acknowledged shooting by its troops, and has also said that most casualties occurred as a result of congestion and incidents of people being run over by trucks.[2]

Al Jazeera Arabic reports that the few aid trucks that come north from Rafa to Gaza City come along the coast up Rasheed Street. Dawar al-Nabulsi (a traffic circle) is at the intersection of Rasheed Street and Tenth Street, which runs east and west through Gaza City.[3] It is at the edge of the Zaytun neighborhood, which is heavily garrisoned by Israeli military units, though most Israeli troops had withdrawn from northern Gaza City. It was at the traffic circle where people converged on an aid delivery that the Israeli military began sniping and shelling.

The Israeli newspaper *Arab 48* reports that on Thursday evening the death toll rose to 112 and the number of injured was confirmed to be at least 760.[4] It says that the Ministry of Health was reporting late Thursday that large numbers of the wounded had still not been moved to hospital. Some of the dead were taken to the al-Shifa Medical Complex, which has been destroyed as a functioning hospital by the Israeli army, in one of its many war crimes. The Israeli Air Force on Thursday also dropped bombs on several neighborhoods in the Strip, and Israeli artillery pieces fired at residential complexes in Khan Younis.

Israel has a responsibility as the occupying power in Gaza to ensure the safety and well-being of the civilian population. That it has not arranged secure methods of providing food relief, and that according to its military spokesman, its soldiers, "afraid" of the resulting scramble by crowds, fired into them, is an indictment, not an excuse. It also does not reflect well on the courage of Israeli soldiers that women and children seeking flour should so terrify them. The civilian noncombatants who risked their lives to get food for loved ones were far braver.

Alas, it is also possible that the "being afraid" story is a falsehood and propaganda. There is a lot of evidence that Israeli soldiers in Gaza have standing orders to shoot down military-age men whenever they are moving around freely outside. That was likely why they shot three Israeli hostages who escaped last fall—they saw military age men moving around. There have also been many reports of Israeli soldiers firing on people approaching aid trucks. This tactic could be intended to ensure that Hamas fighters cannot receive aid. However, there are hundreds of thousands of military age men in Gaza and there were only 30,000 members of the Hamas paramilitary, the Qassam Brigades, so such a policy would penalize hundreds of thousands of innocent noncombatants, who are thereby targeted for death or arbitrary imprisonment.

Eyewitnesses interviewed on Arab satellite channels maintain that the Israeli army sniped at them and bombarded them with no provocation and in "cold blood."[5]

Despite the International Court of Justice's preliminary injunction on January 26 against Israel that it is plausibly committing genocide in Gaza and should immediately cease doing so, the Israeli government has halved the number of aid trucks allowed into the strip in February as compared to January. The January total was already woefully inadequate according to U.N. and other aid workers on the ground, who are reporting widespread hunger, dependence on non-potable water, and lack of essential medicines and medical supplies. Israeli government figures, in and out of office, have spoken of the desirability of reducing the Palestinian population of Gaza and of the usefulness of disease in doing so.

OCHA head Martin Griffiths posted on "X," "Life is draining out of Gaza at terrifying speed."[6]

Al Jazeera Arabic reports that pretty much all major world leaders have condemned Israel's handling of the incident, including regional powers such as Egypt and Saudi Arabia and some European officials, including France.[7] The Secretary General of the U.N., António Guterres, called for a dispassionate and transparent investigation.

Although this incident was dramatic and drew attention, the slow, invisible starvation by Israel of the Palestinians of Gaza has the potential to kill thousands of people, not just hundreds.[8]

Notes

[1] The U.N. Office for the Coordination of Humanitarian Affairs reports on the Great Flour Massacre in Gaza on Black Thursday. https://reliefweb.int/report/occupied-palestinian-territory/hostilities-gaza-strip-and-israel-flash-update-129

[2] Ibid.

[3] *Al Jazeera* Arabic covers the route of aid trucks in Gaza and the location of the massacre. https://tinyurl.com/mpf8vcfk

[4] *Arab 48* details the death toll and the situation of the wounded following the Gaza massacre. https://tinyurl.com/3yadu425

5 See the detailed report by *Al Jazeera* Arabic, which presented much better sequential video than did the Israeli military, showing that the latter abruptly opened fire. https://youtu.be/LR7nHerzpQE?si=bQihwLtfjRrdzbx4

[6] https://twitter.com/UNReliefChief/status/1763215562455359648

[7] Worldwide leaders condemn Israel's handling of the massacre. https://tinyurl.com/pr6tb54n

[8] Details on the invisible starvation of Palestinians in Gaza by Israeli policies. https://www.juancole.com/2024/02/million-starvation-children.html

PART 6

Iran, the Alliance of Resistance, and International Courts

As Israel's campaign of bombing unfolded against all the buildings and civilian infrastructure of Gaza, including schools, mosques, churches, hospitals, shelters and the tent encampments into which it had chased most residents, along with occasional land incursions with tanks and artillery, it became a regional Middle East issue. Hezbollah, the Shiite militia of southern Lebanon, showed symbolic support for Gaza by sending rockets over onto Israeli, though it seemed to be careful not to provoke an all-out war. Thousands of Israelis were forced from the north near the Lebanese border, though it should also be noted that thousands of Shiites were forced from their homes in southern Lebanon, as well. The Iraqi Shiite militias that had sprung up to fight ISIL in 2014, many of them backed with training and funds by the Jerusalem Brigade of the Iranian Revolutionary Guards Corps, as we have seen, engaged in the harassment of U.S. troops in Iraq and Syria. The Helpers of God (Houthi) government in north Yemen took up the cause of Gaza, targeting shipping in the Red Sea and bankrupting the Israeli port of Eilat. Most of the 12 percent of global maritime trade that usually plied the Suez Canal was diverted around Africa, with all the extra costs and time delays that change implied. The increased Israeli recklessness visible in its campaign of ethnic cleansing in Gaza extended to Iranian targets in Syria, where it dared murder from the skies high officers of the IRGC in the Iranian embassy in Damascus, provoking the first Iranian missile barrage directly against Israel. The Biden administration increasingly had to divert scarce resources from the effort to combat the Russian occupation of Ukrainian territory in an attempt to prevent the outbreak of all-out war between Israel and

Iran and its alliance of resistance. I have spent a good deal of my career studying modern Iran and Iraq, and have written on Lebanon and Yemen, so I felt a responsibility to write some journalism on this corner of the conflict.

Even as this conflict between the alliance of resistance and Israel unfolded, the world community increasingly reacted against the open disregard by the Netanyahu government for the norms of International Humanitarian Law and the laws of war enacted by the world community after the horrors of the Second World War and the crimes of the Nazis and their Axis. Some European governments, such as Spain, Ireland, Norway, and Slovakia, recognized Palestine in response. United Nations bodies and courts began ruling against Israel, branding its policies in Gaza plausibly genocidal. By late May, the International Criminal Court, harassed unbearably by Israeli intelligence dirty tricks for years, finally summoned the courage and defiance to request arrest warrants against Benjamin Netanyahu and Yoav Gallant, as well as against three Hamas leaders. The United State swung into motion to attempt to quash the request, pressuring allies such as Britain to join in, and Congress bruited new sanctions on the judges if they followed through. In late May, the International Court of Justice ordered Israel to halt its invasion of Rafah on the grounds that it was committing genocide. The order was predictably ignored by the American and much European mass media, and Netanyahu went on with the operation with impunity. He was by that time not only defying the ICJ but even the Biden administration, which had drawn a red line around Rafah that Israeli tanks simply bulldozed their way through, without drawing so much as a harsh word from the increasingly woolly-minded Biden. In mid-June, the United Nations added Israel, now widely seen as a rogue state, to its blacklist of violators of children, charging it with killing or maiming 20,000 Palestinian minors in 2023 alone. The question began to arise, however, of whether the United States' and other Western powers' commitment to granting the Israeli government absolute impunity would fatally undermine the entire latticework of International Humanitarian Law. As I pointed out, it was rather difficult for Washington to convince the Global South to celebrate the ICC indictment of Russian President Vladimir Putin for his war crimes in Ukraine while objecting to the indictment of Netanyahu for even more severe crimes.

40. Is Tehran Winning the Middle East? How the Gaza Conflict Made Democracy's Name Mud for Millions

March 4, 2024

In the midst of Israel's ongoing devastation of Gaza, one major piece of Middle Eastern news has yet to hit the headlines. In a face-off that, in a sense, has lasted since the pro-American Shah of Iran was overthrown by theocratic clerics in 1979, Iran finally seems to be besting the United States in a significant fashion across the region. It's a story that needs to be told.

"Hit Iran now. Hit them hard" was typical advice offered by Republican Senator Lindsey Graham after a drone flown by an Iran-aligned Iraqi Shiite militia killed three American servicemen in northern Jordan on January 28th.[1] The well-heeled Iran War Lobby in Washington has, in fact, been stridently calling for nothing short of a U.S. invasion of that country, accusing Tehran of complicity in Hamas's October 7th terrorist attack on Israel.

No matter that the official Iranian press has vehemently denied the allegation.[2] American intelligence officials swiftly concluded that the attack on Israel had taken top Iranian leaders by surprise.[3] In mid-November, Reuters reported that Iranian leader Ayatollah Ali Khamenei informed a key Hamas figure, Ismail Haniya, that his country wouldn't intervene directly in the Gaza war, since Tehran hadn't been warned about the October 7th attack before it was launched. He actually seemed annoyed that the leadership of the Hamas paramilitary group, the Qassam Brigades, thought they could draw Tehran and its allies willy-nilly into a major conflict without the slightest consultation. Although initially caught off-guard, as the Israeli counterattack grew increasingly brutal and disproportionate, Iran's leaders clearly began to see ways they could turn the war to their regional benefit—and they've done so skillfully, even as the Biden administration in its full-scale embrace of the most extreme government in Israeli history tossed democracy and international law under the bus.

The gut-wrenching Hamas attacks on civilians at a music festival and those living in left-wing, peacenik Kibbutzim near the Israeli border with Gaza on October 7th initially left Iran in an uncomfortable position. It had allegedly been slipping some $70 million[4] a year to Hamas—though Egypt and Qatar had provided major funding to Gaza at Israel's request through sanctioned Israeli government bank accounts.[5] And after decades of championing the Palestinian cause, Tehran could hardly stand by and do nothing as Israel razed Gaza to the ground. On the other hand, the ayatollahs couldn't afford to gain a reputation for being played like a fiddle by the region's young radicals and so drawn into conventional wars their country can ill afford.

The Adults in the Room?

Despite their fiery rhetoric, their undeniable backing of fundamentalist militias in the region, and their depiction by inside-the-Beltway war hawks as the root of all evil in the Middle East, Iran's leaders have long acted more like a status quo power than a force for genuine change. They have shored up the rule of the autocratic al-Assad family in Syria, while helping the Iraqi government that emerged after President George W. Bush's invasion of that country fight off Islamic State of Iraq and the Levant (ISIL). In truth, not Iran but the U.S. and Israel are the countries that have most strikingly tried to use their power to reshape the region in a Napoleonic manner. The disastrous U.S. invasion and occupation of Iraq, and Israel's wars on Egypt (1956, 1967), Lebanon (1982-2000, 2006), and Gaza (2008, 2012,

2014, 2021, 2024), along with its steady encouragement of large-scale squatting on the Palestinian West Bank, were clearly intended to alter the geopolitics of the region permanently through the use of military force on a massive scale.

Only recently, Ayatollah Khamenei bitterly asked, "Why don't the leaders of Islamic countries publicly cut off their relationship with the murderous Zionist regime and stop helping this regime?"[6] Pointing to the staggering death toll in Israel's present campaign against Gaza, he was focusing on the Arab countries—Bahrain, Morocco, Sudan, and the United Arab Emirates—that, as part of Trump son-in-law Jared Kushner's "Abraham Accords," had officially recognized Israel and established relations with it. (Egypt and Jordan had, of course, recognized Israel long before that.)

Given the anti-Israel sentiment in the region, had it, in fact, been rife with democracies, Iran's position might have been widely implemented. Still, it was a distinct sign of terminal tone deafness on the part of Biden administration officials that they hoped to use the Gaza crisis to extend the Abraham Accords to Saudi Arabia, while sidelining the Palestinians and creating a joint Israeli-Arab front against Iran.[7]

The region had already been moving in a somewhat different direction. Last March, after all, Iran and Saudi Arabia had begun forging a new relationship by restoring the diplomatic relations that had been suspended in 2016 and working to expand trade between their countries.[8] And that relationship has only continued to improve as the nightmare in Israel and Gaza developed.[9] In fact, Iranian President Ebrahim Raisi first visited the Saudi capital, Riyadh, in November and, since the Gaza conflict began, Foreign Minister Hossein Amir-Abdollahian has met twice with his Saudi counterpart. Frustrated by a markedly polarizing American policy in the region, de facto Saudi ruler Crown Prince Mohammed Bin Salman and Iran's Ayatollah Ali Khamenei resorted to the good offices of Beijing to sidestep Washington and strengthen their relations further.[10]

Although Iran is far more hostile to Israel than Saudi Arabia, their leaderships do agree that the days of marginalizing the

Palestinians are over. In a remarkably unambiguous statement issued in early February, the Saudis offered the following: "The Kingdom has communicated its firm position to the U.S. administration that there will be no diplomatic relations with Israel unless an independent Palestinian state is recognized on the 1967 borders with East Jerusalem as its capital, and that the Israeli aggression on the Gaza Strip stops and all the Israeli occupation forces withdraw from the Gaza Strip."[11] Significantly, the Saudis even refused to join a U.S.-led naval task force created to halt attacks on Red Sea shipping by the Houthis of Yemen (no friends of theirs) in support of the Palestinians. Its leaders are clearly all too aware that the carnage still being wreaked on Gaza has infuriated most Saudis.[12]

In late January, President Raisi also surprised regional diplomats by traveling to Ankara for talks on trade and geopolitics with Turkish President Recep Tayyip Erdogan, another sign of his country's changing role in the region.[13] At the end of the visit, while signing various agreements to increase trade and cooperation, he announced: "We agreed to support the Palestinian cause, the axis of resistance, and to give the Palestinian people their rightful rights."[14] That's no small thing. Remember that Turkey is a NATO member and considered a close ally of the United States. To have Erdogan suddenly cozy up to Iran, while denouncing Israeli Prime Minister Benjamin Netanyahu's war on Gaza as a Hitlerian-style genocide, was an unmistakable slap in Washington's face.[15]

Meanwhile, Iran, Turkey, and Russia recently issued a joint communiqué that "expressed deep concern over the humanitarian catastrophe in Gaza and stressed the need to end the Israeli brutal onslaught against the Palestinians, [while] sending humanitarian aid to Gaza."[16] From the Biden administration's point of view, Moscow's bombing of civilian sites in Ukraine and Iran's role in crushing Sunni Arab rebels in Syria had been the atrocities that needed attention until Netanyahu suddenly pulled the rug out from under them by upping the ante from mere atrocities to what the International Court of Justice has ruled can plausibly be labeled a genocide.[17] One thing was clear: Washington's long struggle to exclude Iran from regional influence has now visibly failed.

Iran's Rising Popularity

At the Gulf International Forum (GIF) last November, Abdullah Baaboud, a prominent Omani academic, said that there had been a "very strong condemnation of Israel from Iran and Turkey, embarrassing some Arab countries that are not using the same language. My worry is that this conflict is leading to the empowerment of Turkey and Iran among the Arab public."[18] GIF's executive director, Dania Thafer, concurred. Of that public, she said, "Grief and anger have reached unprecedented levels," and added, "with each photo out of Gaza, Iran gains more influence across the region."[19] In short, at remarkably little cost, Iran is unexpectedly winning the battle for regional public opinion and its standing in the Arab world has risen strikingly. Meanwhile, the reputation of the United States has been indelibly tarnished by Washington's full-throated support for what most in the region do indeed see as a merciless slaughter of thousands of children and other innocent civilians.

A recent opinion poll of Arabs in 16 countries, conducted jointly by the Arab Center in Washington, D.C., and the Arab Center for Research and Policy Studies in Doha, Qatar, found that 94 percent of them considered the American position on Israel's war "bad."[20] In contrast, a surprising 48 percent of them considered the Iranian position positive. To grasp just how remarkable such a finding was, consider that a Gallup poll conducted in 2022 found that Shiite Iran's name was mud in most Sunni Arab countries and approval of its leadership fell somewhere between 1 percent and 20 percent.[21]

In recent months, Iran has made striking use of the weakness of Washington's case in the region. While the State Department likes to contrast Iran's "dictatorship" with Israel's "democratic character," only recently foreign ministry spokesperson Nasser Kanaani observed, "The disaster in Gaza removed the mask from the face of the so-called advocates of human rights and showed the extent of vileness, brutality, and lies hidden within the nature of the Israeli regime, whose supporters used to refer to [it] as a symbol of democracy."[22] Although Iran has among the world's worst human-rights records, Netanyahu has even managed to take the focus off of that.

Losing the Middle East, Washington-Style

Iran's allies in the region include Iraqi Shiite militias like the Party of God Brigades (*Kata'ib Hezbollah*), which first gained prominence in the struggle against the ISIL terrorist group from 2014 to 2018.[23] Those were years when the regular Iraqi army had essentially collapsed and was only gradually being rebuilt. Washington was also focused on destroying ISIL then and so developed a wary de facto alliance with them in its campaign to crush that "caliphate." In January 2020, however, President Trump was responsible for the drone assassination of the group's leader, Abu Mahdi al-Muhandis, along with Iranian General Qasem Soleimani, just after their arrival by plane at Baghdad International Airport in what was evidently an attempt to prevent them, through the Iraqis, from forging an agreement with Saudi Arabia to reduce tensions with Iran.[24]

That assassination led to a long-running, low-intensity conflict between the Shiite militias of Iraq and the 2,500 remaining American troops stationed there. With the onset of the Gaza conflict last October, the Party of God Brigades began launching mortars and drones against Iraqi military bases hosting American soldiers, as well as against small forward operating bases in southeast Syria where some 900 U.S. military personnel are stationed, ostensibly to support the Syrian Kurds in mopping up operations against ISIL. After more than 150 such attacks, on January 28th one of their drones hit Tower 22, a support base where U.S. troops were stationed in northern

Jordan, killing three American soldiers, while wounding dozens more.[25]

Iran's leaders generally back those Shiite militias, but whether they had anything to do with the attack on Tower 22 remains unknown. Officials in Tehran did, however, immediately recognize the danger of escalation once American troops had actually been killed. And indeed, the Biden administration responded with dozens of air strikes on bases and facilities of the Party of God Brigades in Iraq and Syria. *Washington Post* reporters were told by Iraqi and Lebanese officials that Iran had actually urged caution on the militias with clear effect.[26] Their attacks on bases hosting U.S. troops ceased. At the same time, the Iraqi parliament and government complained bitterly about Washington's violation of the country's sovereignty, while heightening preparations to force the withdrawal of the last U.S. troops from their land.[27] In other words, President Biden's fierce backing of Israel's war, his decision to increase weapons shipments to that country, and his bombing of pro-Palestinian militias may have led to the achievement of a longstanding Iranian aim: seeing American troops finally leave Iraq.[28]

Meanwhile, in southern Lebanon, where the militant group Hezbollah has been exchanging occasional fire with Israeli forces in support of Gaza, according to the *Washington Post* reporters, one Hezbollah figure told them that Iran's message was: "We are not keen on giving Israeli Prime Minister Benjamin Netanyahu any reason to launch a wider war on Lebanon or anywhere else."[29] Wars are unpredictable, and the Lebanon-Israeli border could still erupt dramatically. Moreover, Iranian pleas for restraint appear to have had far less effect on the Houthi leadership in Yemen's capital Sanaa, leading to an ongoing American and British bombing campaign on that city and elsewhere in that country that has so far done little to stop Houthi missile and drone attacks against ships in the Red Sea.

So far, however, despite the Republican urge to devastate Iran, that country's leaders have taken deft advantage of the butchery in Gaza (in which the Israeli military has killed more civilian noncombatants each day than belligerents have in any other conflict in this century).[30] The ayatollahs have significantly increased their popularity even among Arab and Muslim publics that had not previously shown them much favor. They have strengthened their relationship with the Shiites of Iraq and may be on the verge of finally achieving their goal of ending the U.S. military missions in Iraq and Syria.

They have also achieved closer ties with Turkey, while improving relations with Saudi Arabia and the other Gulf Arab oil states. In doing so, they have distinctly blunted the Biden administration's aim of isolating Iran while tying the wealthier Arab states ever more firmly to Israel through arms and high-tech deals.

In addition, through its backing of and weaponizing of Israel in these last grim months, Washington has made a mockery of the human rights talking points that the U.S. has long deployed against Iran. In the process, Joe Biden has done more than any recent president to undermine both international humanitarian law and democratic principles globally. With 94 percent of Arab poll respondents viewing American policy in the region as "bad," one thing is clear: for the moment at least, Iran has won the Middle East.[31]

Notes

[1] Lindsey Graham's Twitter Post:
https://twitter.com/LindseyGrahamSC/status/1751657471280652397

[2] Nour News Denial of Allegations:
https://nournews.ir/Fa/News/153901

[3] Reuters Report on American intelligence conclusion:
https://www.reuters.com/world/initial-us-intelligence-shows-hamas-attack-surprised-iranian-leaders-ny-times-2023-10-11/

[4] *Washington Post* on Iranian Financial Support to Hamas:
https://www.washingtonpost.com/national-security/2023/10/09/iran-support-hamas-training-weapons-israel/

[5] CNN Report on Egyptian and Qatari Funding to Gaza:
https://www.cnn.com/2023/12/11/middleeast/qatar-hamas-funds-

israel-backing-intl/index.html

[6] Ayatollah Khamenei's Question about Islamic Countries' Relations with Israel: https://www.leader.ir/fa/content/26998/

[7] *Axios* report on Biden Administration's Middle East Hopes: https://www.axios.com/2024/01/21/biden-middle-east-gaza-palestinian-state-israel

[8] Juan Cole at TomDispatch on the Iran and Saudi Arabia Relationship: https://tomdispatch.com/china-and-the-axis-of-the-sanctioned/

[9] AGSIW Article on Saudi-Iranian Relationship Improvements: https://agsiw.org/why-the-saudi-iranian-pact-is-withstanding-the-gaza-war/

[10] Juan Cole at TomDispatch on China's mediation between Saudi Arabia and Iran. https://tomdispatch.com/china-and-the-axis-of-the-sanctioned/

[11] Juan Cole on Saudi Arabia's unambiguous statement: https://www.juancole.com/2024/02/contradict-blinken-palestinian.html

[12] *The Cradle* article on Saudi Reaction to Gaza: https://thecradle.co/articles-id/21919

[13] *Hurriyet Daily News* report on President Raisi's Ankara Visit: https://www.hurriyetdailynews.com/raisi-in-ankara-for-delayed-gaza-talks-190009

[14] Ibid.

[15] Anadolu Agency report on Erdogan's Comparison of Netanyahu to Hitler: https://www.aa.com.tr/en/middle-east/no-difference-between-actions-of-hitler-israeli-premier-netanyahu-turkish-president-erdogan/3093860

[16] Turkish Ministry Joint Communiqué with Iran and Russia: https://www.mfa.gov.tr/iran--rusya-ve-turkiye-temsilcileri-tarafindan-yapilan-astana-formatindaki-suriye-konulu-21-yuksek-duzeyli-toplanti-ya-iliskin-ortak-bildiri.en.mfa

[17] Juan Cole's Article on the International Court of Justice Ruling: https://www.juancole.com/2024/01/reputation-besmirched-palestinians.html

[18] Washington Report on the Middle East's Gulf GCC Response to Gaza: https://www.wrmea.org/gulf-gcc/the-arab-gulfs-response-to-the-war-on-gaza.html

[19] Ibid.

[20] Arab Center Poll on Public Opinion of Israel's War on Gaza: https://arabcenterdc.org/resource/arab-public-opinion-about-israels-war-on-gaza/

[21] Gallup Poll on Saudi Arabia Soft Power and Iranian Views: https://news.gallup.com/poll/474251/saudi-arabia-soft-power-outshines-iran.aspx

[22] Press TV Coverage on Iranian Foreign Ministry Spokesperson's Remarks: https://www.presstv.ir/Detail/2024/02/19/720366/Iran-Kanani-Gaza-war-Israel-U.S.-human-rights

[23] Juan Cole's Analysis of the Party of God Brigades: https://www.juancole.com/2024/01/inherited-militia-netanyahu.html

[24] Juan Cole's Commentary on Fallout from Soleimani's Assassination: https://www.juancole.com/2020/01/parliament-threatens-sanctions.html

[25] CNN Report on U.S. Troops Killed by Drone Attack in Jordan: https://www.cnn.com/2024/01/28/politics/us-troops-drone-attack-jordan/index.html

[26] Washington Post Coverage of Iran-Proxy Conflict and U.S. Strikes: https://www.washingtonpost.com/world/2024/02/18/

[27] *Baghad al-Yawm* on Iraq's complaint about violation of sovereignty. https://tinyurl.com/39kn9b57

[28] CBS on Biden's emergency dispatch of weapons to Israel. https://www.cbsnews.com/news/biden-administration-emergency-weapons-sale-israel/

[29] *Washington Post* on Iran urging its proxies to avoid a wider war. https://www.washingtonpost.com/world/2024/02/18/iran-proxies-middle-east/

[30] Oxfam on unprecedented Gaza casualties in 21st century. https://www.oxfam.org/en/press-releases/daily-death-rate-gaza-higher-any-other-major-21st-century-conflict-oxfam

[31] Arab Center Poll on Public Opinion of Israel's War on Gaza: https://arabcenterdc.org/resource/arab-public-opinion-about-israels-war-on-gaza/

41. Israel's Lavender Murderbot is Programmed to Kill up to a Third of all Palestinian Civilians in Gaza

April 4, 2024

The incredibly brave and resourceful Israeli journalist Yuval Abraham revealed Wednesday in a hard-hitting piece of investigative journalism that the Israeli military has used two artificial intelligence programs, "Lavender" and "Where's Daddy," to target some 37,000 alleged members of the military wings of Hamas and Palestinian Islamic Jihad.[1] The programs used GPS to discover when a Hamas member had gone home, since it was easiest to hit him there, ensuring that his wife and children would also be killed. If he lived in an apartment building, which most did, then all the civilians in neighboring apartments could also be killed—children, women, non-combatant men.

Science fiction writer Martha Wells has authored a series of novels and short stories about a "Murderbot," a Security Unit artificial intelligence in the body of an armored warrior.[2] Her Murderbot, despite being lethal, is a good guy, and in noir style frees himself from the control of his corporate overlords to protect his friends.

The Israeli army, in contrast, is acting much more robotically.

Lavender is just a program and doesn't have a body attached to it, but uses Israeli fighter jet pilots as an extension of itself.

The AI programs identified the Hamas militants according to vague specifications. It is known to have a 10 percent error rate and in other cases the supposed militant might have only loose connections to the Qassam Brigades paramilitary or the PIJ. There was, Abraham writes, almost no human supervision over the working of the algorithm.

AI Lavender, at a 10 percent error rate, could have identified 3,700 men in Gaza as Hamas guerrillas when they weren't. It could have allowed as many as 20 civilians to be killed in each strike on each of these innocents, which would give a total of 77,700 noncombatants blown arbitrarily away by an inaccurate machine.

One of Abraham's sources inside the Israeli army said, "We were not interested in killing [Hamas] operatives only when they were in a military building or engaged in a military activity," A., an intelligence officer, told +972 Mag. "On the contrary, the IDF bombed them in homes without hesitation, as a first option. It's much easier to bomb a family's home. The system is built to look for them in these situations."

I hope the International Court of Justice, which is considering whether Israel is committing a genocide, is reading +972 Mag.

The AI program included extremely loose rules of engagement on civilian casualties. It was set to permit 15-20 civilians to be killed as part of a strike on a low-level Hamas member, and up to 100 civilians could be killed to get at a senior member. These new rules of engagement are unprecedented even in the brutal Israeli army.

The "Where's Daddy" program identified and tracked the members.

The 37,000 Hamas paramilitary fighters did not carry out October 7. Most of them did not know about it beforehand. It was a tiny, tight clique that planned and executed it. The civilian wing of Hamas was the elected government of Gaza, and its security forces provided law and order (refugee camps are most often lawless). It may be that Lavender and "Where's Daddy" swept up ordinary police in the definition of low-level Hamas fighters, which would explain a lot.

This new video game way of war violates the Rules of Engagement of the U.S. military and all the precepts of International Humanitarian Law. The Marine Corps Rules of Engagement go this way:

Do not strike any of the following except in self-defense to protect yourself, your unit, friendly forces, and designated persons or property under your control:

- Civilians.
- Hospitals, mosques, churches, shrines, schools, museums, national monuments, and other historical and cultural sites.

Do not fire into civilian populated areas or buildings unless the enemy is using them for military purposes or if necessary for your self-defense. Minimize collateral damage.

Do not target enemy infrastructure (public works, commercial communications facilities, dams), lines of communication (roads, highways, tunnels, bridges, railways) and economic objects (commercial storage facilities, pipelines) unless necessary self-defense or if ordered by your commander. If you must fire on these objects to engage a hostile force, disable and disrupt but avoid destruction of these objects, if possible.[3]

None of the Israeli "soldiers" operating Lavender were in danger from the civilians they killed. They made no effort to "minimize collateral damage." In fact, they built very substantial collateral damage into their standard operating procedure.

If the Israeli military killed an average of 20 civilians each time they struck one of the 37,000 alleged militants, that would be 740,000 deaths, or three-quarters of a million. Of babies, toddlers, pregnant mothers, unarmed women, unarmed teenagers, etc., etc. That would be about a *third* of the total Gaza population.

That is certainly a genocide, however you wish to define the term.

And there is no way that Joe Biden and Antony Blinken haven't known all this all along. It is on them.

Notes

[1] Yuval Abraham's article on the use of AI by the Israeli military targeting alleged members of Hamas.
https://www.972mag.com/lavender-ai-israeli-army-gaza/

[2] Martha Wells' Murderbot series.
https://www.marthawells.com/murderbot.htm

[3] The U.S. Marine Corps Rules of Engagement.
https://www.trngcmd.marines.mil/Portals/207/Docs/TBS/B130936%20Law%20of%20War%20and%20Rules%20Of%20Engagement.pdf

42.   Netanyahu, Empowered by Biden's Grant of Impunity baits Iran into his genocidal Gaza War

April 14, 2024

Iran responded to the Israeli bombing of its Syrian diplomatic mission on April 13, 2024. Despite all the hype about Iran's largely symbolic barrage of over 200 drones and cruise and ballistic missiles, unleashed on the thinly populated Negev Desert (where it was mainly Palestinian Bedouins who were put in danger), the military significance of this action was minimal. An Israeli base was hit at Dimona, which houses the country's nuclear warheads, but the government said that the damage was negligible.[1] Almost all of the projectiles were shot down by the U.S. armed forces, and the rest by the Jordanian and Israeli Air Forces, or by anti-missile missiles. The only casualty appears to be a 7-year-old Palestinian Bedouin girl, who was seriously injured by a falling missile.

Iran struck because Israeli Prime Minister Binyamin Netanyahu on April 1 bombed the consular annex of the Iranian embassy in Damascus bombed, killing high-ranking Iranian officials, including Brigadier General Mohammad Reza Zahedi and seven other officers of the Iranian Revolutionary Guards Corps (IRGC). Those officials were there at the invitation of the Syrian government, and embassies are protected from military attack by the Vienna Convention.

Iran cited Article 51 of the United Nations Charter for its counter-strike on Israel, which guarantees states the right of self-defense. Embassies are considered national soil.[2]

Ayatollah Ali Khamenei, Iran's clerical Leader, had said Wednesday at his Eid al-Fitr sermon: "The consulate and embassy institutions in any country are the soil of that country. The evil regime made a mistake and must be punished and will be punished." He added, "The events in Gaza showed the evil nature of Western civilization to the world. They killed thirty-odd thousand defenseless people; aren't they human? Do they not have rights?"[3] He added, "They showed what kind of civilization this is. A child is killed, in the mother's arms. The patient dies in the hospital. Their power cannot touch...the men of the resistance; so they target the lives of family members, the lives of children and the oppressed, the lives of old men."

Iran's permanent mission to the United Nations in New York wrote on X, "Conducted on the strength of Article 51 of the U.N. Charter pertaining to legitimate defense, Iran's military action was in response to the Zionist regime's aggression against our diplomatic premises in Damascus. The matter can be deemed concluded. However, should the Israeli regime make another mistake, Iran's response will be considerably more severe. It is a conflict between Iran and the rogue Israeli regime, from which the U.S. MU.S.T STAY AWAY!"[4]

Tehran is saying that with this exchange, "the matter can be deemed concluded." Ayatollah Ali Khamenei is not looking for an all-out war.

It was not only the strike on the Iranian embassy that set the stage for Iran's barrage, but also the six months of intensive Israeli bombing of the Palestinians of Gaza, in which the vast majority of those killed were innocent noncombatants, with 70 percent being women and children and many others noncombatant men. The death toll in April 2024 stands at 33,686 Palestinians.[5] Only a small clique of militants committed the horrific October 7 attack on Israel, without telling anyone else what they were planning. There is no military or other justification for using an artificial intelligence program to identify all members of Hamas's paramilitary (some of which is the equivalent of a neighborhood watch for local security) and to murder them from the skies along with their spouses, children, extended families, and neighbors.

Iran is pledged to defend the Palestinians and has been made to look ineffectual and foolish by the ongoing Israeli atrocities, which have set the blood of the publics in the Middle East to boiling and much raised the esteem in which they hold Iran.[6] The embassy strike was the last straw. If Iran did not reply to it at least symbolically, its credibility, and any deterrence it was perceived to have, became a joke.

Netanyahu for his part was attempting to provoke Iran, in the hope that Tehran would take the bait. He knew that even Washington had come to see Israel as the aggressor in Gaza, and that he was losing support in Congress. He knew that if the issue became an Iranian attack on Israel, the Western capitals would all rally around him and forgive him at least for a while for having brought the Israeli equivalent of Neo-Nazis into his cabinet and then gone Amalek on tens of thousands of innocent Palestinians.

In the end, Khamenei and the Revolutionary Guards let their devotion to the late Gen. Zahedi sway their emotions and they fell for Netanyahu's trick.

Earlier on Saturday the naval section of the Iranian Revolutionary Guards Corps boarded and confiscated a container ship in the Gulf of Oman that belongs to the company of one of Netanyahu's billionaire backers. While this action violated the law of the sea and can't be condoned, it was a wiser way of replying to the embassy attack than sending missiles against Israel. It hit Netanyahu where it hurts and no one would have cared about it in the outside world.

Now, we have to suffer with Netanyahu proclaiming his victimhood (he started it) and suffering through statements of solidarity with his fascist government in the face of the ayatollahs, with the ongoing genocide in Gaza cast into the shade.

As many observers are pointing out, this very dangerous situation was caused by President Joe Biden's mishandling of the

Gaza crisis. He should have cut Netanyahu off at the knees by January 1, once it became clear that the Israelis were implementing their notorious Amalek imperative, which implied genocide. By vetoing 3 United Nations Security Council resolutions demanding a ceasefire and by undercutting the only one he allowed to pass by branding it nonbinding, Biden let the butchery continue apace. It continued the past week, during which Israel continued to bomb the bejesus out of Gaza, to kill hundreds of innocents, and to starve them (despite phony pledges to let more aid in, on which Netanyahu did not follow through.)[7]

Biden, UK PM Rishi Sunak and other leaders could also have defused the deliberate provocation of Iran by Netanyahu by simply condemning the embassy attack of April 1 and defending the Vienna convention. Again, the Iranian mission to the U.N. said this plainly: "Had the U.N. Security Council condemned the Zionist regime's reprehensible act of aggression on our diplomatic premises in Damascus and subsequently brought to justice its perpetrators, the imperative for Iran to punish this rogue regime might have been obviated."[8]

Instead, Biden and his allies declined to condemn Netanyahu's action, continuing the North Atlantic insouciance toward Israeli war crimes and continuing the implementation of their double standard whereby International Humanitarian Law applies only to white people. That is, there is not as much difference between Trumpian white nationalism and Biden's foreign policy as it might seem on the surface, though Trump is of course far worse.

Notes

[1] Israeli government's statement on the minimal damage caused by Iran's missile strike, according to AP.
https://whnt.com/news/international/ap-international/ap-british-military-warns-of-possible-vessel-being-boarded-near-strait-of-hormuz/

[2] Iran's citation of Article 51 of the United Nations Charter for its counter-strike on Israel in *Aftab*. https://tinyurl.com/5n7k37ve

[3] Ayatollah Ali Khamenei's statement on the protection of embassies and the nature of Western civilization in *Jamaran*. https://tinyurl.com/5f8erjwz

[4] Statement from Iran's permanent mission to the United Nations in New York regarding the military action. https://twitter.com/Iran_U.N./status/1779269993043022053

[5] The toll of Palestinian casualties as a result of Israeli strikes according to Asharq. https://tinyurl.com/3fpm7sr2

[6] Juan Cole's article in *Tomdispatch.com* discussing the raised esteem of Iran in the Middle East. https://tomdispatch.com/is-tehran-winning-the-middle-east/

[7] CNN article detailing Netanyahu's failure to follow through on pledges to allow more aid into Gaza. https://www.cnn.com/2024/04/12/middleeast/gaza-aid-israel-ramping-up-un-famine-mime-intl/index.html

[8] Iranian mission to the U.N.'s statement on potential U.N. Security Council actions that could have prevented the Iranian counter-strike. https://twitter.com/Iran_U.N./status/1778434597954470241

43. Lawless: Washington Celebrates ICC ruling against Russia, Condemns Warrant Request for Israel

May 21, 2024

Karim A.A. Khan, Prosecutor of the International Criminal Court (ICC), said Monday that he is asking the ICC to issue arrest warrants for several Hamas leaders as well as Israeli Prime Minister Benjamin Netanyahu and Secretary of Defense Yoav Gallant.[1]

It is the first time the ICC has sought warrants against leaders of a parliamentary government. Most of the officials indicted have been from African dictatorial regimes. If the warrants are approved, in a process that may take several months, Netanyahu and Gallant will join a rogues gallery featuring deposed Libyan strongman Moammar Gaddafi, deposed Sudanese dictator Omar al-Bashir, and Russian President Vladimir Putin.

In March, 2023, just a year ago, Secretary of State Antony Blinken asked all countries that are parties to the ICC to detain Vladimir Putin if they could, after the court issued an arrest warrant for him.[2] Russia is not a signatory to the Rome Statute that authorizes the court, but in 2015 Ukraine (also not a signatory) granted jurisdiction to the court over Ukrainian territory. It was for crimes committed in Ukraine that Putin was indicted.

The reaction in Washington to the warrant request for Netanyahu and Gallant has been the opposite. This reaction shows that the Biden administration does not respect international law and does not care that Putin committed crimes under it, but just wants to stick it to Putin. It is personalistic, not a matter of law. Because if the law was at issue, it should apply to everyone, including (especially) Benjamin Netanyahu, the Butcher of Gaza.

Everything Washington officials said in response to the request for warrants was wrong. I mean, incorrect. It isn't a matter of opinion or a difference in values. They are spewing falsehoods. It is as though they have all contracted Trumpitis and now keep compulsively telling serial lies.

President Biden, apparently now the chief defense attorney for Netanyahu, denounced any "equivalence" between Hamas and the Israeli leadership and said that he rejects charges of genocide against it. Biden's spokespeople questioned whether the ICC has jurisdiction to charge the Israeli leaders. Secretary of State Antony Blinken condemned the announcement as "outrageous" and said that it threatened the success of negotiations toward a ceasefire and a hostage release. Mr. Blinken did not explain why the ICC request for warrants should delay a ceasefire. The Biden administration vetoed three ceasefire calls at the U.N. Security Council earlier this year, and abstained on a fourth, which it undercut by falsely damning it as "non-binding." Speaker of the House of Representatives Mike Johnson said he and his colleagues would look into the possibility of placing sanctions on the ICC judges and their families.[3]

The 18 judges are elected to nine-year terms by an assembly of the 124 states that are signatories to the Rome Statute, finalized in 2002, which authorizes the court and lays out International Humanitarian Law.[4] The ICC therefore represents nearly two-thirds of the countries in the world. Mike Johnson represents a district in Louisiana.

The parties to the International Criminal Court include Britain, Canada, France, Belgium, Germany, Italy, the Netherlands, Norway, Denmark, Ireland, Switzerland, Japan, Spain, Sweden, as well as the State of Palestine and large numbers of countries in Asia, Africa, Latin America, and the Pacific. It took some courage to sign the Rome Statute, since the officials of the signatory country place themselves under the authority of the judges. It is not a courage that the United States, Israel or Russia displayed, and it is disgraceful that the United States has not signed the major human rights instrument of the twenty-first century.

So why is everything Washington is saying about the decision of Karim Khan wrong?

First, the request for warrants does not make an equivalence between Israel and Hamas. The court does not judge countries, it judges individual officials.

These are the charges against the three Hamas leaders, aside from just killing a lot of innocents:

- Taking hostages as a war crime, contrary to article 8(2)(c)(iii)
- Rape and other acts of sexual violence as crimes against humanity, contrary to article 7(1)(g), and also as war crimes pursuant to article 8(2)(e)(vi) in the context of captivity
- Torture as a crime against humanity, contrary to article 7(1)(f), and also as a war crime, contrary to article 8(2)(c)(i), in the context of captivity
- Other inhumane acts as a crime against humanity, contrary to article 7(1)(k), in the context of captivity
- Cruel treatment as a war crime contrary to article 8(2)(c)(i), in the context of captivity
- Outrages upon personal dignity as a war crime, contrary to article 8(2)(c)(ii), in the context of captivity

Note that rape, torture, and hostage-taking all bulk large here.

These are the charges against Netanyahu and Gallant:

- Starvation of civilians as a method of warfare as a war crime contrary to article 8(2)(b)(xxv) of

the Statute
- Wilfully causing great suffering, or serious injury to body or health contrary to article 8(2)(a)(iii), or cruel treatment as a war crime contrary to article 8(2)(c)(i)
- Wilful killing contrary to article 8(2)(a)(i), or Murder as a war crime contrary to article 8(2)(c)(i)
- Intentionally directing attacks against a civilian population as a war crime contrary to articles 8(2)(b)(i), or 8(2)(e)(i)
- Extermination and/or murder contrary to articles 7(1)(b) and 7(1)(a), including in the context of deaths caused by starvation, as a crime against humanity
- Persecution as a crime against humanity contrary to article 7(1)(h)
- Other inhumane acts as crimes against humanity contrary to article 7(1)(k)

The charges aren't the same or equivalent at all. The Israeli officials are charged with starving the civilian population, blowing up the civilian population, and exterminating the civilian population. There is no mention of rape or torture or hostage-taking. In each case, the officials are being charged for their specific actions. The Israeli officials are not charged with genocide by the ICC, contrary to what Mr. Biden alleged.

The reason that the ICC has jurisdiction is that the State of Palestine has very doggedly and brilliantly arranged for that jurisdiction. First, Palestine sought to be admitted as a non-member observer state of the United Nations, the same status that the Vatican has. The U.N. General Assembly voted Palestine in some 12 years ago. As an observer state, it gained the right to become a signatory to the Rome Statute, which it did in 2015. Then Palestine asked the ICC to exercise jurisdiction over the Occupied Palestinian Territories, which had de jure been granted to the State of Palestine by the 1993

Oslo Peace Treaty, signed by Bill Clinton, Yitzhak Rabin, and Yasser Arafat.

On February 5, 2021, the ICC concluded that it does have jurisdiction over actions taken in the Occupied Territories. Gaza is included in that jurisdiction. Hence, the ICC can issue the request for warrants against Hamas war criminals as well as against Israeli officials who commit war crimes or crimes against humanity in the Occupied Territories. It most definitely has jurisdiction. In fact, since Palestine is a party to the ICC, the case for jurisdiction here is much stronger than for Ukraine and Putin.

Prime Minister Netanyahu has repeatedly rejected the whole notion of a ceasefire and contrary to Mr. Blinken's flagrant toadying there is no prospect of any such ceasefire. Hamas offered a hostage deal on the eve of the invasion of Rafah, and Netanyahu invaded precisely in order to torpedo any deal. That is why Israelis are demonstrating in the tens of thousands against Netanyahu. If Blinken had any shame he'd fly to Tel Aviv and join them. The ICC decision is completely irrelevant to negotiations, which have in any case collapsed and are not ongoing. Blinken is trying to blame Karim Khan for his own egregious failure as a diplomat. Unlike Khan, Blinken has done nothing practical to hold Netanyahu to account for repeatedly violating the Biden administration's toothless red lines.

As for Mike Johnson and his merry band of GOP troglodytes, he should be careful if he'd ever like to vacation in Rio or in most of Europe.

Article 70 of the Rome Statute[5] has these paragraphs prohibiting:

- Impeding, intimidating or corruptly influencing an official of the Court for the purpose of forcing or persuading the official not to perform, or to perform improperly, his or her duties
- Retaliating against an official of the Court on account of duties performed by that or another official

The Court should play hardball with politicians who try to sanction its judges and should issue warrants against them. Wouldn't it be lovely to see Mike Johnson arrested while on vacation at Copacabana Beach in Rio de Janeiro and unceremoniously flown to the Hague in handcuffs? And Mike Pompeo and Trump, who did sanction ICC judges, should also have warrants out. Though with Trump the ICC would have to get in line behind a whole gaggle of prosecutors waving warrants for an endless list of crimes.

Notes

[1] Statement by Karim A.A. Khan, Prosecutor of the ICC: https://www.icc-cpi.int/news/statement-icc-prosecutor-karim-aa-khan-kc-applications-arrest-warrants-situation-state

[2] Secretary of State Antony Blinken asks countries to detain Vladimir Putin: https://www.reuters.com/world/us-top-diplomat-blinken-urges-all-icc-members-comply-with-putin-arrest-warrant-2023-03-22/

[3] Biden administration reaction to ICC warrant for Israeli leaders: https://www.cnn.com/2024/05/20/politics/biden-denounce-icc-warrant-israel-hamas/index.html; SpeakervMike Johnson's plans to sanction ICC judges and their families: https://www.axios.com/2024/05/20/icc-netanyahu-arrest-warrant-congress

[4] Parties to the ICC: https://asp.icc-cpi.int/states-parties

[5] Rome Statute prohibitions: https://www.icc-cpi.int/sites/default/files/Publications/Rome-Statute.pdf

44. International Court of Justice Orders Israel to Halt Rafah Invasion

May 25, 2024

The International Court of Justice ruled Friday that Israel must immediately cease its ongoing invasion of Rafah governorate in southern Gaza on the grounds that it is having a genocidal impact. The court's ruling went this way:

> The State of Israel shall, in conformity with its obligations under the Convention on the Prevention and Punishment of the Crime of Genocide, and in view of the worsening conditions of life faced by civilians in the Rafah Governorate:
>
> (a) By thirteen votes to two,
>
> Immediately halt its military offensive, and any other action in the Rafah Governorate, which may inflict on the Palestinian group in Gaza conditions of life that could bring about its physical destruction in whole or in part;
>
> IN FAVOUR: President Salam; Judges Abraham, Yusuf, Xue, Bhandari, Iwasawa, Nolte, Charlesworth, Brant, Gómez Robledo, Cleveland, Aurescu, Tladi;
>
> AGAINST: Vice-President Sebutinde; Judge ad hoc Barak.[1]

Some observers were disappointed that the court did not order an immediate ceasefire but limited itself to forbidding the Rafah campaign. Apparently, the judges were concerned to distinguish firmly between war-fighting and its inevitable toll, and genocidal actions having the effect of bringing about the destruction of a people in whole or part. They judged that a full-scale Rafah invasion would have that effect but did not go so far as to see the war itself in that light. It is a determination that they have yet to make.

President Joe Biden had also said that invading Rafah would be a red line because there is no way to ensure the welfare of the civilian, noncombatant population. Israel had ethnically cleansed northern Gaza and forced over a million Palestinians to the south, where they were living in tents or impossibly crowded tenement buildings amidst squalor. The population of Rafah had only been about 300,000 but it swelled to a million and a half. Shooting into their midst or bombing these dense settlements, as Israel is now doing, is sure to inflict massive killing and wounding on women, children, and noncombatant men.

Biden, having set a red line, however, has watched helplessly as Prime Minister Benjamin Netanyahu and his rogue's gallery of ultra-right cabinet members have ordered several brigades into Rafah. Some 900,000 civilians have now again been ethnically cleansed and are seeking shelter in largely destroyed cities in the middle of the Strip or are being forced with no food or water into the wilderness. Israel has largely halted food and aid shipments as part of the invasion.

If Biden is serious about his red line, he will abstain when the U.N. Security Council takes up the ICJ ruling and allow it to place sanctions on Israel for showing contempt of court.

The likelihood, however, is that Israel will continue to enjoy impunity, guaranteed by the United States.

The ICJ was set up after WWII to adjudicate disputes between United Nations members. South Africa prevailed in convincing the court last winter that since both Israel and South Africa are signatories to the 1948 Genocide convention, Pretoria has standing to sue the government of Prime Minister Benjamin Netanyahu over its actions in the Gaza Strip.

In January, South Africa sought what we in this country would call a preliminary injunction. For instance, say you sue a company for polluting a river, but you know that it will take years for the court to issue a verdict. You can ask the judge to issue a preliminary injunction against the company spewing pollution into the river until the case can be decided. On January 26, the court ruled again in South Africa's favor, judging that there is a plausible case that Israel is committing genocide and it should cease immediately those war strategies that would potentially come under that heading.

The Netanyahu government has thumbed its nose at these rulings, and despite some tut-tutting, the Biden administration has fully backed the continuation of the war, resupplying Israel with arms and ammunition for it in real time.

Aid NGOs active in Gaza now say that as a result of the Israeli attack on Rafah, people are thirsting to death or getting sick because they are being denied potable water and hygiene.

The U.N.'s OCHA reports,

On 22 May, the International Rescue Committee (IRC) and Medical Aid for Palestinians (MAP) reported that some displaced people in central Gaza are surviving on just three percent of the internationally recognized minimum requirements. According to humanitarian standards, the minimum amount of water needed in an emergency is 15 litres [about 4 gallons], which includes water for drinking, washing, and cooking. For survival alone, the estimated minimum is three litres per day. This is the case, for instance, at a shelter visited by the IRC [International Rescue Committee] that houses 10,000 people and receives just 4,000 litres of water per day, translating to about 0.4 litres per person, for drinking, washing, cooking, and cleaning.[2]

The IRC stressed that this situation is forcing people to rely on unsafe water sources like seawater and agricultural wells, and the lack of adequate water quantities is contributing to dehydration.

In the absence of sanitation facilities, displaced people are also building their own makeshift latrines, with up to 600 individuals sharing a single latrine, a situation exacerbated by the scarcity or unaffordability of hygiene supplies.

Within this context, communicable diseases, including diarrhoea and suspected Hepatitis A, continue to increase, with children under the age of five being particularly affected.

If you do not think putting hundreds of thousands of people in this situation is genocidal, then frankly there's nothing I can do for you because you are either not being honest with yourself and the world, or you are a sociopath lacking basic empathy.

CARE reports that the new flood of refugees to places such as Deir al-Balah lack basic medical facilities for maternal and pediatric care, and there is a danger of a lot of dead babies and mothers.[3]

Interfering in a people's ability safely to reproduce themselves is an element of genocide to which the International Court of Justice referred in its January 26 ruling.

The likelihood is that despite the court ruling, Washington will run interference for the genocidal policies of Tel Aviv, and that this carnage will continue for months to come. In the next stage, more people will die of disease, given the lack of hygienic facilities, than have been killed by Israel's indiscriminate bombing and shelling -- over 35,000 at present not counting thousands more under the rubble, the majority of them women and children.

Notes

[1] ICJ ruling on Rafah governorate invasion: https://www.icj-cij.org/sites/default/files/case-related/192/192-20240524-pre-01-00-en.pdf

[2] International Rescue Committee (IRC) and Medical Aid for Palestinians (MAP) reports on water and hygiene: https://reliefweb.int/report/occupied-palestinian-territory/hostilities-gaza-strip-and-israel-flash-update-170-enarhe

[3] CARE report on maternal and pediatric care in Deir al-Balah: https://careevaluations.org/evaluation/rafah-governorate-deception-destruction-death-in-the-safe-zone-rapid-gender-analysis/

45. Israel on U. N. Blacklist of Violators of Children, Killing or Maiming 20,000 Last Year

June 14, 2024

The United Nations has added Israel to its blacklist of nations that commit harms against children.[1] It joins Russia, DR Congo, South Sudan, Somalia, Sudan, Syria, Yemen, and Myanmar. Non-state actors in this category include ISIL, the Taliban, and the Lord's Resistance Army. Hamas and the Palestinian Islamic Jihad have been added to this category this year as well, especially for their attacks on Israeli children on October 7, 2023.

In 26 conflicts throughout the world, the United Nations counted almost 33,000 grave violations against more than 22,500 children, according to the U.N. report.[2] Israel and the Palestinian Occupied Territories witnessed an alarming rise in violations against children. The report found a 155 percent increase in violations against children in Israel and Palestine.

As bad as the situation was there, it was even worse in Sudan. Hamas and the Palestinian Islamic Jihad were responsible for killing 43 Israeli children on Oct. 7, by live fire, or by rockets and other means. Militant Palestinian groups also killed or maimed Israeli children in the Occupied West Bank, East Jerusalem, and northern Israel. Some three thousand cases of alleged injuries to Israeli children have yet to be verified.

The report says that for 2023, the U.N. verified 3,029 Israeli violations against children in Gaza, and over 4,800 in the Occupied

West Bank, including East Jerusalem. About 5,698 of these violations were committed by the Israeli armed and security forces. Last year, Israel detained 906 Palestinian children, mostly in the Palestinian West Bank and East Jerusalem. Some remained imprisoned without charge at the end of the year. In some instances, the Israelis attempted to turn minors into informants. Among the most alarming sentences in the report is that "the United Nations received reports of the detention of Palestinian children in the Gaza Strip, compounded by multiple forms of sexual violence."

My lord.

The Israeli Security Forces killed thousands of children in the Gaza Strip with explosive weapons: "Some 19,887 Palestinian children were reported killed or maimed and the reports are pending verification." The U.N. was able to verify that another 1,975 children were maimed, including 166 girls, mainly in the Palestinian West Bank and East Jerusalem. Some 10,787 children in Gaza were reported maimed by Israeli forces, but the verification process is ongoing.

Harms to children included not only bodily harm but also on schools and hospitals serving children, as well as on teachers and physicians. Some 340 such attacks were carried out by Israeli security forces, 45 on schools and 326 on hospitals. Some 106 teachers, physicians, or other staff in schools and pediatric clinics and hospitals were harmed by Israeli troops.

The report says, "A total of 3,227 permit applications (1,895 for boys, 1,332 for girls) to Israeli authorities for children to exit the Gaza Strip through the Erez crossing point, or from the occupied West Bank, to gain access to specialized medical treatment were denied or not approved in time to reach scheduled hospital appointments." This number represented about 18 percent of such applications, so almost a fifth were turned down. Of course, in the last quarter of 2023, children in Gaza with medical conditions needing outside treatment were simply trapped, and many have died of cancer or kidney disease.

The report adds that in Israel's war on Gaza, "all critical infrastructure, facilities and services have been attacked, including shelter sites, United Nations installations, schools, hospitals, water and sanitation facilities, grain mills, and bakeries." As a result of lack of electricity and lack of these destroyed facilities, "Children are at risk of famine, severe malnutrition and preventable death." In fact, the U.N. just reported that 8,000 Palestinian children in Gaza have been diagnosed with malnutrition.[3]

The report is also scathing about the crimes against Israeli children committed by Hamas' Izz al-Din al-Qassam Brigades and Palestinian Islamic Jihad's Al-Quds Brigades. But they also harmed Palestinian children and last year they "organized 'summer camps,' including for children, exposing them to military content and activities." The U.N. called for all sides to release child hostages and to abide by the laws of war in avoiding harm to innocent children in the prosecution of their war aims.

- *Informed Comment*

Notes

[1] United Nations adds Israel to blacklist:
https://news.un.org/en/story/2024/06/1151001

[2] U.N. report on violations against children:
https://documents.un.org/doc/undoc/gen/n24/095/07/pdf/n2409507.pdf?token=MS5mz4Zc9uXdsX6U13&fe=true

[3] U.N. report on Palestinian child malnutrition:
https://news.un.org/en/story/2024/06/1150996

46. The Gaza War Paralyzes Red Sea Shipping

July 2, 2024

The Associated Press announced in mid-June that the U.S. Navy has engaged in the most intense naval combat since the end of the second world war in the Red Sea, which surely would come as a surprise to most Americans.[1] This time the adversary is Yemen's Shiite party-militia, the Helpers of God (Ansar Allah), often known for their leading clan as the Houthis. They are supporting the Palestinians of Gaza against the Israeli campaign of total war on that small enclave, and their weapons of choice are rockets, drones and small ships rigged with explosives, with which they have targeted Red Sea shipping. The Houthis see the U.S. Navy as an adjunct to the Israeli war effort.

The Gate of Lamentation

The Yemenis have managed to launch a challenge to the prevailing world order, despite being poor, weak and brown, attributes that usually make people invisible to the U.S. Establishment. One asset the Houthis have is the emergence of micro-weaponry, of small drones and rockets that cannot at the moment easily be wiped out even by sophisticated armaments. Another asset is geographical. The Houthis command the Tihamah coastal plain, the eastern littoral of the Red Sea. It stretches between the Bab el-Mandeb Strait (the entry point to the Red Sea from the Gulf of Aden and the Indian Ocean) and the Suez Canal, which connects it to the Mediterranean and Europe. The Bab el-Mandeb, known for being treacherous to navigate, is said to mean "the Gate of Lamentation," and it is living up to its name these days. Some 10 percent of world trade flows through the Suez Canal, and 12 percent of the world's energy supplies.

What we might call the Battle of the Tihamah has already lasted seven months, and its outcome remains in doubt. AP quotes Brian Clark, a senior fellow at the Neoconservative Hudson Institute and a former Navy submariner, as expressing concerns that the Houthis are on the verge of being able to penetrate naval defenses with their missiles, raising the possibility that they could inflict major damage on a U.S. destroyer or even an aircraft carrier.[2] Repeated U.S. and British bombing of Houthi weapons sites in the capital, Sanaa, have failed to halt the war on shipping. Even the hi-tech American Reaper drones are no longer assured of dominating Middle Eastern air space, as they did in Iraq, since the Houthis have shot down four of the $30 million weapons so far.[3]

Idling the Suez Canal

The Houthi movement has its roots in Zaydi Shiism, which took hold in northern Yemen in the 890s. Today's Zaydis are protesting Israeli atrocities against the Palestinians of Gaza. Last December, large crowds came out in the Zaydi stronghold of Saadeh and other northern towns to protest the Israeli bombing of Gaza, waving Yemeni and Palestinian flags. They pledged support against "the armies of tyranny," and shouted, "We closed Bab el-Mandeb, O Zionist, do not approach" and "The Yemeni response is legitimate, and the Red Sea is forbidden."[4]

Houthis have hit commercial container ships in the Red Sea and seized the Galaxy Leader cargo ship. They have sunk two cargo ships and killed three crew members.[5] Although they maintain they are hitting Israeli-owned vessels, most of their attacks have targeted unrelated third parties such as Greece. Their strikes have caused a major disruption in world trade. The Houthis have also fired large numbers of ballistic missiles at the Israeli Red Sea port of Eilat, idling it since November.[6] Some five percent of imports had come into Israel through Eilat. Now, trade has been rerouted to Mediterranean ports, but at a higher cost, while southern Israel's economy has taken a big hit. Gideon Golber, the CEO of the Port of Eilat, demanded that the United States intervene. Israel is not the only country to suffer. Ports in the Horn of Africa have also become ghost towns, and the traffic through the Suez Canal is so light that Egypt, which collects transit tolls, is suffering significant economic damage.[7]

The Houthi strikes have had an impact on global supply chains. Insurance costs are high. War risk premiums have been as high as 100 percent of the value of the cargo earlier this year and are still at 70 percent. Spot prices for ocean container ship rates have surged this spring, as companies have been forced to go around the Cape of Good Hope and ply the Atlantic coast of Africa in Asian-Europe trade instead of going through the Suez Canal.[8] Even the addition of more ships has not much reduced carriage costs because of the longer, expensive routes. Shanghai to Rotterdam rates skyrocketed from $1452 per forty foot container in July of last year to $5270 in late May, 2024.[9]

Revolutionary Shiite Islam

Abdul-Malik al-Houthi situates himself in a Shiite revolutionary tradition. The militia commander last year observed the death in battle of the founder of his tradition, Zayd b. Ali (d. 740), "whose movement, renaissance, jihad, and martyrdom," he said, "made a great contribution to the continuity of the authentic Islam of Muhammad . . . He faced tyranny [the Umayyad Kingdom] and had an impact on instituting change."[10]

A generation of Americans involved in the Middle East has come to understand that there are two major branches of Islam, the Shiite and the Sunni. Neither is monolithic, with each branch having several denominations. The division goes back to questions about the succession to the Prophet Muhammad (d. 632). One faction of early believers invested leadership thereafter in senior disciples of the Prophet from his Quraysh clan. Over the centuries, these became the Sunnis.

Another faction, which gradually evolved into the Shiites, favored Muhammad's son-in-law and first cousin, Ali ibn Abi Talib, seeking a dynastic succession. They invested leadership thereafter in Ali's descendants through the Prophet's daughter, Fatimah. Most Shiites acknowledge twelve Imams or leaders from the dynasty. The Zaydis only recognized Ali and four descendants, the last being, Zayd b. Ali.[11]

Unlike the Twelver Shiites of Iran and Iraq, Yemen's rationalist Zaydis never had ayatollahs. Nor did they curse Sunnis, with whom they often had good relations. The leadership of the Zaydi branch of Shiism in Yemen was provided by court judges or qadis, typically hailing from a caste of putative descendants of the Prophet Muhammad, the Sayyids or Sadah, who emerged as mediators in tribal feuds. Critics of today's Helpers of God government in North Yemen allege that despite its populist rhetoric, it is dominated by a handful of clans who consider themselves descendants of the Prophet, including the Houthis themselves.[12]

Arab Nationalism

Forms of Arab nationalism and a rhetoric of anti-imperialism are not new for Yemen. After World War II, a desire for independence swept the Global South as the European empires were weakened. Col. Gamal Abdel Nasser of Egypt emerged as a nationalist leader who finally kicked the British out of his country, inspiring the Third World masses. Egypt-backed young officers in Sanaa staged a coup in 1962 against the hidebound Zaydi Imam, a theocratic leader who had kept Yemen isolated. They thereby threw the country into a civil war between republican nationalists and royalists. Britain, Saudi Arabia and Israel backed the royalists. Some 100,000 crack Egyptian troops won the day for the young officers in the North before withdrawing in 1970. In 1978 Ali Abdallah Saleh made an internal coup within the officer corps in North Yemen, appointing himself president for life.

The Helpers of God party-militia arose among the Zaydi Shiites of northern Yemen in the 1990s as a backlash to the inroads that neighboring, wealthy Wahhabi Saudi Arabia had made.[13] The corrupt government of Ali Abdallah Saleh, putatively a secular Arab nationalist, received billions in strategic rent from fundamentalist, royalist Riyadh.

Saudi Arabia's Wahhabism had been founded as a puritan reformist movement in the eighteenth.[14] Although now grouped with Sunnis, it began as a critique of both Sunnism and Shiism. Angered by Saudi Wahhabi proselytizers' challenge to Zaydi identity, Badr al-Din al-Houthi established the "Believing Youth Movement" in the 1990s to combat it. He gradually came into conflict with Saleh's government, which killed him and tried to crush the movement in 2004.

Saudi Hegemony and the Rise of the Houthis

Zaydi militiamen based in Saadeh in the hardscrabble north turned radical, coming into frequent conflict with the Yemeni army in the first decade of this century. When the Arab Spring youth revolt overthrew Saleh in 2012, the Party of God used its civil political wing to seek influence in the subsequent government. But impatient with an interminable reform process aimed and drafting a new constitution and electing a new parliament, in September 2014 the Houthis marched into Sanaa and took it over. They had allied behind the scenes with the deposed president, Saleh, and the army faction still loyal to him, which gave them access to billions in American-supplied weaponry. By early 2015 the Houthis had expelled Saleh's successor, Abdrabbuh Mansur Hadi, from the capital and made a bid to take all of Yemen from Saadeh in the north to Aden in the south.

Houthi dominance of North Yemen proved unacceptable to their old rival, Wahhabi Saudi Arabia, and to the United Arab Emirates, whose secular potentate, Mohammed Bin Zayed, despises movements of political Islam. They launched a war from the air on the Helpers of God in the spring of 2015.[15] The ruinous Seven Years War displaced millions and endangered more millions with food insecurity and disease, but it failed to dislodge the Helpers of God, and by 2022 a truce had been reached. Perhaps for this reason, the Saudis have declined to join the U.S. in the Battle of Tihamah against the Houthis this year. In some ways the tactics of Saudi Arabia and the UAE in Yemen, of intensive aerial bombing of even civilian infrastructure, prefigured Israeli procedures in Gaza, which is one reason for Houthi sympathy for the latter.

Alliance of Resistance

Both the Saudis and the Emiratis saw the Houthis as a mere cat's paw of Iran, and although Iran was drawn into providing some sorts of support for them, this is a misreading both of the significant Zaydi-Twelver differences in Shiism and of the relationship of Sanaa and Tehran. Iranian aid certainly was dwarfed by the billions in U.S. weaponry provided to Riyadh and Abu Dhabi. The Houthis are largely a form of homegrown Yemeni nationalism, and they have attracted some Sunni tribes into their coalition. Still, current leader Abdul-Malik al-Houthi has clearly been influenced by aspects of Iran's political radicalism, chanting death to America and death to Israel just as does Iranian clerical leader Ali Khamenei. Like the clerical regime in Iran, the Houthi government has no respect for human rights or dissent. Although there is no command line from Tehran to Sanaa, the Houthis loosely form part of Iran's alliance of resistance against Israel and the United States.[16] It is not clear, however, that Iran, which is close to Russia and China and covertly exports its U.S.-sanctioned petroleum, wanted international shipping costs to double, which hurts all three.

Despite the Houthi appeal to religious identity, it is also a movement of Arab nationalism, helping to explain its deep sympathy for the Sunni Palestinians, fellow Arabs. In an interview at the beginning of June, Abdul-Malik al-Houthi condemned Israel for its genocide against the Palestinian people in Gaza and its targeting of Palestinian East Jerusalem with Israeli squatter-settlements.[17] He denounced the United States as a full imperial partner in and enabler of Israeli crimes and as a hypocrite that talks a good game about respecting the rule of law but in fact dismisses or even threatens international courts and cracks down on domestic universities when they protest Israeli policies. He praised the resistance of his loose allies, Lebanon's Hezbollah and the Iraqi Shiite militias. He vowed that however intense the U.S. and British attacks on Yemen became, he and his movement would not back down from their support for the Palestinian people.

The situation in the Red Sea is among the more dangerous in the world today, rivaling that in Ukraine and Taiwan. It is at least somewhat of a drag on the world economy, contributing to stubborn inflation and supply chain problems. Major Houthi damage to a U.S. naval vessel could plunge the United States into war and would risk direct conflict with Iran. President Joe Biden could lower the temperature by intervening to end the Israeli total war on the people of Gaza, an intolerable affront to norms of international humanitarian law that is calling forth vigilantism such as that of the Houthis. The war should be ended to prevent further mass death and looming starvation. But it should also be ended to forestall yet another ruinous American war in the Middle East.

This essay appeared in a slightly different from at Tomdispatch.com

Notes

[1] The Associated Press report on U.S. Navy combat in the Red Sea. https://apnews.com/article/us-navy-yemen-houthis-israel-war-7a9997f9d84ac669fae69ecf819913fb

[2] AP quoting Brian Clark on the naval threat posed by the Houthis. https://twitter.com/HudsonInstitute/status/1801621975812464813

[3] An account of how the Houthis have shot down American Reaper drones. https://www.thenationalnews.com/news/mena/2024/06/19/drone-dilemma-multimillion-dollar-aircraft-no-longer-rule-skies-above-war-zones/?utm_medium=Social&utm_source=Twitter#Echobox=1718772690

[4] Yemeni protests against Israeli actions featuring nationalist slogans. https://www.alahednews.com.lb/article.php?id=63049&cid=123

[5] Report on Houthis sinking cargo ships in the Red Sea. https://english.alarabiya.net/News/gulf/2024/06/19/action-should-be-taken-in-the-red-sea-as-houthis-sink-second-vessel-shipping-groups

[6] Houthis firing missiles at the Israeli Red Sea port of Eilat. https://themedialine.org/top-stories/eilat-still-shipless-houthis-strangle-port-city/

[7] The economic impact on ports in the Horn of Africa due to Houthi strikes. https://www.juancole.com/2023/12/houthis-support-container.html

[8] Increase in ocean container ship rates due to the disruption caused by Houthis in the Red Sea. https://www.scdigest.com/ontarget/24-06-16_drewry_4_factors_higher_ocean_rates.php?cid=21459

[9] Surge in prices for container shipments due to alternative routes taken to avoid the Red Sea. https://www.drewry.co.uk/supply-chain-advisors/supply-chain-expertise/world-container-index-assessed-by-drewry

[10] Houthi leader Abdul-Malik al-Houthi's observations on the Shiite revolutionary tradition. https://www.saba.ye/ar/news3257538.htm

[11] The Zaydi branch of Shiism and its differences with other sects. Alexander Knysh, "Twelver Shi`ism and Zaydism," in Alexander Knysh, *Islam in Historical Perspective* (Abingdon, Oxon: Routledge, 2017), 185-210.

[12] Criticism of the Houthi-led government's power structure in Yemen. https://tinyurl.com/3cv227vj

[13] Background of the rise of the Helpers of God (Houthis) in Yemen. Marieke Brandt, *Tribes and Politics in Yemen* (Oxford: Oxford University Press, 2024).

[14] Overview of Saudi Arabia's Wahhabism and its impact on the region. Peter Mandaville, ed., *Wahhabism and the World: Understanding Saudi Arabia's Global Influence on Islam* (Oxford: Oxford University Press, 2022).

[15] The Saudi and UAE campaign against the Houthis in Yemen. Juan Cole, "Terraforming Yemen: Geoeconomic imperialism, the UAE and the southern secessionists," *Journal of Gulf Studies*, 1, 1 (Jan 2024): 59 - 79.

[16] Iran's alliance of resistance in the Middle East, including the Houthis' role. https://tomdispatch.com/is-tehran-winning-the-middle-east/

[17] Interview with Abdul-Malik al-Houthi condemning actions against Palestinians. https://tinyurl.com/3kph8z8a

47. The Sphinx and the Sultan:

How Biden's Bear Hug of Netanyahu Caused Washington's Mideast Policy to Crash and Burn

September 17, 2024

At least one thing is now obvious in the Middle East: the Biden administration has failed abjectly in its objectives there, leaving the region in dangerous disarray. Its primary stated foreign policy goal has been to rally its partners in the region to cooperate with the extremist Israeli government of Benjamin Netanyahu while upholding a "rules-based" international order and blocking Iran and its allies in their policies. Clearly, such goals have had all the coherence of a chimera and have failed for one obvious reason. President Biden's Achilles heel has been his "bear hug" of Netanyahu, who allied himself with the Israeli equivalent of neo-Nazis, while launching a ruinous total war on the people of Gaza in the wake of the horrific October 7th Hamas terrorist attack on Israel.

Biden also signed on to the Abraham Accords, a project initiated in 2020 by Jared Kushner, the son-in-law and special Middle East envoy of then-President Donald Trump. Through them the United Arab Emirates, Bahrain, and Morocco all agreed to recognize Israel in return for investment and trade opportunities there and access to American weaponry and a U.S. security umbrella. Not only did Washington, however, fail to incorporate Saudi Arabia into that framework, but it has also faced increasing difficulty keeping the accords themselves in place given increasing anger and revulsion in the region over the high (and still ongoing) civilian death toll in Gaza. Typically, just the docking of an Israeli ship at the Moroccan port of

Tangier this summer set off popular protests that spread to dozens of cities in that country. And that was just a taste of what could be coming.

Breathtaking Hypocrisy

Washington's efforts in the Middle East have been profoundly undermined by its breathtaking hypocrisy. After all, the Biden team has gone blue in the face decrying the Russian occupation of parts of Ukraine and its violations of international humanitarian law in killing so many innocent civilians there. In contrast, the administration let the government of Prime Minister Benjamin Netanyahu completely disregard international law when it comes to its treatment of the Palestinians. This summer, the International Court of Justice ruled that the entire Israeli occupation of Palestinian territories is illegal in international law and, in response, the U.S. and Israel both thumbed their noses at the finding. In part as a response to Washington's Israeli policy, no country in the Middle East and very few nations in the Global South have joined in its attempt to ostracize Vladimir Putin's Russia.

Worse yet for the Biden administration, the most significant divide in the Arab world between secular nationalist governments and those that favor forms of political Islam has begun to heal in the face of the perceived Israeli threat. Turkey and Egypt, daggers long drawn over their differing views of the Muslim Brotherhood, the fundamentalist movement that briefly came to power in Cairo in 2012-2013, have begun repairing their relationship, specifically citing the menace posed by Israeli expansionism.

The persistence of Secretary of State Antony Blinken in pressing Saudi Arabia, a key U.S. security partner, to recognize Israel at a moment when the Arab public is boiling with anger over what they see as a campaign of genocide in Gaza, is the closest thing since the Trump administration to pure idiocracy. Washington's pressure on Riyadh elicited from Saudi Crown Prince Mohammed Bin Salman the pitiful plea that he fears being assassinated were he to normalize relations with Tel Aviv now. And consider that ironic given his own past role in ordering the assassination of Saudi journalist Jamal Khashoggi. In short, the ongoing inside-the-Beltway ambition to secure further Arab recognition of Israel amid the annihilation of Gaza has America's security partners wondering if Washington is trying to get them killed — anything but a promising basis for a long-term alliance.

Global Delegitimization

The science-fiction-style nature of U.S. policy in the Middle East is starkly revealed when you consider the position of Jordan, which has a peace treaty with Israel. In early September, its foreign minister, Ayman Safadi, warned that any attempt by the Israeli military or its squatter-settlers to expel indigenous West Bank Palestinians to Jordan would be considered an "act of war." While such anxieties might once have seemed overblown, the recent stunning (and stunningly destructive) Israeli military campaign on the Palestinian West Bank, including bombings of populated areas by fighter jets, has already begun to resemble the campaign in Gaza in its tactics. And keep in mind that, as August ended, Foreign Minister Israel Katz even urged the Israeli army to compel Palestinians to engage in a "voluntary evacuation" of the northern West Bank.

Not only is the expulsion of Palestinians from there now the stated policy of cabinet members like Jewish Power extremist Itamar Ben-Gvir; it's the preference of 65% of Israelis polled. And mind you, when Israel and Jordan begin talking war you know something serious is going on, since the last time those two countries actively fought was in the 1973 October War during the administration of President Richard Nixon.

In short, Netanyahu and his extremist companions are in the process of undoing all the diplomatic progress their country achieved in the past half-century. Ronen Bar, the head of Israel's domestic Shin Bet intelligence agency, warned in August that the brutal policies the extremists in the government were pursuing are "a stain on Judaism" and will lead to "global delegitimization, even among our greatest allies."

Turkey, a NATO ally with which the U.S. has mutual defense obligations, has become vociferous in its discontent with President Biden's Middle Eastern policy. Although Turkey recognized Israel in 1949, under President Recep Tayyip Erdogan of the pro-Islam Justice and Development Party interactions had grown rocky even before the Gaza nightmare. Still, until then their trade and military ties had survived occasional shouting matches between their politicians. The Gaza genocide, however, has changed all that. Erdogan even compared Netanyahu to Hitler, and then went further still, claiming that, in the Rafah offensive in southern Gaza in May, "Netanyahu has reached a level with his genocidal methods that would make Hitler jealous."

Worse yet, the Turkish president, referred to by friend and foe as the "sultan" because of his vast power, has now gone beyond angry words. Since last October, he's used Turkey's position in NATO to prohibit that organization from cooperating in any way with Israel on the grounds that it's violating the NATO principle that harm to civilians in war must be carefully minimized. The Justice and Development Party leader also imposed an economic boycott on Israel, interrupting bilateral trade that had reached $7 billion a year and sending the price of fruits and vegetables in Israel soaring, while leading to a shortage of automobiles in the Israeli market.

Erdogan's Justice and Development Party represents the country's small towns and rural areas and its Muslim businesses and entrepreneurs, constituencies that care deeply about the fate of Muslim Palestinians in Gaza. And while Erdogan's high dudgeon has undoubtedly been sincere, he's also pleasing his party's stalwarts in the face of an increasing domestic challenge from the secular Republican People's Party. In addition, he's long played to a larger Arab public, which is apoplectic over the unending carnage in Gaza.

The Alliance of Muslim Countries

Although it was undoubtedly mere bluster, Erdogan even threatened a direct intervention on behalf of the beleaguered Palestinians. In early August, he said, "Just as we intervened in

Karabakh [disputed territory between Azerbaijan and Armenia], just as we intervened in Libya, we will do the same to them." In early September, the Turkish president called for an Islamic alliance in the region to counter what he characterized as Israeli expansionism:

"Yesterday, one of our own children, [Turkish-American human rights advocate] Ayşenur Ezgi Eygi, was vilely slaughtered [on the West Bank]. Israel will not stop in Gaza. After occupying Ramallah [the de facto capital of that territory], they will look around elsewhere. They'll fix their eyes on our homeland. They openly proclaim it with a map. We say Hamas is resisting for the Muslims. Standing against Israel's state terror is an issue of importance to the nation and the country. Islamic countries must wake up as soon as possible and increase their cooperation. The only step that can be taken against Israel's genocide is the alliance of Muslim countries."

In fact, the present nightmare in Gaza and the West Bank may indeed be changing political relationships in the region. After all, the Turkish president pointed to his rapprochement with Egypt as a building block in a new security edifice he envisions. Egyptian President Abdel Fattah al-Sisi made his first visit to Ankara on September 4th (following a February Erdogan trip to Cairo). And those visits represented the end of a more than decade-long cold war in the Sunni Muslim world over al-Sisi's 2013 coup against elected Muslim Brotherhood Egyptian President Mohamed Morsi, whom Erdogan had backed.

Despite its apparent embrace of democratic norms in 2012-2013, some Middle Eastern rulers charged the Brotherhood with having covert autocratic ambitions throughout the region and sought to crush it. For the moment, the Muslim Brotherhood and other forms of Sunni political Islam have been roundly defeated in Egypt, Syria, Tunisia, and the Persian Gulf region. Erdogan, a pragmatist despite his support for the Brotherhood and its offshoot Hamas, had been in the process of getting his country the best possible deal, given such a regional defeat, even before the Israelis struck Gaza.

Netanyahu's Forever War in Gaza

For his part, Egypt's al-Sisi is eager for greater leverage against Netanyahu's apparent plan for a forever war in Gaza. After all, the Gaza campaign has already inflicted substantial damage on Egypt's economy, since Yemen's Houthis have supported the Gazans with attacks on container ships and oil tankers in the Red Sea. That has, in turn, diverted traffic away from it and from the Suez Canal, whose tolls normally earn significant foreign exchange for Egypt. In the first half of 2024, however, it took in only half the canal receipts of the previous year. Although tourism has held up reasonably well, any widening of the war could devastate that industry, too.

Egyptians are also reportedly furious over Netanyahu's occupation of the Philadelphi Corridor south of the city of Rafah in Gaza and his blithe disregard of Cairo's prerogatives under the Camp David agreement to patrol that corridor. The al-Sisi government, which, along with Qatar's rulers and the Biden administration, has been heavily involved in hosting (so far fruitless) peace negotiations between Hamas and Israel, seems at the end of its tether, increasingly angered at the way the Israeli prime minister has constantly tacked new conditions onto any agreements being discussed, causing the talks to fail.

For months, Cairo has also been seething over Netanyahu's charge that Egypt allowed tunnels to be built under that corridor to supply Hamas with weaponry, insisting that the Egyptian army had diligently destroyed 1,500 such tunnels. Egypt's position was given support recently by Nadav Argaman, a former head of Shin Bet, who said, "There is no connection between the weaponry found in Gaza and the Philadelphi Corridor." Of Netanyahu, he added, "He knows very well that no smuggling takes place over the Philadelphi Corridor. So, we are now relegated to living with this imaginary figment."

In the Turkish capital, Ankara, al-Sisi insisted that he wanted to work with Erdogan to address "the humanitarian tragedy that our Palestinian brothers in Gaza are facing in an unprecedented disaster that has been going on for nearly a year." He underscored that there was no daylight between Egypt and Turkey "regarding the demand for an immediate ceasefire, the rejection of the current Israeli escalation in the West Bank, and the call to start down a path that achieves the aspirations of the Palestinian people to establish their independent state on the borders of June 4, 1967, with East Jerusalem as its capital." He also pointed out that such positions are in accord with U.N. Security Council resolutions and pledged to work with Turkey to ensure that humanitarian aid was delivered to Gaza despite "the ongoing obstacles imposed by Israel."

To sum up, the ligaments of American influence in the Middle East are now dissolving before our very eyes. Washington's closest allies, like the Jordanian and Saudi royal families, are terrified that Biden's bear hug of Netanyahu's war crimes and the fury of their own people could, in the end, destabilize their rule. Countries that, not so long ago, had correct, if not warm, relations with Israel like Egypt and Turkey are increasingly denouncing that country and its policies. And the alliance of U.S. partners in the region with Israel against Iran that Washington has long worked for seems to be coming apart at the seams. Countries like Egypt and Turkey are instead exploring the possibility of forming a regional Sunni Muslim alliance against Netanyahu's geopolitics of Jewish power that might, in the end, actually reduce tensions with Tehran.

That things have come to such a pass in the Middle East is distinctly the fault of the Biden administration and its position — or lack of one — on Israel's nightmare in Gaza (and now the West Bank, too). Today, all too sadly, that administration is wearing the same kind of blinkers regarding the war in Gaza that President Lyndon B. Johnson and his top officials once sported when it came to the Vietnam War.

- Tomdispatch

Conclusion

As I write, in October 2024, the war continues and has expanded to include an Israeli invasion of southern Lebanon, with heavy bombardment of civilian infrastructure and residential buildings reminiscent of the tactics used by the Israeli military on Gaza. As for Gaza, in the summer of 2024 the Israeli military conducted major ground operations in Gaza City and in southern districts such as Tal al-Hawa, Sabra and Shujaiyya. Regular Israeli airstrikes struck targets such as the Nuseirat refugee camp. The Israelis launched repeated bombardments of civilian objects, including schools. The military claimed that it found weapons caches and a Hamas command center in a building of the United Nations Relief and Works Agency (UNRWA). UNRWA officials had investigated Israeli claims of connections of some of their employees to Hamas in spring 2024 and found them to be baseless, leading European governments to restore UNRWA funding. The majority of hospitals continued to be closed, and the ones still operating faced a severe shortage of fuel and medical supplies. On July 19, the International Court of Justice found the Israeli military occupation of the Occupied Palestinian Territories to be illegal.

On July 29, an Israeli mob attempted to rescue Israeli military personnel at the Sde Teiman base, whom military police arrested on grounds of systematically raping and torturing Palestinian prisoners. The issue split the country, though many members of parliament and cabinet members defended the actions of the rogue unit. On the diplomatic plane, Prime Minister Netanyahu was accused by Israeli officials and the public of derailing talks with Hamas after an Israeli operation assassinated Hamas civilian politburo chief Ismail Haniyeh in Tehran on July 31, with whom Israel had been indirectly negotiating for a hostage release.

In August, the Israeli army redoubled its efforts in the south at Khan Younis, including ground operations and drone strikes on al-Qassam Brigades units, tunnels and weapons caches. Soldiers recovered the bodies of six Israeli hostages from a tunnel in Khan Younis, though critics blamed heavy-handed military tactics, charging that al-Qassam Brigades operatives had murdered the hostages at the approach of Israeli troops. Schools used as shelters continued to be bombed, killing civilians. Although Israeli authorities gave it out that these impromptu refugee shelters were "Hamas command centers," it seems likely they were hit because of the presence of al-Qassam Brigades personnel there, without regard to civilian life, in accordance with the directives of the Lavender and Go Daddy automated attack systems. Those systems, it bears repeating, permitted 15 to 20 civilian deaths for every militant killed, astonishing rules of engagement that were one of the grounds for Israel's exclusion from NATO activities in 2024, at Turkey's insistence, since the resultant high rate of deaths of women, children and non-combatant men violated NATO's ROE. It states: "NATO recognizes that all feasible measures must be taken to avoid, minimize and mitigate harm to civilians. When planning and implementing such measures, NATO should give consideration to those groups most vulnerable to violence within the local context. NATO recognizes that, in general, children constitute a particularly vulnerable group during conflict and women are often disproportionately affected by violence."

After the Haniyeh assassination, Hezbollah increased the number of rockets it fired from southern Lebanon into Israel, and the Israeli Air Force replied with strikes on Hezbollah positions. On September 18 and 19, Israel detonated pagers used by Hezbollah personnel in Lebanon, killing at least 42 people, including several civilians, and wounding some 3,000 individuals. Many observers criticized the use of booby traps as a contravention of international law, and the exploding pagers did kill and wound civilians and children. The operation demonstrated that Israel had penetrated Hezbollah decision-making and equipment supply chains at a high level. About two weeks later, Israeli bunker-busting bombs were deployed against a building complex in Beirut's Shiite-majority Dahiyeh neighborhood, killing Hezbollah leader Hassan Nasrallah. This strike, as well, attested that Israeli intelligence had high level assets within the party-militia, who could inform Mossad of Nasrallah's movements in real time. Hezbollah, however, gave evidence of resilience in the face of these attacks, with new leaders swiftly emerging and evidence of discipline in the ranks and continued ability to hit Israel with rockets and missiles. In Gaza, Israeli forces fought Hamas guerrillas in Rafah.

On October 1, Iran sent some 200 ballistic missiles against Israel, but as with the similar attack in the spring, most were shot down by the United States military in the region. The Iranians were retaliating for the assassinations of Haniyeh (killed in Tehran the previous summer) and Nasrallah, and attempting to reestablish deterrence with Israel, which had broken down because of the Iron Dome and U.S. anti-missile defenses. Israeli officials pledged a robust counterstrike.

At the beginning of October, Israel launched a ground invasion of Lebanon, forcing hundreds of thousands of Lebanese to flee north or to Syria. The grim milestone of the anniversary of the October 7 attacks by Hamas on Israeli targets was solemnly commemorated in Israel and the West, though protesters also demonstrated on that day and after against the subsequent carnage. Israel launched airstrikes against areas such as Jabalia and Khan Younis, where many civilians remained trapped, resulting in high casualties. Hospitals and shelters, often housing displaced people, continued to be hit by bombing raids, adding to the humanitarian crisis. Israeli officials ordered the expulsion of the entire remaining population of Palestinians in Gaza from the north of the Strip, some 400,000 persons, and repeatedly bombarded refugee camps. They little food into the north in October and ordered the patients and staff in the few remaining hospitals in the region to leave, though it was not clear how they could do so or where they would go. Secretary of State Antony Blinken and Secretary of Defense Lloyd Austin threatened Netanyahu with a cut-off of military supplies within thirty days if he did not cease targeting civilians, which violates the Leahy Act forbidding supplying U.S. weaponry to states that use it in a way contrary to U.S. law. Critics complained that the deadline given was far off, and that Blinken had already demonstrated an unwillingness to hold Netanyahu's feet to the fire over the massive civilian death toll, regardless of the Leahy Act

On October 16, 2024, an Israeli drone killed Hamas leader Yahya Sinwar, the mastermind of the October 7 attacks. Netanyahu was quick to underline, however, that this blow to the Hamas leadership did not signal an end to hostilities. The war continues as I write because the extremist Netanyahu government views the October 7, 2023, attacks as a warrant for reshaping its security environment in the Middle East. This government apparently hopes to cleanse North Gaza of its Palestinians and crowd all residents of the Strip into a small enclave in the south. The government has accelerated state-backed squatting on Palestinian land in the West Bank and some extremists on the Cabinet dream of expelling the 3 million Palestinians there to Jordan. Jordan warns that such an action would be viewed in Amman as an act of war.

Netanyahu seeks to reestablish an Israeli buffer zone in south Lebanon, occupying water-rich Lebanese territory in the south. He appears to hope he can coerce Lebanon into electing a president favorable to Israel and into marginalizing Hezbollah, which is a party as well as a militia. Netanyahu's game with Iran is unclear. He appears to desire to provoke a war with that country because an Iranian counterattack will always reliably generate American support for Israel. Despite American hopes of rallying Arab partners against Iran, the latter have grown wary of Israel instead. Egypt began improving its relationship with Turkey in fall 2024, in a bid to defend itself from Israeli aggressiveness. Turkey, a NATO member, sought a rapprochement with Iran on the basis of defending Palestinian rights. Saudi Arabia's crown prince, Mohamed Bin Salman, rejected American pressure to recognize Israel on the grounds that Tel Aviv would first have to agree to a Palestinian state and that he was afraid of being assassinated by an angry populace were he to normalize relations with Israel while it was attacking the Palestinians of Gaza so fiercely.

American policy in the Middle East, a little over a year into the Gaza War, lies in tatters, while, as I argued above, Iran has been able to improve its standing in the region substantially. That the Biden administration allowed Netanyahu to commit a genocide with impunity has perhaps fatally weakened the entire structure of International Humanitarian Law. The Gaza atrocities will likely foment further terrorism against the United States, which the U.S. right wing will use to deprive Americans of more of their civil liberties. The biggest danger is that when the shooting finally stops, the US will enable Israel to continue its unsustainable occupation of the Palestinians, with no clear path to rescuing them from statelessness. Without basic rights and dignity, they will continue to throw up resistance movements, and they will be championed by important sections of the two billion-strong Muslim world community.

About The Author

Juan Cole

Juan Cole is the Richard P. Mitchell Collegiate Professor of History at the University of Michigan Cole has devoted his career to understanding the Middle East and the Muslim world more generally, and to critically evaluating its relationship with the North Atlantic states.   He has appeared widely on media, including the PBS News Hour, ABC World News Tonight, Nightline, the Today Show, Anderson Cooper 360, Rachel Maddow, Chris Hayes' All In, CNN, the Colbert Report, Democracy Now! and many others. He has written about Egypt,  Iran, Iraq, the Gulf and South Asia and about both extremist groups and peace movements. He is proprietor of the Informed Comment news and analysis site. Cole conducts his research in Arabic, Persian, Urdu and Turkish as well as several European languages. He knows both Middle Eastern and South Asian Islam. He lived in various parts of the Muslim world for more than a decade, and continues to travel widely there. He has written, edited or translated 22 books and authored over 100 articles and chapters.

Books By This Author

Muhammad: Prophet Of Peace Amid The Clash Of Empires

In the midst of the dramatic seventh-century war between two empires, Muhammad was a spiritual seeker in search of community and sanctuary.

Many observers stereotype Islam and its scripture as inherently extreme or violent-a narrative that has overshadowed the truth of its roots. In this masterfully told account, preeminent Middle East expert Juan Cole takes us back to Islam's-and the Prophet Muhammad's-origin story.

Cole shows how Muhammad came of age in an era of unparalleled violence. The eastern Roman Empire and the Sasanian Empire of Iran fought savagely throughout the Near East and Asia Minor. Muhammad's profound distress at the carnage of his times led him to envision an alternative movement, one firmly grounded in peace. The religion Muhammad founded, Islam, spread widely during his lifetime, relying on soft power instead of military might, and sought armistices even when militarily attacked. Cole sheds light on this forgotten history, reminding us that in the Qur'an, the legacy of that spiritual message endures.

A vibrant history that brings to life the fascinating and complex world of the Prophet, Muhammad is the story of how peace is the rule and not the exception for one of the world's most practiced religions.

The Rubáiyát Of Omar Khayyam: A New Translation From The Persian

A repository of subversive, joyous and existentialist themes and ideas, the rubaiyat (quatrains) that make up the collected poems attributed to the 12th century Persian astronomer Omar Khayyam have enchanted readers for centuries. In this modern translation, complete with critical introduction and epilogue, Juan Cole elegantly renders the verse for contemporary readers. Exploring such universal questions as the meaning of life, fate and how to live a good life in the face of human mortality, this translation reveals anew why this singular collection of poems has struck a chord with such a temporally and culturally diverse audience, from the wine houses of medieval Iran to the poets of Western twentieth century modernism.

Napoleon's Egypt

In this vivid history, master storyteller and world-renowned historian Juan Cole tells the story of Napoleon's invasion of Egypt in 1798. Revealing Napoleon's reasons for leading the expedition against Egypt and showcasing the young general's fascinating views of the Orient, Cole delves into the psychology of both the military titan and his entourage. He paints a multifaceted portrait of the daily travails of the soldiers in Napoleon's army, including how they imagined Egypt, how their expectations differed from what they found, and how they grappled with military challenges in a foreign land. Cole explains how Napoleon's invasion, the first modern attempt to conquer the Arab world, invented and crystallized the rhetoric of liberal imperialism.

Engaging The Muslim World

With clarity and concision, Juan Cole disentangles the key foreign policy issues that America is grappling with today--from our dependence on Middle East petroleum to the promotion of

Islamophobia by the American right--and delivers his informed advice on the best way forward. Cole's unique ability to take the true Muslim perspective into account when looking at East-West relations make his insights well-rounded and prescient as he suggests a course of action on fundamental issues like religion, oil, war and peace. With substantive recommendations for the next administration on how to move forward in key countries such as Iraq, Pakistan, Afghanistan, and Iran, Engaging the Muslim World reveals how we can repair the damage of the disastrous foreign policy of the last eight years and forge ahead on a path of peace and prosperity.

Peace Movements In Islam

Contrary to the distorted and in many places all-too prevalent view of Islam as somehow inherently or uniquely violent, there is a dazzling array of Muslim organizations and individuals that have worked for harmony and conciliation through history. The Qur'an itself, the Muslim scripture, is full of peace verses urging returning good for evil and wishing peace upon harassers, alongside the verses on just, defensive war that have so often been misinterpreted.
This groundbreaking volume fills a gaping hole in the literature on global peace movements, bringing to the fore the many peace movements and peacemakers of the Muslim world. From Senegalese Sufi orders to Bosnian women's organizations to Indian Muslim freedom fighters who were allies of Mahatma Gandhi against British colonialism, it shows that history is replete with colorful personalities from the Muslim world who made a stand for peaceful methods.

Sacred Space And Holy War: The Politics, Culture And History Of Shi'ite Islam

Juan Cole examines Shi'i Islam as a world religion that has faced modernity on its own terms. He explores the little known history of Shi'i communities as far afield as Bahrain and India, giving attention as well to important centers such as Lebanon , Iraq, and Iran. He demonstrates the way in which the Shi'is have sought to define space and time as sacred, and to defend those spaces from encroachment by the Other, whether that other be Sunni Arab, Hindu, or European Christian.